Sons of the South

C L A Y T O N R A N D

Sons of the South

P O R T R A I T S B Y

Dalton Shourds

Harry Coughlin

Constance Joan Naar

H O L T , R I N E H A R T A N D W I N S T O N · N E W Y O R K

Published simultaneously in Canada by Holt, Rinehart
and Winston of Canada, Limited.

FIRST EDITION

Library of Congress Catalog Card Number: 61-8069

87334-0111
Printed in the United States of America

DEDICATED TO

Daughters of the South,

Mothers of Its Sons

Foreword

IT IS MY belief that in no given geographical area or equal period of time has any part of the world or any breed of men produced the character, statesmanship, and political genius that the South sired from Virginia to Texas. Patrick Henry cried out for liberty or death. George Washington led the forces of the American Revolution, struggling for freedom and independence, to victory. Thomas Jefferson wrote the Declaration of Independence. James Madison was the father of the Constitution and George Mason was the author of the Bill of Rights. John Marshall, first Chief Justice of the United States Supreme Court, construed that covenant for posterity. All were of the Virginia Dynasty.

Not only was this government formed by sons of the South, dedicated to the independence of the republic and the sovereignty of its several states, but the nation itself expanded under Southern statesmanship. The English colonies were first converted into the United States of America under the leadership of Washington. Under the administration of Thomas Jefferson, the geographic area of the republic was doubled in size with the Louisiana Purchase—out of which fifteen independent states were carved in whole or in part. Florida was purchased from Spain under the administration of James Monroe.

The independence of Texas was achieved through the leadership of Sam Houston and Stephen Austin, of Virginia, and the spirit of Texas was born in the Alamo under the heroism of Southern patriots.

The war with Mexico in 1846 was won under the generalship of Winfield Scott and Zachary A. Taylor, and with the heroism of Jefferson Davis, John A. Quitman, and Robert E. Lee. And the Treaty of 1848, in which Mexico ceded claims to Texas, California, Arizona, New Mexico, Nevada, Utah, and part of Colorado, was negotiated under the presidency of James K. Polk of Tennessee. Under this same administration and the statesmanship of John C. Calhoun, the Oregon Claims were settled with Britain, expanding the republic into an empire.

Immediately following the Civil War, when President Andrew Johnson, a Democrat from Tennessee, had been impeached and was being tried before the United States Senate, one of the grievances against him was that he had squandered $7,200,000 of the people's money in the purchase of Alaska.

Certainly the picturesque personalities presented in these pages represent a superior type of man. To begin with, the American explorers, colonizers, and pioneers were adventuresome spirits. These original homeseekers must have been endowed with great vision and courage to have braved uncharted seas and a trackless wilderness. And their descendants thrived in the face of adversity.

The Periclean Age, with its surpassing science and art, sprang from a rocky, thin soil and an economy of grapes and goats. The ancient Mesopotamians who flourished between the Tigris and Euphrates achieved their golden age on an economy of clay and irrigation. The culture of the South, like that of the ancients, was agrarian and reached its zenith on an economy of tobacco, cotton, and sugar—and later, coal, iron, oil, and gas. In all the ancient civilizations, even in Palestine's, which excelled in ethics and religion, the institution of slavery was a contributing influence.

Though the original sons of the South were transplantations, environment had its wholesome effect upon their character. Just as the longhorns on southwest ranges evolved into a breed different from the Spanish cattle that strayed from the herds of Cortez and De Soto and the wild mustangs were a departure from the ponies imported by the explorers, the Southern plantation produced a type peculiar to the South, and the wild frontier fashioned a rugged individual not duplicated in history.

From George Washington, "Father of the Country," to Cordell Hull, "Father of the United Nations," one hundred *Sons of the South* are presented here as a compilation for the Centennial of the Civil War. No other such epic in heroism, human sacrifice, and suffering is recorded in the experiences of mankind.

The Confederates believed themselves to be the political and spiritual heirs of the founders of the republic. That faith prompted them to center the image of Washington in the Great Seal of the Confederacy, and to inscribe there the date of February 22, 1862, as the official birthday of the Confederate States of America.

As a casual student of history it has long been the belief of this author that historians have too often made the most interesting and exciting of all subjects dull with too many dates, battles, and events. Primarily, history is people. This biographical approach to history is not an innovation. Early in our Christian Era, the philosopher Plutarch interpreted the history of ancient Greece and Rome to succeeding generations through his *Lives.*

So this inspiring story of a superior breed of stalwarts is inscribed to mark the Civil War Centennial, that it may enrich the lives of all who pause to review the records of these men that God made for the New World, men to match its seas and its rivers, its deserts and wilderness, its valleys and its mountains.

—C.R.

Gulfport, Mississippi

CONTENTS

I

Founding Fathers of the Republic

George Washington	James Madison
Patrick Henry	James Monroe
Thomas Jefferson	George Mason
John Randolph	John Marshall

George Washington

THE "FATHER of his country," first president of the United States, "first in war, first in peace and first in the hearts of his countrymen," was born at Wakefield, Westmoreland County, Virginia, February 22, 1732, the son of Augustine Washington and Mary Ball. His great-grandfather had come to Virginia from Northamptonshire, England, about 1658. George Washington was eleven years of age when his land-poor father died, and so he spent most of his childhood at Mount Vernon, the home of his half brother, Lawrence.

Taught at home, he studied mathematics with care and at sixteen was included in a party surveying the lands of Lord Fairfax on the Shenandoah, after which he became surveyor for the county of Culpeper. At nineteen he accompanied his brother Lawrence, who was dying of consumption, to the Barbados, where George contracted smallpox and became deeply scarred. Upon the death of Lawrence, he inherited Mount Vernon.

Washington's military career began at the age of twenty-one, when Governor Dinwiddie made him lieutenant colonel of militia and sent him against the French who were connecting their settlements on the Great Lakes with those on the Mississippi. After suffering great hardships, he was forced to surrender Fort Necessity. Later he served under General Braddock in an expedition during which two horses were shot from under him. After Braddock's death, he was appointed as an aide; to determine the authority for his command, he went to Boston, covering the entire distance from Winchester, Virginia, on horseback.

In 1759 Washington married Martha (Dandridge) Custis, a rich and charming widow, and settled down to the quiet life of a gentleman farmer at Mount Vernon. He raised tobacco, fruit, and wheat, bred horses and cattle, and experimented with domesticating the American buffalo. He practiced crop rotation and expanded his holdings, which at the time of his death exceeded seventy thousand acres.

During the Stamp Act agitation, Washington sided with Massachusetts and Virginia. "Parliament," he said, "hath no more right to put their hands into my pocket without my consent than I have to put my hands into yours." He had already served in the House of Burgesses when made a delegate to the First Continental Congress. At the Second Continental Congress he was elected commander-in-chief of the armies, taking command at Cambridge, Massachusetts, on July 3, 1775. For eight years Washington led the revolutionary forces in the fight for American independence. With its bloodshed, hunger, and rags, it provides one of the most agonizing and heroic chapters in human history. Largely through his tenacious generalship and consecrated faith, his Continentals were triumphant.

When the war was over the commander was called upon to become the statesman. Washington favored the formation of a federal government. Depressed over the prevailing apathy, he appealed to George Mason, "Where, where are our men of abilities? Why do they not come forth and save the country?" He was chairman of the Constitutional Convention of 1787 and helped get the constitution ratified. He was unanimously elected president and inaugurated April 30, 1789, taking the oath of office on the balcony of New York's Federal Hall at Broad and Wall Streets. A Federalist, Washington appointed Alexander Hamilton, a member of his own party, Secretary of the Treasury and Thomas Jefferson, the leading Democrat, Secretary of State. As he had refused to accept compensation for his services as commander-in-chief, so he refused to accept any pay as president. He retired at the end of his second term and could not be persuaded to be renominated.

After an absence of nine years as a soldier and eight as chief executive, he returned to the management of his plantation which Martha had supervised in his absence. His death came suddenly after an acute attack of laryngitis and high fever following a ride in the snow and rain around his estate. As was the prevailing practice, he was bled by the doctors and died on December 14, 1799. The strains of the Revolution and his responsibilities as president had much to do with his collapse. A giant of a man over six feet in height, weighing two hundred pounds, and of unusual strength and tireless energy, he drove himself unsparingly in the public service. Half his life was spent doing what he conceived to be his duty. With his compatriots, he had placed his "life, fortune, and sacred honor" upon the altar of liberty.

Though Washington lacked the eloquence of Patrick Henry and the literary flair of Thomas Jefferson, he stood above all his contemporaries as commander and chief executive. Foremost among the makers of America, there is no major problem of state, internal or external, for which one will not find the answer in his words or acts. If his admonitions to the Congress on preparation for war and the need for cherishing public credit, if his warnings in his Farewell Address on the dangers of entangling foreign alliances had been heeded, many of the world's woes would not have been passed on to posterity. Under his surpassing leadership the great American venture in freedom became one of the foremost political achievements in history.

There must be something enduring in a personality that after a century and a half finds millions still testifying to his greatness. The stone obelisk which pierces the sky in the capital city that bears his name is as much a tower proclaiming eternal truth as a monument to his memory.

Patrick Henry

AT A CRITICAL time in the excitement over the British Stamp Act, Patrick Henry, a new member of Virginia's House of Burgesses, introduced resolutions in the assembly declaring the act unconstitutional and void, along with all other parliamentary decrees which encroached upon the rights of the colonies.

Only nine days after he had taken his seat, on May 29, 1765, his twenty-ninth birthday, the young spokesman shocked the dignified burgesses when he said: "Tarquin and Caesar each had his Brutus, Charles the First his Cromwell, and George the Third. . . ." Interrupted by the presiding officer and members with cries of "Treason! Treason!" the young orator continued, "may profit by their example. If *this* be treason, make the most of it." The resolutions were adopted by a majority of one vote.

Patrick Henry was born in Hanover County, Virginia, on May 29, 1736, the son of John Henry and Sarah (Winston) Henry. His father had come to the province from Aberdeen, Scotland, before 1730, and his mother, a woman of marked ability, was of English extraction. From his father he learned enough Latin to read with ease the Roman classics.

Averse to farm work, which included deworming tobacco, Patrick became a country store clerk at fifteen. Later, in partnership with his brother, he failed in the business. He was hardly eighteen when he married Sarah Shelton, who brought a small dowry. The young couple started out with six slaves and three hundred acres of sandy, worn-out land. A fire destroyed their house and its contents, and Patrick returned to storekeeping. Facing ruin again, he began to study law and obtained a license to practice in 1760. Within three years he took part in 1,185 suits and established his reputation as a lawyer.

Henry became a freeholder in Louisa County and was sent to the House of Burgesses from that frontier region. After the adoption of his anti-Stamp Act resolutions, he became a recognized revolutionary leader. Colonial committees of correspondence were formed, and Massachusetts notified Virginia that the port of Boston was closed. A continental congress and a Virginia convention were called. Henry arrived in Philadelphia on September 4, 1774, and made the first speech, one of fiery eloquence, before the assembly. The declaration of grievances and the association of the colonies for the purpose of boycotting British goods received his hearty support.

When Henry returned to Virginia, his prominence was further enhanced by his work in the provincial convention. He introduced resolutions to have the colony prepare for defense. Randolph and others sought to delay action, but Henry, pressing for action, cried out: "What is it that the gentlemen wish? What would they have? Is life so dear, or peace so sweet as to be purchased at the price of chains and slavery? Forbid it, Almighty God! I know not which course others may take, but as for me, give me liberty, or give me death!"

Under the spell of his impassioned appeal, the convention capitulated. Henry was selected to attend the Second Continental Congress. He was about to leave for Philadelphia when messengers brought news of the battle of Lexington. The American Revolution had begun. When Lord Dunmore, royal governor of Virginia, seized the gun powder in the arsenal at Williamsburg, Henry collected a militia and marched toward the capital. The governor delivered the ammunition and then issued a proclamation outlawing "a certain Patrick Henry" for disturbing the peace.

Henry took his seat in the Second Continental Congress and had a share in the legislation under which a continental army was organized and Washington made general-in-chief. From the anxious deliberations in Philadelphia Henry hurried to Richmond where a second Virginia convention met to draft a constitution and bill of rights for an independent state. Henry was the first governor and was reëlected four times.

In 1777 he planned and sent out an expedition to conquer the vast territory northwest of the Ohio. At the close of the war he advocated the return of the banished Tories and opened the state's ports to immigration and commerce. He declined appointment as delegate to the convention that framed the constitution of the United States, but he was a member of the state convention that finally ratified it.

At fifty, his health broken, his fortune depleted, and with a score of children and grandchildren around him, Henry withdrew from public life, after twenty-six years of service, and turned to the practice of his profession. He was an old, broken man at sixty years of age and retired to Red Hill, his plantation on the Staunton River, where he died on June 6, 1799. He had never held federal office. Washington offered him the portfolio of Secretary of State and the office of Chief Justice of the Supreme Court, both of which he declined. In his last days, at Washington's insistence, he was a candidate for the Virginia House of Delegates. Although in poor health, he campaigned, and he made his last speech on a cold March day at the Charlotte Courthouse in a debate with young John Randolph. Though he was elected, death intervened and he did not take his seat.

Patrick Henry's transcendent genius has been testified to by so many men of quality that patriots will ever rank him among the gifted orators of the ages. He was our great awakener.

Thomas Jefferson

"I HAVE *sworn upon the altar of God eternal hostility against every form of tyranny over the mind of man.*"

With these words of resolve Thomas Jefferson, third President of the United States of America, summarized his political philosophy. Author, architect, inventor, scientist, diplomat, planter, philosopher, statesman, apostle of freedom, he was born on April 13, 1743, at Shadwell, Albemarle County, Virginia. His father, Peter Jefferson, of Welsh descent, a farmer and civil engineer, died when Thomas was fourteen years of age; his mother was Jane Randolph, daughter of one of Virginia's first families.

Thomas was the third child and eldest son in a family of ten children. At seventeen, he entered William and Mary College from which he was graduated two years later; throughout his life he was a diligent student. An amateur violinist, good singer and dancer, and skilled horseman, he never used tobacco nor played cards and was never a party to a personal altercation.

On his graduation, Jefferson began to study law and after five years was admitted to the bar. He inherited 2,750 acres from his father. In his thirtieth year he married Martha Wayles Skelton, a beautiful and childless young widow. Their married life was exceedingly happy, and he never remarried after her death ten years later. Upon the death of his father-in-law, Jefferson inherited extensive holdings in land and slaves.

He was six feet two inches in height, large-boned, slim, strong, and erect. He had angular features, a ruddy complexion, sandy hair, and hazel eyes. At the time of the American Revolution he was a thriving young planter operating in three counties with a household of thirty-four whites and eighty-three blacks. Shadwell having burned in 1770, he began building Monticello, overlooking Charlottesville, on which he worked for years. A country gentleman of erudition, he was practicing law when chosen as a delegate to the House of Burgesses.

As a member of the Virginia Committee of Correspondence and the Continental Congress he denied Britain's right to tax her colonies. On the committee to draw up a Declaration of Independence, he wrote the basic draft. He was in the Virginia House of Delegates in 1776, was elected governor to succeed Patrick Henry in 1779, and wrote the state statute on religious freedom. In the Continental Congress, he drew up the ordinance for the Northwest Territory, forbidding slaves after 1800. He was sent to Paris with Benjamin Franklin and John Adams to negotiate treaties of commerce in 1784, and later, as minister to France, he witnessesd the destruction of the Bastille.

Washington appointed him Secretary of State in 1789. Jefferson's strong faith in the consent of the governed as opposed to executive control favored by Hamilton, Secretary of the Treasury, led to official friction and Jefferson resigned. He was the Democratic-Republican candidate for president in 1796, was defeated by John Adams, and became vice-president. He opposed Adams' alien and sedition laws, reiterating his concept of the basic right of the states. In 1800 when Jefferson and Aaron Burr received equal votes for president, the House of Representatives elected Jefferson with the help of Hamilton. Jefferson cancelled levies and titles, ignored diplomatic precedence, turned the Federalists out of office, and opposed a strong navy.

During his first term he curbed the Barbary pirates, who had long exacted tribute in Mediterranean waters, and completed the Louisiana Purchase to double the size of the country. In his second term, the duel between Hamilton and Vice-President Burr was a sensational episode, and the killing of Hamilton and the trial of Burr for treason shocked and angered the nation.

After nearly continuous public service for forty-four years, Jefferson retired to private life in 1809 to devote his talent and energy to the building of the University of Virginia and to agricultural pursuits. The embargo on foreign trade, which prevented the exportation of tobacco, had reduced his private income. Along with his own financial distress, he had endorsed a note of twenty thousand dollars for a friend, which he was forced to pay. After the destruction of the Library of Congress by the British in 1814, he sold his rare collection of thirteen thousand volumes to the nation for $23,950, which provided temporary relief only. With a house full of relatives and invited and uninvited guests, he was forced to retire to a second home, constructed as a refuge. He died there believing his creditors would be satisfied. Monticello with its priceless contents was sold to discharge his debts.

Jefferson died on July 4, 1826, on the fiftieth anniversary of the signing of the Declaration of Independence; he died on the same day as John Adams, his political foe and personal friend. With unimpaired influence and unclouded fame, he saw infinitely deeper into the principles of the rising democracy and farther into the future than any man of his time. He was buried at Monticello, inscribed on the simple monument over his grave is an epitaph he wrote: "Here was buried Thomas Jefferson, author of the Declaration of Independence, of the Statute of Virginia for Religious Freedom, and Father of the University of Virginia."

John Randolph

STATESMAN and orator, "John Randolph of Roanoke," was the third son of John Randolph and great-grandson of William Randolph of Turkey Island," progenitor of the most noted of Virginia families. His mother was also descended from William Randolph.

John was born at Cawsons, Prince George County, the home of his mother's father on June 2, 1773. His father died when he was two, and his mother married St. George Tucker. John's father left him his land on the Staunton River, which he did not occupy until 1810. His early education was under the direction of his stepfather until he was sent to school in Orange County where, according to a statement by him, he "was tyrannized over and tortured by the most peevish and ill-tempered of pedagogues."

Randolph made full use of an excellent library he had inherited and was sent to Princeton to attend its grammar school, a stay cut short by the death of his mother. At seventeen he read law in the office of Edmund Randolph, a cousin, who was Attorney-General in the cabinet of President Washington. His two brothers having died, he inherited Bizarre, the family plantation, and for a time squandered his substance following the races. He was at William and Mary College for a short term, where he had a duel with Robert Barrand Taylor.

Described as a "tall, gawky-looking, flaxen-haired stripling . . . with a complexion of a good parchment color," and beardless chin, he apparently led a gay life until he settled down to a political career. The rupture of his engagement to Maria Ward, a famous beauty of the time, provided one of the tragic chapters in his life.

Randolph was a candidate for Congress in 1799 and made his political debut by audaciously speaking in opposition to Patrick Henry, who was a Federalist candidate; Randolph was a Jeffersonian. The controversy was over the alien and sedition laws under which the president had power to expel foreigners from the country without trial; Randolph opposed such acts as unconstitutional.

Elected to Congress at the age of twenty-seven he served there for thirteen years. He opposed a large standing army and called the regular soldiers "mercenaries." He supported the Louisiana Purchase, claiming Jefferson had "extraconstitutional" powers to consummate the transaction. He resisted any compromise on the Yazoo fraud which grew out of an act of the Georgia legislature granting the greater part of the territory now forming Alabama and Mississippi to four land companies for the sum of five hundred thousand dollars.

At twenty-eight years of age, he was chairman of the committee on ways and means and was in effect administration leader. Because of his hostility to the War of 1812 he suffered his only defeat in the House of Representatives in 1813. Later he served an unexpired term in the United States Senate. He was defeated for a full term by John Tyler but was returned to the House in 1827. After the election of Andrew Jackson in 1828, he announced he would not be a candidate for reëlection. With the rise of the Missouri question, Randolph became a sectional leader. Suspicious of Henry Clay and bitterly hostile to John Adams, he described their alliance as a combination "of the puritan and black lėg." Clay challenged him for using insulting language in a speech. Clay's second shot pierced the skirt of Randolph's coat, but he himself fired into the air.

On most public questions Randolph was a member of the opposition. He was a constitutional purist, an unsparing critic, a merciless foe. In 1815, he was an ardent member of the states' rights party. "Asking one of the States to surrender part of her sovereignity," he said, "is like asking a lady to surrender part of her chastity." A keen student of the past, he said, "the lust for innovation" has caused the death of all republics. He went down in history as the great champion of lost causes. Endowed with poetic eloquence he was an incomparable orator, whose "flute-like voice irritated and fascinated, pouring upon his audience shafts of biting wit, literary allusions, epigrams, parables, and figures of speech redolent of the Virginia countryside."

He went to Russia in 1830 as Andrew Jackson's minister in an effort to negotiate a treaty of commerce but returned home because of poor health. He had added to his inheritance until he owned eight thousand acres, four hundred slaves, and a valuable stud of blooded horses. He spent much time in his log-house retreat in the wilderness, which he called "Roanoke." He liked the place because he said it never belonged to anyone except to the Indians and his ancestors.

Randolph suffered most of his life from bad health. In 1833 he decided to go to England where on past visits he had been relatively happy. In Philadelphia to take a packet, he was stricken and died on May 24, 1833.

He was buried at "Roanoke" with his face to the west, in order, it was said, that he might keep his eye on Henry Clay. In 1879 his remains were removed to Richmond. Dauntless in spirit, a brilliant but pathetic figure, he was, according to Hugh A. Garland, his biographer, Virginia's "wisest statesman, truest patriot and most devoted son."

James Madison

FATHER of the federal Constitution and fourth president of the United States, James Madison was born at Port Conway, Virginia, on March 16, 1751. He was the eldest of ten children and our smallest president; he stood only five feet four inches and weighed one hundred pounds.

After receiving his bachelor of arts degree from the College of New Jersey (Princeton) in 1771, he continued another year studying Hebrew, with the idea of entering the ministry. On returning home, he studied history, law, and theology while teaching his brothers and sisters. He was first elected to the Committee of Safety for Orange County, then in 1776 to the Virginia convention to help frame the state's constitution. He was a member of the first Assembly and was elected by it to the governor's Council. In 1780 he was a delegate to the Continental Congress.

Madison, who took his seat in Congress in 1780, was a consistent advocate of raising federal revenue by levying duties. In the controversy over the proposal to change the basis of state contributions to the federal government from land values to population, he broke the deadlock by suggesting that five slaves be counted as three free persons, originating the "federal ratio" later incorporated in the Constitution of the United States.

Madison returned to Montpelier, his home in Virginia, in 1783, to pursue the study of law so that he might have a profession in which he could "depend as little as possible on the labour of slaves." He was elected to the Virginia House of Delegates where he took an active interest in Kentucky, Virginia's western district, and insisted on the free navigation of the Mississippi. He participated in efforts to modernize Virginia's laws, develop its resources, improve its commerce, and defend its credit. He defeated a project of Patrick Henry and others to impose a general assessment for the support of religion.

Madison went as a delegate to the Annapolis convention and was named to represent Virginia at the Philadelphia convention. He contended for a strong central government and was recognized as "the master builder of the Constitution." He was not only the dominating spirit of the Convention but recorded its proceedings.

While attending Congress in New York he collaborated with Alexander Hamilton in a series of essays later published under the title of *The Federalist.* Although the philosophy of *The Federalist* was based upon the idea of popular sovereignity, it placed emphasis upon the protection of persons and their property against popular majorities. "It is of great importance in a republic," Madison said, "not only to guard the society against the oppression of its rulers, but to guard one part of the society against the injustice of the other part."

Madison had a thin, almost inaudible voice, but his quick, cogent reasoning was often effective against Patrick Henry's eloquence. Though Governor Patrick Henry blocked Madison's way to a seat in the Senate, he was three times in Congress. In the first Congress he played a leading role in the passage of revenue legislation, in the creation of the executive departments, and in the framing of the first ten amendments to the Constitution. He opposed assumption of state debts by the federal treasury, though this opposition was in a measure silenced by the agreement to relocate the capital on the Potomac. The overthrow of the Federalists in the election of 1800 and the inauguration of Jefferson brought Madison again into prominence as Jefferson's Secretary of State and chief adviser, a position he held for eight years.

Madison's marriage to Dolly Payne Todd, a young widow of Philadelphia, on September 15, 1794, was the beginning of an extraordinarily happy union that lasted forty-two years. She was the daughter of a boardinghousekeeper, twenty-two years Madison's junior, lively, warmhearted, and charming, with a penchant for pretty hats. Jefferson and his vice-president both being widowers, she became the first lady long before her husband became president. Jefferson chose Madison as his successor, and he entered office March 4, 1809.

During the War of 1812, called "Mr. Madison's War," the British burned Washington. When they put the torch to the White House, the Madisons fled to the hills and were never able to reoccupy it. There was some consolation in the victorious battle of New Orleans, on January 8, 1815, though it was fought two weeks after the war was over.

At the close of his second term as President, Madison retired to Montpelier where he spent nearly twenty years with his books and friends until his death on June 28, 1836. He was a prominent supporter of Jefferson in the founding of the University of Virginia and after Jefferson's death became its rector. He was interested in the work of the American Colonization Society as the most promising solution of the Negro problem, that "dreadful calamity."

The greatest part of Madison's career was finished before he became President. What he had achieved even before he became Secretary of State placed him in the foremost rank of men who have built nations. His genius in providing for dual systems of state and federal law and in devising the division of and checks and balances for the legislative, executive, and judicial powers was one of the longest reaches of constructive statesmanship ever known to the world.

James Monroe

DURING the first thirty-six years of the republic, four of its presidents were native Virginians, Washington, Jefferson, Madison, and Monroe. Its fifth president, James Monroe, was born in Westmoreland County, April 28, 1758. His parents, Spence and Elizabeth (Jones) Monroe, were of good but not distinguished stock. James attended the private school of Parson Archibald Campbell, and at sixteen he entered the College of William and Mary. His academic career was soon interrupted by the American Revolution.

Monroe was commissioned a lieutenant in the Third Virginia regiment and was present at several battles, receiving a shoulder wound while leading the advanced guard at Trenton. As a volunteer aid with the rank of major, he later took part in the battles of Brandywine, Germantown, and Monmouth. From 1780 to 1783 he had a connection as a student of law with Thomas Jefferson, then governor of Virginia, that was the beginning of a lifelong friendship.

Monroe was elected to the Assembly of Virginia in 1782 and the following year to the Congress of the Confederation, where he served until 1786. He was a member of the Virginia convention that considered the ratification of the constitution. With Patrick Henry, he opposed ratification, fearing federal encroachment. He was a member of the United States Senate from 1790 to 1794 and was four times governor of Virginia. He was twice appointed minister to France and was also accredited to the court of St. James and subsequently to Madrid. He served as Secretary of State, then Secretary of War in the cabinet of Madison and was for two terms President of the United States. While attending Congress in 1786, he married Elizabeth Kortright of New York, the daughter of a captain in the British army.

As a member of the Virginia Assembly and as congressman, Monroe, an anti-Federalist, resisted the centralization of political powers in the federal government. He predicted ultimate conflict between the state and national authorities as inevitable. He was among the first to perceive the importance of free navigation of the Mississippi and on his second trip to Paris helped negotiate the purchase of Louisiana, in collaboration with Robert M. Livingston. Though his mission to Madrid for the cession of the Floridas was unsuccessful they were acquired while he was president, giving the United States control of our present Atlantic and Gulf seaboards.

While he was Secretary of War under Madison, the fall of Plattsburg and the still greater victory at New Orleans did much to enhance Monroe's prestige. He was elected President by the Democratic-Republican party and was inaugurated in 1817.

As President, Monroe followed the conservative course of Madison. He vetoed a bill authorizing the federal government to erect tollhouses, gates, and turnpikes on the Cumberland Road, accompanying his veto with a formidable state paper on internal improvements. He declared that Congress had unlimited power to raise money, "restricted only by the duty to appropriate it to purposes of common defense and of general, not local, national, not State, benefit." His resistance to foreign interference in American affairs was formulated in a declaration known as the Monroe Doctrine.

With the enunciation of this doctrine the young republic came of age, proclaiming that the Americas were for Americans. Europe was informed that the American continents were not to be considered for further colonization and that the United States would consider any attempt on the part of European powers to extend their systems to any portion of this hemisphere as dangerous to our peace and safety.

Monroe's administration was known as "the era of good feeling." Lafayette made a return visit, and Monroe made a ceremonious tour of the nation's principal cities. The Seminoles were suppressed. The United States and Great Britain agreed to disarm along the Canadian border. The Missouri Compromise on slavery provided an interim of peace. The first link of the Cumberland Road was finished, and restless Americans pushed across the Alleghenies. The *Savannah,* the first steamship to cross the Atlantic, reached Liverpool from Georgia in twenty-nine days. The United States enjoyed the admiration and respect of the world.

On the expiration of his second term, Monroe retired to his home at Oak Hill, Virginia, and became a regent at the University and a member of the state constitutional convention. Having neglected his private affairs during his prolonged public service, he suffered business reverses. In 1826 Congress voted him thirty thousand dollars in settlement of certain claims against the government for expenses he incurred during his missions abroad. After the death of his wife, and still in financial straits, he took up residence with his daughter and her husband in New York City where he died on July 4, 1831.

Monroe was described as a tall, lanky, blue-eyed man, with a big mouth and well-shaped nose. Unpretentious in appearance, lacking in imagination, and without any genuine graces, he achieved distinction and success through dogged determination. He was never discouraged by failure and never lost the loyal support of friends. Making many personal sacrifices in his service to his country, he is numbered among the nation's good and great as one who deserved and won the full confidence of his compatriots.

George Mason

MORE than any other planter-statesman, George Mason of Virginia was responsible for the first ten amendments to the Constitution, known as the Bill of Rights. He was the author of the Virginia Declaration of Rights and co-author of its Constitution. The former was drawn upon generously by Jefferson in drafting the Declaration of Independence and became the basis for the constitutional amendments that guaranteed to the individual freedom of speech, press, religion, and public assembly.

The fourth of his name in Virginia, George Mason was born in Dogue's Neck in 1725. When he was ten, his father died, and he grew up under the guardianship of his mother, Ann (Thompson) Mason, and an uncle, John Mercer of Marlborough. Though given some instruction by private tutors, he was mostly self-educated in Mercer's excellent library of fifteen hundred volumes. At twenty-five Mason married Anne Eilbeck of Mattawoman, Charles County, Maryland. Soon thereafter he established Gunston Hall on the Potomac where his five sons and four daughters were born. Here Mason managed his large and self-sufficient plantation and resided until his death on October 7, 1792.

Mason served for a time as trustee of the recently founded town of Alexandria, Virginia, and as vestryman of Truro Parish; he was one of the overseers of the poor after relief became a lay function. He was inactive in the American Revolution. His chronic ill health and the death of his wife in 1773, left him, as he wrote in 1775, with a sense of "the duty I owe to a poor little helpless family of orphans to whom I must now act the part of Father and Mother."

After his marriage to Sarah Brent in 1780, Mason accepted a seat in the federal convention in Philadelphia. He put a low rating on human nature in committee. He had served with Washington in the House of Burgesses in 1759, but at the end of his first term withdrew, with an opinion of that body that did not change when he returned to take the place of the newly elected commander-in-chief in the convention of 1775. He wrote Washington that the "babblers" caused him "vexation and disgust."

Off stage, however, he was a dedicated defender of rights of the individual and one of the foremost founders of the republic. He was an outstanding constitutionalist. Jefferson had such respect for his ability that he referred to him as "a man of the first order of wisdom, of expansive mind, profound judgment, cogent in argument, learned in the lore of our former constitution, and earnest for the republican change in democratic principles."

In a perilous period he was the young republic's troubleshooter, collaborating with Thomas Jefferson and Patrick Henry. He was a member of the committee of five entrusted with the revision of the laws. He was active in the organization of military affairs and was one of Governor Henry's secret committee that authorized the conquest of the west by George Rogers Clark. As a result, he was in a measure responsible for fixing the American-British boundary at the Great Lakes rather than Ohio in the treaty of 1783. For a number of years he was a member of the Ohio Company, serving as treasurer. He was among the liberal churchmen who effected disestablishment.

During the early eighties Mason was among those whom disgust at public affairs drove into retirement. Not until 1786 did he emerge to appear in the Virginia Assembly to prevent an orgy of inflation. In the debates at Philadelphia at the federal convention he was one of the most frequent and effective speakers. His decision not to sign the document was made during the last two weeks. Until the final days of the convention he struggled for the inclusion of clauses guaranteeing individual rights. He and Henry conducted a campaign against ratification by Virginia. Their insistence on the necessity of incorporating a Bill of Rights in the Constitution finally prevailed in the adoption of the first ten amendments.

As a firm believer in individual rights, Mason looked upon slavery as a diabolical institution. However, he believed that life, liberty, and the use of property are central human rights, that a man should not be deprived of his property without due compensation, and that education and preparation should precede manumission.

Mason never sought political office. He was elected the first United States senator from Virginia but declined to accept. Though he never knocked for admittance to the bar nor engaged in legal practice, he was one of the foremost legal minds of his time whose counsels were coveted by lawmakers and lawgivers. He was the layman scholar and legal light of his generation. At fifty he was described as of commanding presence and lofty bearing, of robust build, and swarthy complexion. His black hair, sprinkled with gray, crowned a serious countenance enlivened with dark, bright eyes.

George Mason pioneered in the promulgation and preservation of the freedom of man. He subscribed to the English common-law concept of government that individual rights exist in themselves as inborn, given by God. But he would acknowledge and reassert them periodically, as was done in the Magna Charta, the Petition of Rights, and the Bill of Rights. As a leading advocate of the inalienable rights of the individual, the influence of Mason found expression in the constitutions of the several states and spread throughout the English-speaking world.

John Marshall

FOUNDER and foremost exponent of the American system of Constitutional law, Chief Justice John Marshall was born in a log cabin on the Virginia frontier near Germantown on September 24, 1755. On his father's side, he was of humble origin. On his mother's, his ancestors were also the ancestors of Thomas Jefferson, Robert E. Lee, and of many noted Randolphs.

For his education, John Marshall was primarily indebted to his father, a farmer, who snatched a little time from his exacting calling to instruct his fifteen children. At fourteen John was placed under the tutelage of the Reverend Archibald Campbell for one year.

By the time he was eighteen his formal schooling was all over. He was struggling with Blackstone's *Commentaries* when the shadow of the Revolution was cast across the land. Young Marshall joined the Virginia militia and as lieutenant and captain in the Continental army was in active service during the entire war. He fought at Brandywine, Germantown, and Monmouth and was half starved and half frozen at Valley Forge. His legal studies were continuously interrupted by his stints with the military until the close of the war when he attended a brief course of law lectures by Chancellor Wythe of William and Mary College. He procured his license and began practice in 1781.

In the wake of the War of Independence, questions of vital moment were resolved, and Marshall was a part of every controversy and struggle. He was a member of the Virginia Assembly, an executive councilor, general of militia, delegate to the state convention which adopted the federal Constitution, member of Congress, envoy to France, and when he was appointed Chief Justice in 1801, he was Secretary of State in John Adams' cabinet.

At the time he was a member of the House of Burgesses in 1782, he was married to Mary Willis Ambler, daughter of the state treasurer, with whom he lived for nearly fifty happy years.

The new republic of thirteen small states strung along the Atlantic seaboard comprised a population of four million souls. Marshall first called it the "American Empire." This great experiment in free government, with its confederation of sovereign states, its Constitution, Congress, President and Supreme Court, was in dire need of an interpreter, and Marshall assumed that role for thirty-five years to give it the stamp of his wisdom and personality. He made the Supreme Court the keystone of the arch that supported the Republic, and to him the Constitution was the ark of the covenant.

As Chief Justice, he administered the presidential oath of office to Thomas Jefferson. When he died on July 6, 1835, Andrew Jackson was President. Marshall was the last of the Federalists; Jefferson and Jackson were Democrats, and his opinions and theirs did not conform. Jefferson was not satisfied with Marshall's conduct of the trial of Aaron Burr for treason, and in a decision involving the unconstitutionality of state acts, President Jackson said, "John Marshall has made his decision, now let him enforce it."

The conflict over the sovereignty of the federal government and the sovereignty of the state governments was from the beginning a lively issue. Marshall was the consistent constitutionalist, and as Chief Justice he had the last word. Under him, however, court procedures were conducted more or less leisurely. In the argument of *Fletcher* v. *Peck* the Court adjourned to enable Luther Marshall to sober up. On another occasion he permitted William Pinkney to go back and repeat part of an argument in order that several ladies who had just entered the courtroom might not miss some especially choice tropes.

Of a total of 1,215 cases that came before the court over which he presided, he delivered the opinion in 1,106; so the precedents he followed in his judicial reviews were mostly his own. No doubt his meticulous research in compiling *The Life of George Washington* in five volumes gave him a knowledge of the intentions of the framers of the Constitution that stood him in good stead. To him the Constitution with its checks and balances and division of political powers charted the course of the Republic . . . an indestructible union of indestructible states. In his interpretations the Constitution was a covenant with posterity, to endure for the ages, the everlasting bulwark of the liberties, the lives, and the possessions of the people against all aggression.

His contemporaries described him as tall, meager, emaciated, "loose-jointed, inelegant in dress, attitudes, gesture," and looking beyond his years. His countenance was small in proportion to his size; he had dark eyes, an amiable temper, and irradiating spirit. Biographers note that he enjoyed the fellowship of friends and was convivial on occasion.

In 1833, Justice Story, in publishing *Commentaries on the Constitution of the United States,* dedicated the work to John Marshall with the tribute: "Your expositions of constitutional law enjoy a rare and extraordinary authority. They constitute a monument of fame far beyond the ordinary memorials of political and military glory. They are destined to enlighten, instruct and convince future generations, and can scarcely perish but with the memory of the constitution itself."

2

Colonizers and Builders of the Republic

Leonard Calvert
Jean Baptiste le Moyne de Bienville
James Oglethorpe
Etienne de Boré
John Sevier
William Dunbar
Daniel Boone
William Richardson Davie
Andrew Jackson
Pushmataha
William C.C. Claiborne
Sequoyah
Samuel Dale
William Harris Crawford
Henry Clay
John Caldwell Calhoun
John McDonogh
William Wyatt Bibb
Zachary Taylor
John James Audubon
William E. Woodruff
John Tyler
John Anthony Quitman
John Ross
Opothleyahola
John Gorrie
Alexandre Mouton
Seargent S. Prentiss
Albert Pike
Crawford Williamson Long
Samuel Houston
Stephen Fuller Austin
William Barrett Travis
James Bowie
David Crockett
Mirabeau Buonaparte Lamar
James Sevier Conway
Isaac Shelby

Leonard Calvert

IN THE colonization of the New World some men sought adventure, others came seeking civil and religious liberty. Among England's religious dissenters was a sect of Pilgrims who first settled in Leiden, Holland, to escape the persecution of the Established Church. Later they obtained a charter from the Virginia Company, the first English colony established in America.

Until freedom of religion was proclaimed by George Mason, Patrick Henry, and others, the church of England presided exclusively over the spiritual lives of the colonists in Virginia.

And while the Episcopalians and Pilgrims contended with one another in England and Virginia, England's Roman Catholics also sought a sanctuary. Sir George Calvert, first Baron of Baltimore and first Lord Proprietor of Maryland, a Roman Catholic and friend of King James, was issued a royal patent to a province in the New World, where those of his persuasion might worship according to conscience.

A small colony was first founded at Ferryland, Newfoundland, but finding the climate too severe, Lord Baltimore, after spending twenty-five thousand pounds of his own money there, prevailed upon King James's successor, King Charles I, to grant him a royal charter to lands in Virginia, which he had visited en route to England. Overcoming the opposition of Virginia Episcopalians who did not wish to share their colony with Roman Catholics, Lord Baltimore was granted a portion of Virginia that became the Maryland Palatinate.

Sir George Calvert projected an American colony, blessed by conciliation, where all men might cherish religious peace, foster industry, and promote unity. Before he could realize his dream he died, and his son, Cecilius, fell heir to his title and charter. Though in his twenties, the second Lord Baltimore undertook the colonization of a Roman Catholic community in Maryland plantations.

Sir Cecilius never visited Maryland but remained in England to defend the family charter and finance the project. His brother Leonard, second son of Sir George and his wife, Anne Wynne, was commissioned by him to carry on with the project. Leonard Calvert had gone with his father to Newfoundland and returning to England with some French prizes petitioned King Charles for letters of marque. Governor Calvert sailed from Cowes, Isle of Wight, on November 22, 1633, with three hundred persons in two small vessels, the "Ark" and the "Dove." After encountering rough weather, the expedition reached St. Clements (now Blackstone) Island in Maryland on March 25, 1634, and took "solemn possession of the country for our Savior and our Sovereign Lord the King of England."

Assisted by two commissioners, Governor Calvert established the seat of government at St. Mary's. He was commander in chief of armed forces, chief magistrate, chancellor, and chief justice, with power to grant patents for lands, locate ports, fairs, and markets. Supreme authority, however, remained with Sir Cecilius in London.

Governor Calvert had been instructed by his brother to give no offense to Protestant members living in the colony and to keep peace with the Episcopalians in Virginia. This liberal spirit led afterwards to the famous Act of Religious Toleration in Maryland. He gave early attention to the promotion of trade with the native Pascataways, a peaceable tribe, and sent the "Dove" with a cargo of corn to Boston to trade for codfish and notions. He called the first assembly of freemen to meet at St. Mary's. The laws which it passed he sent to their proprietor in England for approval; Sir Cecilius at first rejected them, and then wrote later, "I am persuaded."

In 1637 Governor Calvert headed a small force that reduced to submission a rebellious trading post on Kent Island, established in 1631 and claimed by William Claiborne of Virginia. The governor went to England in 1643 to confer with his brother. Shortly after his return, Claiborne, incited an insurrection of Protestants against Catholics and seized St. Mary's. Governor Calvert was forced to take refuge in Virginia but two years later returned to subdue the rebels, recover possession, and restore order.

Leonard Calvert died on June 9, 1647, leaving two children by his marriage to Anne Brent, who had died some time before. He named Thomas Green as his successor. In 1648 Sir Cecilius, at a time when England was having religious troubles of its own, appointed William Stone, a Protestant and friend of the English Parliament, governor of Maryland in the place of Green. He also reorganized the council so that half the members were Protestants. In order to preserve the principles of religious liberty, which he had consistently maintained in the province from the beginning, he embodied in the oath of office a provision that no inhabitant would be disturbed on account of his religious affiliations.

Governor Calvert and Sir Cecilius together "raised up a community unsurpassed in the western world for order, harmony, and general prosperity; and the scanty materials of its early history are in no small measure owing to the fact that, as history deals principally in wars and calamities, the happiness of the early inhabitants of Maryland left little to record."

H.C.

Jean Baptiste le Moyne de Bienville

FOUNDER of Mobile and the Father of New Orleans, Jean Baptiste le Moyne de Bienville spent twenty-six years in the American wilderness in the service of his country and his king.

Bienville was the eighth child of that remarkable Canadian family who did so much to change the map of the world. His father, Charles le Moyne, was ennobled by his king in 1676 for heroic service and granted the seigneury of Longueuil. There Jean Baptiste was born on February 23, 1680. His mother was Catherine Tierry. Both parents died when Bienville was young, and he aspired to emulate the career of Iberville, his illustrious brother who was nineteen years his senior. At the age of twelve he became gardemarine in the royal navy on his brother's vessel. In the naval battles in the north Atlantic and Hudson Bay in 1697 he so distinguished himself for bravery under British fire that he won the lifelong admiration and confidence of Iberville, who commanded the victorious frigate, "Pelican." Bienville was seriously wounded in the engagement.

When Iberville was commissioned by the king to relocate the mouth of the Mississippi, discovered by La Salle, and to colonize New France, Bienville at nineteen was put second in command under Sauvolle, the first governor of the French colony at Biloxi. Sauvolle, the first known victim of yellow fever in the province, soon died, and Bienville at twenty-one was in command.

Bienville saw seven years of active service in the French navy and participated in seven major sea engagements. He helped build Fort Maurepas at Old Biloxi, Fort Rosalie at Natchez, Fort St. Louis de la Mobile, posts at Ship Island, Baton Rouge, and on the lower Mississippi. He established the capital of the province at Mobile in 1702 and founded New Orleans in 1718. He established the town of Mobile on the present site of the city in 1711.

Bienville surveyed the country, charted its waters, and made maps that are still impressive for their accuracy. He explored the Red River as far as Natchitoches, mastered the language of various tribes, and waged wars against the Indians. After de Tonti and Iberville both died from yellow fever, the colony declined, and Bienville had to contend with enemies within and without. In 1712 the king granted Louisiana to a company founded by Antoine Crozat, who replaced commander Bienville with Governor Cadillac. But John Law later made Bienville governor of the province. Bienville was summoned to France in 1724 to answer charges against his administration, was degraded and deprived of all offices, but Louisiana having been brought to the verge of ruin by the inadequacy of its new governor and the rebellion of the Natchez, Bienville was implored to return in 1733 as royal governor and was received "with a joy and satisfaction without parallel." He went into voluntary retirement in 1743 and spent his declining years in Paris on a pension. He was decorated with the Cross of the Order of St. Louis.

In 1766, at the age of eighty-six, he came out of twenty-four years' obscurity and appeared before the minister with Jean Milhet from Louisiana to implore his government not to transfer "his province" to the king of Spain. He suffered the pain of seeing France cede the colony he had striven to build.

His patience and tenacity are without parallel in colonizing history. Despite an indifferent court, jealousies within the colony, and marauding tribes, he became a stabilizing influence in the development of the province.

In all his dealings with the Indians, in the councils of the tribes, and on the field of battle he fathomed the barbarian mind and matched its cunning. He once demanded the heads of Natchez chiefs responsible for the murder of French traders, and they were delivered to him. An eye for an eye, a life for a life, was in keeping with primitive experience, and even the most unfriendly Indians had profound respect for him.

His was no vain search for the fountain of youth, no conquest of strange tribes for silver or gold. A practical explorer, Bienville saw the productive soil of the new province and initiated the plantation idea. He introduced the first cattle, hogs, and chickens. He grew and shipped the first cotton and tobacco. He experimented with the cultivation of indigo and silk.

Bienville operated the first lumber mills in the province and exported the first timber and turpentine. He first saw the natural advantages of the ports of New Orleans and planned the deepening of the mouth of the Mississippi. He capitalized upon the commercial advantages of a rich valley and colonized a new dominion.

As one explores the fertile mind and follows in the bold footsteps of this intrepid Canadian in his pursuit of an idea, it is uncanny how true to his original design has become the final reality that surrounds us. His faith, his genius, his tenacity, his fortitude, and his frugality, even now, provide the underlying inspiration for industrial and agricultural development.

Sailor, soldier, explorer, colonizer, statesman, and patriot, Bienville was primarily the "Great Builder."

James Oglethorpe

NEAR the city hall on Bay Street, Savannah, Georgia, there is a marble seat bearing the inscription: "On this spot one hundred and seventy-three years ago James Oglethorpe, the founder of the colony, pitched his tent and here rested. . . ."

Oglethorpe and his bold band of thirty-five English families, including a few gentlemen who were in reduced circumstances, and sundry mechanics and indigent farmers, did pitch their tents there on February 12, 1733, and began building their log cabins on the bluff where now stands the city of Savannah.

James Oglethorpe, the father of Georgia, was born in London on December 21, 1698, of a very old and noble family. His father, Sir Theophilus, was a soldier under James II and went into temporary exile with that monarch. His mother was Lady Eleanor (Wall) Oglethorpe.

James was educated at Eaton and Corpus Christi College, Oxford. He held a succession of army commissions until 1715 when he migrated to Paris. In 1717 he took service under Prince Eugene of Savoy against the Turks. Upon his return to England, he succeeded his elder brother as incumbent of the family estate at Surrey and later emerged from his rural retreat as a candidate for Parliament, of which body he remained a member for thirty-two years. He was a high churchman, a deputy governor of the Royal African Society, a gentleman of position, independent means, and genuine piety.

While giving attention to the wretched condition of unfortunate debtors, who languished in London prisons in large numbers when the laws for the imprisonment of debtors were rigidly enforced, Oglethorpe projected a colony in the New World for the distressed. He sought new surroundings and new opportunities for the victims of depressed times, and his scheme met with public favor.

Parliament granted ten thousand pounds for the purpose, and additional funds were raised by subscription. King George II granted to Oglethorpe and nineteen other persons the territory that lies between the Savannah and Altamoha rivers, which was named Georgia in his honor. The colonists were not to be indentured servants, but proprietors; they were to have small farms which they could not sell. No strong liquors were to be allowed. No African slaves would be introduced. They were to have a clergyman and schoolmaster and all provisions for their sustenance for one year.

With Oglethorpe as their governor, the one hundred fifty colonists landed safely, and the foundations of the settlement known as Savannah were laid on Yamacraw bluff overlooking the river. Oglethorpe returned to England in April, 1734, taking with him the Yamacraw chief and several members of his family. During the visit he sent out one hundred fifty Scottish Highlanders as protection for the colonists and arrived a year later with five hundred additional emigrants, among whom were John and Charles Wesley who were to look after the spiritual needs of his company.

Oglethorpe established a fort on the Ogeechee called Fort Argyle and extended the boundary to build Fort Augusta near the falls of the Savannah River. Spanish outposts became a menace; so Oglethorpe hastened to England, where he raised a regiment of seven hundred men, obtained a grant of twenty thousand pounds, and in 1738 was back in Georgia. On a journey to make peace with the Creeks and Chickasaws he crossed the Ogeechee, the Oconee, the Ocmulgee, and the Flint and rested on the banks of the Chattahoochee, a distance of three hundred miles through unbroken wilderness.

War having been declared by England against Spain, Oglethorpe made an unsuccessful attack on St. Augustine in 1741; the following year Oglethorpe defeated the Spaniards when they attempted to drive the English out of their colonies in Georgia and South Carolina. Twelve years after Oglethorpe made his first expedition, he was charged with incompetency. A court-martial resulted in which the charges were dismissed as "frivolous . . . and without foundation."

The affairs in the new colony had by no means prospered. The general said the people were to blame; they said the fault was his. The silk culture did not pay, the wine-making project failed, and it is not surprising that the Wesley brothers could not control the thirst of the colonists under the circumstances.

General Oglethorpe did not return to Georgia. He married Elizabeth Wright, heiress of Crantham Hall, Essex, on September 15, 1744, and participated in a campaign against the Young Pretender that lead to another court-martial at which he was acquitted. He resigned his Georgia charter and retired from Parliament to his seat in Essex where as a quiet country gentleman, he entertained his many friends, among whom were Samuel Johnson, Boswell, Goldsmith, Horace Walpole, Edmund Burke, and the Georgian Ladies' Clubs. His death on June 30, 1785, closed a career full of promise and replete with achievement in the expansion of the British Empire beyond the seas. He founded an English colony from which he aimed to secure no gain and received none, but had the satisfaction of knowing he had laid the foundations of a proud and prosperous state.

H.C.

Etienne de Boré

THERE was general distress in Louisiana in 1795. High winds and insects had laid waste the crops of the country, and no satisfactory staple had been discovered to provide the colonists a ready market.

Rice and corn were produced for home consumption only. Eli Whitney's gin was not yet perfected, and the cultivation of cotton was still unprofitable. The manufacture of sugar had been abandoned since 1766 as unsuited to the climate and the production of indigo had yielded a harvest of disappointments.

This was the dark outlook in Louisiana when Jean Etienne de Boré abandoned the cultivation of indigo on his plantation just north of New Orleans in 1795 and against the advice of friends and family risked his all on sugar.

Iberville had imported the first sugar cane to the province from Santo Domingo in 1700, but it had turned yellow and sour before it could be seeded. The Jesuits brought cane to the colony in 1751, but being of a late maturing variety it failed to ripen for sugar-making purposes.

In 1758, Dubreuil, a wealthy planter, built the first sugar mill in the province, but the sugar he made turned back to syrup almost as fast as it was crystallized. It melted and leaked out of the barrels in which it was shipped to Europe. Some Louisiana syrup was used in the making of an inferior grade of rum called tafia for which there was little demand and in which there was no profit.

This was the unpromising picture when de Boré turned his lands to cane and in spite of the discouragement of neighbors and planters undertook his great experiment.

His crop was harvested, the kettles began to boil, and a dubious audience gathered about him on his plantation. When the sugar-maker cried, "It granulates!" the news was heralded from house to house and plantation to plantation; there was a new crop and a new industry for Louisiana.

De Boré realized twelve thousand dollars for his sugar crop the first year, and within five years the province was exporting a million pounds of sugar annually.

Etienne de Boré of noble Norman descent was born in the Illinois district of the Louisiana province on December 27, 1741. Members of his family had been high in the service of French kings for generations. His great-grandfather was *conseiller de roi* and postal official under Louis XIV. When Boré was four, his parents took him to France where he received his education.

On coming of age he joined the king's household troops in which only the nobility could qualify. In the tenth year of his service he accepted the command of a company of cavalry.

Prompted no doubt by his marriage to the daughter of Destrehan, former royal treasurer of the Louisiana colony under the French, he returned to the land of his birth where his wife had inherited much property.

De Boré settled on a plantation six miles above New Orleans where Audubon Park is now located and planted indigo which the insects repeatedly destroyed, while his slaves sickened of fever and died.

A number of expert sugar-makers were among the refugees who had escaped from Santo Domingo in the bloody massacres of 1791 and arrived in the province. de Boré determined to risk what there was left of his modest savings on sugar. As he prospered in his undertaking, his fame and his fortune expanded.

As de Boré's plantations spread, his Negroes, under semi-military supervision, increased in number and contentment. His great house, surrounded by a moat and ramparts, opened its doors with equal hospitality to the exiled brothers of Louis XVI and to the officers who served under General Jackson. In 1798 three princes of the royal blood found refuge from France's reign of terror on his estate. They were the great-great-grandsons of the Duke of Orleans, in honor of whom Bienville had named the city eighty years before.

It is one of the coincidences of history that one of these princes later became king and entertained the historian, Charles Gayarré, grandson of de Boré, in his royal palace.

When Louisiana was transferred from Spain to France in 1803, de Boré was appointed mayor of New Orleans and served in that capacity into the American period. He was then appointed a member of the first legislative Council, but, consistent with his opposition to the form of government imposed, he refused to serve and repaired to his plantation.

He died at the age of seventy-nine, requesting that his funeral be conducted in simplicity so that the money saved might be given to the Charity Hospital of New Orleans.

To the manor born, Etienne de Boré was a gentleman of character and culture. During his lifetime he was revered as the agricultural savior of his people, and his plantation was the social center of Louisiana.

The plantation system of his day was a comprehensive, self-sustaining unit and he presided over its operations with a discipline and benevolence that won the love and respect of his humblest slave.

De Boré pioneered in both agriculture and industry and balanced the two in the creation of an enterprise that lifted the hopes of a people crushed by economic despair. His discovery changed the economy of Louisiana as completely as Eli Whitney's cotton gin transformed the Deep South.

John Sevier

AT THE AGE of twenty-eight John Sevier moved with his wife and seven children from the Shenandoah Valley to the Watauga settlement in what is now east Tennessee. He was born near New Market, Virginia, on September 23, 1745, was married at sixteen, and engaged in farming and trading on his own.

Tennessee's most prominent pioneer and its first governor sprang from a restless strain; his grandfather had emigrated from France to England, and his father, Valentine Sevier, from London to Baltimore and then to the Shenandoah Valley. The eldest of seven children, by the time John Sevier reached the Watauga frontier in 1773, he was ready to offer courageous leadership. He took an active interest in the community, was a member of the local committee of safety in 1776, and urged that North Carolina extend its jurisdiction over the Watauga and Holston settlements. He was elected a representative to its provincial congress, which appointed him lieutenant colonel of militia.

In 1780 Sevier won undying fame by leading two hundred and forty men across the Smokies to the victory of the backwoodsmen over the British in the Battle of King's Mountain. A companion in arms said of him in this attack, "His eyes were flames of fire, and his words electric bolts crashing down the ranks of the enemy." The legislature presented him with a sword and pistol in appreciation of his heroism.

Immediately upon his return home he led an expedition against the Cherokees at Boyd's Creek to gain a reputation as a savage Indian fighter. In all he was the hero of some thirty-five battles and skirmishes. He fought against the British in the Carolinas and Georgia in 1781. About this time he married Catherine Sherrill, his first wife, Sarah Hawkins, having died. At the close of the Revolution he joined William Blount and others in a project for the establishment of a colony at Muscle Shoals.

East Tennessee, a political stepchild in that critical period, was undergoing rapid development, and its settlers clamored for independence. North Carolina first ceded the territory to the general government, then organized it into a district under her jurisdiction, but the people were determined to form a government of their own.

A convention was called in 1784, and the state of Franklin was formed with John Sevier as governor. Within sixty days after he took the oath of office he established a superior court and reorganized the militia. Later the charter of Martin Academy was confirmed, the first institution of higher learning west of the Alleghenies. Among peculiarities of the constitution of the state of Franklin was the provision that lawyers, doctors, and preachers were precluded from membership in the state legislature. During the short and precarious life of this phantom state, it dissolved in a feud between the Sevier and Tipton families in 1788. In its collapse much bitterness was engendered. Sevier was arrested, released on bail, and with friends fled to the mountains, a member of what the governor of North Carolina called "a lawless banditti."

At forty-three he seemed to have ended his spectacular career, but a year later he came out of seclusion to be elected to the North Carolina state senate. He was pardoned, seated, and made a brigadier general of the state militia. He rode into public favor on the burning issue of the ratification of the federal Constitution which he approved. When North Carolina finally ceded its western territory to Congress in 1791, Sevier was commissioned brigadier general under the federal government. He also served a brief term in Congress from North Carolina's western district, which became the Territory of Tennessee.

Sevier's purpose was to retire from the public scene. He fought his last Indian campaign in 1793. He speculated in land, supervised his plantations, and presided over his iron works, his store, and his slaves for the benefit of his wife and his eighteen children. In 1795 he patented sixty-six thousand acres of land in the Cumberland Valley. He was trustee of both Washington College in Tennessee (formerly Martin Academy) and Blount College (the University of Tennessee).

Sevier was elected the first governor of the state of Tennessee in 1796 and, with one term intervening, was six times chief executive. The choice was a natural one; he was a military hero, a dashing figure, an experienced public officer, and bound by ties of friendship to many families throughout the state. His late years were embittered by a quarrel with Andrew Jackson, a younger man rising to political power, who challenged the old veteran to a duel and defeated him in an election to the office of major general of the state militia.

After Sevier's retirement from the governorship, he was elected to the state senate and served in Congress from 1811 until his death on September 23, 1815. He died in a tent near Fort Decatur, Georgia, surrounded by soldiers and Indians. President Monroe had commissioned him to settle a boundary line with the Creeks. His remains were removed to Knoxville, where a monument was erected to his memory. Tennessee placed his statue in Statuary Hall in Washington, and Sevier County built a shrine to perpetuate his name.

William Dunbar

BORN near Elgin in Morayshire, Scotland, in 1749 in the manorhouse of Thunderson that had long sheltered his titled ancestors, William Dunbar became the foremost scholar and scientist of the American Southwest.

Educated at Glasgow he continued his advanced studies in mathematics and astronomy in London. Breaking under the strain, he sailed for the New World when he was twenty-two to regain his health and find fortune. He arrived in Pittsburgh in 1771 with goods valued at five thousand dollars to trade with the Indians.

In 1773 he formed a partnership with John Ross, a Scotch merchant of Philadelphia, to establish a plantation in the British province of West Florida. Dunbar came down the Ohio and Mississippi in a flatboat and repaired to Jamaica to buy slaves. At Pensacola, the seat of government, he secured title to lands near New Richmond, now Baton Rouge, Louisiana. But for the unsettled condition of the times, which repeatedly swept away his accumulations, he would have prospered there.

In 1775 he lost many of his slaves in an insurrection. In 1778 bandits raided his premises. In 1779 Spanish soldiers plundered his plantation, burned his fences, and destroyed his crops. In 1792, after twenty years spent at Baton Rouge, he opened up a plantation called The Forest and moved to his new location, nine miles south of Natchez.

At Baton Rouge, along with the cultivation of various crops, he had manufactured staves for the West Indies trade. From Natchez he shipped ochre to Boston. He grew tobacco, experimented with indigo, and pioneered in cotton.

He applied his knowledge of chemistry and mechanics to make his plantation a self-sustaining unit. He forged plows and harrows to his own patterns. He improved the cotton gin that was coming into common use to produce a cleaner staple. He introduced the square cotton bale as more suitable for packing and shipping and invented a screw-press, which he had forged in Philadelphia according to his original design at a cost of one thousand dollars. He extracted oil from cotton seed one hundred years before it was done commercially, described the product, and prophesied its future.

Dunbar prospered, purchased his partner's interest in the plantation, and pursued his scientific researches. He took the oath of allegiance to the American flag and became the friend of Thomas Jefferson with whom he carried on an active correspondence. He exchanged ideas with Sir William Herschell, David Rittenhouse, John Swift, and other well-known scientists within the states and abroad.

He was the friend and collaborator of Andrew Ellicott, an American civil engineer, who said of Dunbar that he was "a gentleman whose extensive information and scientific attainments would give him a distinguished rank in any place or any country."

Dunbar imported rare books from abroad, bought an expensive telescope, a microscope, surveying instruments, and other scientific equipment. He set up a chemical laboratory and an observatory at The Forest.

He served as astronomer to the Spanish crown, defined the boundary lines between the United States and Spain, and in 1798 was appointed surveyor general of the district of Natchez.

As a member of the American Philosophical Society, Dunbar made twelve lasting contributions to its published *Transactions.* He wrote about animal and plant life. He made the first meteorological report on the Mississippi Delta. He was first to observe an elliptical rainbow and offer a plausible explanation for it. He solved the problem of finding the longitude by a single observer without any knowledge of precise time. He advanced the theory that a profound calm exists within the vortex of a cyclone. He kept careful records of temperature, rainfall, barometric readings, and the rise and fall of the Mississippi River.

In 1804 President Jefferson appointed Dunbar to explore the Ouachita River country. He gave the first scientific account of Arkansas' Hot Springs and an analysis of their waters. He collected the various Indian vocabularies and made a study of the sign language by which remote tribes speaking different tongues could communicate.

Indifferent to politics, Dunbar was for a time, nevertheless, chief justice of the court of Quarter Sessions and later became a member of the territorial legislature of Mississippi.

He traced the courses of the stars, observed comets, and was happiest when the moon or sun was in eclipse. He uncovered the fossilized remains of a mammoth and wrote a scientific description of it. In his late years, he retired to his laboratory, his observatory, and his technical books.

In 1799 Daniel Clark, prominent merchant of New Orleans, wrote Thomas Jefferson of Dunbar, "For Science, Probity, & general information (he) is the first character in this part of the world."

When he died at The Forest in Natchez in 1810, he was survived by a widow and several children, each of whom was left financially independent. But Dunbar left a legacy far richer than worldly goods . . . he added to mankind's ever-increasing accumulation of useful information. In the field of scientific research he parted the curtain to a more abundant future.

Daniel Boone

KENTUCKY'S famed Indian fighter and pioneer was born in Bucks County, Pennsylvania, on November 2, 1734, the son of Squire and Sarah (Morgan) Boone. His grandfather, George Boone, a Quaker, weaver and farmer, brought his wife and eleven children to Philadelphia from Exeter, England, in 1717. His father, a blacksmith-farmer, moved his family to Buffalo Lick on the Yadkin in North Carolina in 1751.

Daniel, who had little if any schooling, became a hunter and trapper at the age of twelve. He went with a North Carolina contingent in General Braddock's expedition against the French in 1755 and met John Finley, a hunter, who fired him with tall tales of the Kentucky wilderness. He returned to his father's farm, married Rebecca Bryan, the young daughter of a neighbor, and built his own log cabin.

The gradual encroachments of civilization upon his solitude, depressed Daniel, who seeking a home went first to Florida and then answered that irresistible call, diagnosed in his day as "Kentucky fever." In 1767, with two companions, Boone reached a point in the present Floyd County. They returned to North Carolina, and two years later, a party consisting of Daniel, his brother-in-law John Stuart Finley, and three others traversed Cumberland Gap, entered the present Estill County, locating their quarters at Station Camp Creek. After many wild adventures experienced by Daniel and his brother Squire, who had joined the party, they returned to their home in 1771. Twice they had been captured by the Indians and escaped.

In 1775 Boone served as an agent of Colonel Richard Henderson, of the Transylvania Company, who planned a Kentucky colony. They reached what was to become Boonesborough where they built a stockade. Though Dr. Thomas Walker, discoverer of the Cumberland Gap, is credited with having ridden the first horse into Kentucky, Daniel Boone and his comrades herded the first horses into the Blue Grass Country.

Boone returned home to bring back his family and a party of young men and spent two years hunting, fighting Indians, and exploring. On the organization of Kentucky as a Virginia county, he was made captain of militia, later becoming a major. He was captured by the Shawnees, escaped, rendered service in the defense of Boonesborough, and spent a year in the East to return in 1779 with a new party of settlers. The repudiation by Virginia of Henderson's land titles sent Boone back east with twenty thousand dollars collected from the settlers for the purchase of land warrants, but he was robbed en route of the whole amount. Upon the division of Kentucky into three Virginia counties, Boone was made lieutenant colonel of Fayette county, a delegate to the legislature, and later sheriff and deputy surveyor.

Boone moved to Maysville in 1786 and was elected to the legislature. He had taken up a number of tracts of land which had been improperly entered, and following the first of a series of ejection suits he abandoned Kentucky in 1788 and moved to Point Pleasant, at the mouth of the Great Kanawha in what is now West Virginia. He was appointed lieutenant colonel and was chosen legislative delegate. Sometime in 1799, having lost the last of his Kentucky holdings, Boone moved to what is now Missouri, where his son, Daniel Morgan, had preceded him, and obtained a grant at the mouth of Femme Osage Creek. He was appointed magistrate of the district, a post he held until this French territory was ceded to the United States in the Louisiana Purchase. His title was voided by the United States land commissioners but after many delays was confirmed by Congress in 1814. Boone journeyed to Kentucky to pay off his debts, which he did in full, leaving him, according to tradition, only 50 cents. His wife died in 1813, and he spent his remaining years mostly in the home of his son Nathan, where he died at eighty-six.

Men could not agree upon Boone's appearance. To Audubon his stature "appeared gigantic"; Daniel Bryan, a kinsman, said he was "about five feet eight or nine inches." His head was large, his eyes blue, and his look sharp and alert. He had light hair, a wide mouth, thin lips and a Roman nose. In his prime, he was a man of great strength, quick of movement, and fleet of foot.

No biographer has been able to separate fiction from fact in the Boone legend. He first came to general notice in 1784 through John Filson's *Discovery, Settlement, and the Present State of Kentucke,* which had wide circulation in the United States and England. Lord Byron devoted seven stanzas to him in *Don Juan* to make him a worldwide celebrity, foremost figure of the American frontier. Historians acclaimed him the discoverer of Kentucky, its first settler, its chief protector, and Timothy Flint, in his biography, hailed him as "The First White Man of the West." None of these distinctions belonged to him, but he had his own claims to fame and posterity.

Boone had all the sterling qualities that fit him into the frontier, courage, fortitude and endurance. He was a skilled craftsman and an expert rifleman. He was intelligent, loyal, honest, and modest. He was a hunter to his last days and like all woodsmen was serene of spirit. Though often wronged he never sought revenge. It is for these reasons that he is revered as one of the nation's beloved heroes. An expert wood carver, he made his own coffin, which he kept under his bed, and after he died he was laid to rest in it.

William Richardson Davie

North Carolina's Revolutionary soldier and scholar, the founder of its state university, William Richardson Davie was an Englishman born in Egremont, near Whitehaven, Cumberlandshire, on June 20, 1756. He came to this country with his father in 1763 and was adopted by his maternal uncle, William Richardson, a Presbyterian clergyman, who lived near Catawba, South Carolina.

Young Davie attended Queen's Museum College at Charlotte and was graduated from Princeton with first honors in the autumn of 1776, having served for a short time with a party of his fellow students as a volunteer with the Revolutionary forces in New York. He began to study law at Salisbury, North Carolina, and was licensed to practice in 1780, but spent the greater part of the next seven years in the American Revolution.

Davie served a few months under General Allen Jones in the Camden region. He then helped organize a company of dragoons and was commissioned lieutenant, captain, and then major. Serving with Pulaski's legion, he was seriously wounded in the thigh at the battle of Stono Ferry, near Charleston. After a slow recovery, he raised another troop, partly equipping it from the small estate bequeathed to him by his uncle. Davie kept the patriot cause alive in western North Carolina where loyalists were numerous. He was in the battles of Hanging Rock and Rocky Mount, fought a reckless but brilliant rear guard action at Charlotte on September 26, 1780, to save valuable equipment for Gates in his flight from Camden, and continued to harass Cornwallis until the latter retreated into South Carolina.

Davie, now a colonel, sought a separate command but was enlisted by General Green to serve as commissary general for the Carolina campaign. Though he detested his assignment and was almost without funds, he succeeded in feeding Green's army and the state militia to the general's satisfaction.

After the war Davie settled at Halifax, North Carolina, and in 1782 he married Sarah Jones, daughter of General Allen Jones, his old commander; she brought him a fine farm as a dowry and bore him six children. Davie rode the circuits of the state for fifteen years in the practice of law thus attaining a position of eminence. Tall, eloquent, commanding, sonorous in speech with a flowing style, he charmed juries and enraptured audiences. As a leading advocate, he served almost continuously in the legislature of North Carolina from 1786 to 1798.

Davie's contributions to the state and to the young republic were substantial. He was a member of the convention that framed the federal constitution, favoring equal representation of the states in the national senate and the enumeration of slaves in assigning representatives to the south. Called home because of illness, he was not a signer of the Constitution, but he was one of its earnest defenders in the North Carolina convention that followed.

More than any one else Davie was responsible for the action taken in the state legislature ordering the revision and codification of the laws. He was influential in securing the cession of the present state of Tennessee to the Union and served three times as commissioner in settling boundary disputes between the Carolinas. He was elected governor of the state in 1799, but before he could complete his term, he was sent by President Adams as a peace commissioner to France.

Davie was chiefly responsible for the establishment and location of the University of North Carolina, which was authorized by the legislature in 1789. The erection of its buildings, the choice of its professors, and the arrangement of its studies received his personal attention. He saw to it that its elastic curriculum included literary and social studies as well as the familiar mathematics and classics. The university, in turn, awarded him its first honorary degree and dubbed him "father," years before Jefferson founded the University of Virginia.

Davie's singular achievements are all the more remarkable when it is realized that he was not a Jefferson Democrat in a thoroughly Democratic state. He favored the election of senators and presidential electors by the legislature. Though he negotiated a treaty with the Tuscarora Indians in 1802, under presidential appointment, he waived aside all political overtures from "that man" Jefferson.

In 1803 Davie was an unsuccessful candidate for Congress. He refused either to modify his aristocratic habits or to solicit personally for votes. He believed that the office should seek the man, not the man the office. When he was defeated by the Jefferson-Macon combination, he became thoroughly disgusted with politics.

Saddened by the death of his wife, he retired in 1805 to his plantation Tivoli on the Catawba River, in Lancaster County, North Carolina, to enjoy his farm, friends, horses, and books. There he served as the first president of the South Carolina Agricultural Society and cultivated his land until he died on November 29, 1820. A plantation statesman, he did much to lay the foundation for an economy and culture of independence and freedom . . . an aristocracy of the soil.

Andrew Jackson

CHILD of adversity, Andrew Jackson was born in 1767 of Irish parents who had migrated to the Carolinas in 1765. His father died a few weeks before he was born. His mother and two brothers were victims of the American Revolution.

Alone in the world at the age of fourteen, Andrew was a veteran in his own right. He saw service in the battle of Hanging Rock, suffered smallpox and hunger in prison, and wore the scars from the saber of a British officer whose muddy boots he refused to clean.

At sixteen, untutored, he attempted to teach school. At eighteen, untamed, he managed to read enough law, between horse races, cockfights, drinking sprees and duels, to hang out his shingle at Jonesboro, Tennessee, a frontier settlement. At Nashville he met and wooed Rachel, the abandoned wife of a jealous husband; she was to bring him forty years of joy and grief. They married at Natchez in 1781.

At twenty-one he was public prosecutor for a turbulent district that was to become Tennessee. He helped frame the new state's constitution, became its first representative in Congress, its United States senator, and a judge of its Supreme Court.

When war was declared against Great Britain in 1812, Jackson led 2,007 volunteers to Natchez, returned to Nashville, fought a duel, was severely wounded, and with his fractured arm in a sling took the field against the Creeks. He closed this arduous campaign in a decisive victory at the battle of Horseshoe Bend in present Alabama and was made major general in the regular army in command of the Department of the South. Because of "Andy's" endurance in his march from Natchez to Nashville, he was named "Old Hickory" by his soldiers.

In the battle of New Orleans, with 5,500 militiamen, Creoles, Negroes, and pirates, he crushed an army of 10,000 seasoned soldiers. The British counted 2,600 dead; Jackson's losses were only eight killed and thirteen wounded. Though the battle was fought after peace with Britain had been declared, it gave world-wide prestige to American arms and made Jackson a national hero.

In 1818 Jackson invaded Spanish Florida where he made war upon the Seminoles and captured Pensacola. Following the purchase of Florida, Jackson was appointed its first governor by President Monroe. He soon resigned to become United States senator from Tennessee again. In 1828 he was elected President of the United States on the Democratic ticket and was re-elected in 1832.

Between his military exploits and political campaigns he fought several duels and developed the broad acres that surrounded The Hermitage, his plantation retreat near Nashville.

A persistent fighter, a man of strong loves and hot hates, he enjoyed a political career as tempestuous as his conflicts upon the field of battle. He turned Washington upside down by introducing the political spoils system, and the capital city swarmed with new faces. He used the veto power with a vengeance and destroyed the Bank of the United States which had become a political issue. He humbled the rich and the arrogant, eclipsed the power and influence of Webster, Clay, and Calhoun, and initiated a democracy in fact as well as name.

Jackson paid off the national debt, distributed surplus revenues to the several states, collected a five million dollar obligation from France by employing pressure, and succeeded so well in foreign affairs that America won the respect of the world.

He opposed the use of federal funds for state projects, and defended states' rights while he proclaimed the preservation of the Union.

Racked through life by dysentery and tuberculosis, suffering many wounds, Andrew Jackson carried his heaviest burden in his heart.

He had unwittingly married Rachel at Natchez before her divorce had been legally granted, and his political opponents made capital of it. Rachel, like Andrew, was a product of the frontier. She possessed few of the refinements of polite society, but she was the only woman he ever loved, and for forty years he kept his dueling pistols loaded for any man who dared speak evil of her. Her virtue was above reproach, and her devotion to him complete. Three times she sent him away to war, and twice he returned wounded to be nursed to health again.

When during the first presidential campaign the gossips made capital of her irregular marriage, she died with a broken heart. The great general walked alone after that and knew little peace until his death in 1845. His grave, beside that of Rachel in the garden at The Hermitage, is a shrine where patriots pay homage to his memory.

Andrew Jackson possessed to a lofty degree the two elements essential to a successful general or chief executive, initiative and leadership. A man of steel and spirit, tall, lean, and strong, with an explosive temperament, he was the republic's most popular and picturesque personality during the period that separates the lives of Washington and Lincoln. Fearless, loyal, practical, and aggressive, colossal in his integrity, he conquered the heart of the world. With sandy-colored hair, flaming blue eyes, a tongue that spit words of liquid fire, his meteoric and amazing career blazed its way into immortality. He lifted the republic to a new glory and the eyes of mankind to new horizons.

H.C.

Pushmataha

NOTHING is known of the strange origin of the warrior Pushmataha, except that he first saw the sun his tribe worshipped somewhere near the sacred city of Naniah Waiya in what is now Winston County, Mississippi, in about 1764.

Often asked about his birth he was wont to say, "I had no father, no mother, no brother, no sister. The winds howled, the rain fell, the thunder roared and the lightning flashed; an oak tree was shivered, and from its splinters stepped forth Pushmataha."

His ashes lie in the Congressional Cemetery of the city of Washington, with other of our glorious dead. This simple epitaph is inscribed upon the shaft that marks his resting place: "Pushmataha, a Choctaw Chief, lies here. This monument to his memory is erected by his brother chiefs. . . . Pushmataha was a warrior of great distinction. He was wise in council, eloquent in an extraordinary degree; and on all occasions, and under all circumstances, the white man's friend. He died in Washington, on the 24th day of December, 1824, of the croup, in the sixtieth year of his life."

At about the age of twenty, escaping from an engagement with the Collegeheahs west of the Mississippi, Pushmataha found refuge in a Spanish settlement where he lived for five years.

He returned to the Red River four times for revenge upon the Collegeheahs, bringing back to his people the scalps of his victims. Some time before 1812 a party of Creeks burned the house of Pushmataha while he was away, and again and again he waged war upon the Creeks.

In the Creek War, primarily fought in the Mississippi Territory, he led a band of five hundred Choctaw braves against the British and their Indian allies. In a war in which Sam Houston, David Crockett, and Andrew Jackson of Tennessee, and F. L. Claiborne, Thomas Hinds, and Sam Dale of Mississippi made history, Pushmataha gave a good account of himself. Following this war, General Claiborne bought Pushmataha a uniform of regimentals, with gold epaulettes, a sword, and silver spurs, and he was breveted a brigadier general in the United States Army.

Pushmataha was one of the two chiefs who represented the Choctaw Nation at the all important Treaty of Doak's Stand in 1820, ceding to Mississippi five and a half million acres out of which nine counties in the heart of the state were carved. He also signed the treaty of Mount Dexter that ceded a large tract of land to Alabama and Mississippi.

In 1824 Pushmataha led a delegation of Choctaw chiefs to Washington, where he had once gone as a younger man to see Thomas Jefferson. His visit to Washington coincided with the triumphant tour of General Lafayette. In speaking before that venerable Frenchman, the chief of the Choctaws, said, "Nearly fifty snows have melted since you drew the sword as a companion of Washington. With him you fought the enemies of America. You . . . proved yourself a warrior. . . . We have heard these things told in our distant villages and . . . longed to see you."

Pushmataha was received by President James Monroe and Secretary of War John C. Calhoun and was royally entertained by others. Unaccustomed to the rich food and strange drinks in such abundance, he fell sick and never recovered.

While ill he spoke to his warriors, gathered around him, "I shall die, but you will return to our brethren. As you go along the paths you will see the flowers, and hear the birds sing, but Pushmataha will see them and hear them no more. When you shall come to your home, they will ask you, 'Where is Pushmataha?' and you will say, 'He is no more.' They will hear the tidings like the sound of the fall of a mighty oak in the stillness of the woods."

President Monroe sent a medal to his eldest son as a tribute to his father's memory, and Senator John Randolph of Virginia eulogized him in the Senate.

He was the most picturesque man the Choctaw Nation ever produced. Colorful, courageous, he was a strange mixture of the savage and the statesman. He stood six feet two, was Herculean in strength, and in single combat never met his equal. The Choctaw chiefs were chosen because of their valor in war or eloquence in council; Pushmataha was doubly qualified.

He knew Spanish, some French, used fluent English, but when he spoke in his mother tongue he was the personification of all the elements. Those who heard him woo his audience with seductive phrases and utter explosive words of fierce defiance testify that only Tecumseh, the great Shawnee chief, could match his eloquence. Majestic in his barbarian mien, animated in voice and gesture, he brought forth a flow of words that was as the thunder of the clouds, the murmur of rustling leaves, the patter of falling rain. Andrew Jackson said that "Push," as he affectionately called him, was "the greatest and the bravest Indian I have ever known."

When Senator Jackson rushed to the bedside of the dying chief, he asked, "Warrior, what is your wish?" And Pushmataha answered, "When I am dead, fire the big guns over me." His funeral procession was more than a mile in length. He was given a military burial, and the big guns were fired.

Great hunter, brave warrior, Choctaw chief, matchless orator and fearless fighter, Pushmataha was proud that neither he nor his people ever "drew bows against the United States."

H.O.

William C.C. Claiborne

HE DIED at forty-two when the careers of most men have just begun; yet, William Charles Coles Claiborne had already directed the fortunes of four states and helped change the course of an empire.

A son of William and Mary (Leigh) Claiborne, he was born in Sussex County, Virginia, in 1775. His formal education was limited to brief periods at Richmond Academy and William and Mary College.

A precocious child, William was employed as a clerk in the national House of Representatives at sixteen; he read law on the side. In 1795, at the age of twenty, he hung out his shingle in Tennessee. At twenty-one he was a delegate to that state's first constitutional convention, was elevated to the State Supreme Court, and at twenty-two represened Tennessee in the national Congress, completing Andrew Jackson's unexpired term and serving one other. President Thomas Jefferson commissioned him when he was twenty-six Governor of the Mississippi Territory, which embraced Alabama, a region torn by internal strife and external fears. There was a rumor that Spain was preparing to return the Province of Louisiana to France which could precipitate British intervention. This, along with the Aaron Burr excitement, kept the border in a panic.

It was into this political turmoil that a lad, burning with the patriotic fires of a new nationalism, was sent to establish peace. Claiborne organized a militia, established Jefferson College, opened a mail route along the Natchez Trace, surveyed boundaries, settled land claims, established a trading house and fort at St. Stephens on the Tombigbee, pacified the Indians, reconciled feuds, and won the confidence of the people.

With the transfer of Louisiana from Spain to France and its simultaneous purchase by the United States, Claiborne was appointed by the President as one of the commissioners to receive this vast domain for his country.

At twenty-eight he was, at one and the same time, Governor of the Mississippi Territory and Governor General of the Province of Louisiana, receiving the latter commission in 1805.

His first wife, Eliza W. Lewis of Nashville, died just one year before he received his appointment as governor. His second wife, Clarissa Duralde, and his third wife, Suzette Bosque, were of prominent Creole families. These domestic alliances did much to remove initial handicaps under which the young American executive suffered in administering an alien rule among a resentful people.

In 1812, when Louisiana was admitted as a state, he became its first governor and was elected to the United States Senate in 1817. He died within the year, just as he was on the threshold of a national career.

The frontier was in a perilous plight when Tennessee, Louisiana, Mississippi, and Alabama were taking form. Even after the Louisiana purchase there remained some doubt as to which of the world powers would ultimately embrace this vast and unpeopled empire. England knocked at the gates of New Orleans, to be met by Andrew Jackson in a battle that was fought after the end of the War of 1812, and during Claiborne's incumbency.

The plots and schemes of men ran rank and thick when Claiborne assumed executive, legislative, and judicial authority. His intensive nationalism had swept from his native Virginia across Tennessee, Mississippi, and Alabama to Louisiana. His influence with Thomas Jefferson may have been the deciding factor in the Louisiana Purchase, for he, an expansionist, often begged the federal government to let him extend the nation's boundaries to the sea.

Schooled in statecraft, Claiborne implanted the republican ideal in far places and prepared a people for self-government. "Rely upon it, my friend," he wrote, "that the danger that menaces us, and our institutions, in the future, is from executive interference, and its tendency to usurp and accumulate power."

A man of culture, common sense, and character, he was primarily a great peacemaker. Criticized on one occasion for an appointment, he said, "The circumstance of his not having been born an American cannot be received by me as an objection. He was strongly recommended as a man of honor, probity and good character."

He gave the best he had within him and accepted men for their real worth. Thus it was that his political personality brought order out of a chaotic community and determined to a large degree the destinies of this republic. He believed that no group could prosper divided against itself, and at a time when we were at loose ends he labored for a united people. Through him Virginia made its contribution to the Americanization of Louisiana.

Before he had hardly passed the meridian of a useful life, William C.C. Claiborne had served as justice of the State Supreme Court and as United States representative from Tennessee, as territorial governor of Mississippi and Louisiana, and as governor of Louisiana and as its senator. As pacemaker and peacemaker, he helped change the course of an empire and consolidate its expanding domains.

H.C.

Sequoyah

THE EXACT time, place, and circumstances of Sequoyah's birth and death are unknown. He was born somewhere in the old Cherokee country, probably in East Tennessee, about 1770.

His mother was a Cherokee. Nothing is known of his father except that he was a white man whose name was Guess, that he spoke English, and abandoned Sequoyah's mother before Sequoyah was born.

Sequoyah spent his childhood on an eight-acre farm. An early attack of "white swelling" left him lame for life. Upon the death of his mother he married Sallie, a Cherokee, and moved to Wills Valley in Alabama where he operated a trading post.

Sequoyah's reputation grew with his trade. Congenial and convivial, his trading post became a popular gathering place. After having become a dissolute drunkard, losing both goods and credit, he abruptly reformed, and influenced the Council to pass prohibition measures. He embraced neither the pagan faith of his mother nor the religion of the whites. The cause of the Cherokees was his only purpose. Following his reform, Sequoyah gave expression to his talents as a blacksmith, silversmith, and artist of charcoal sketches.

His interest in written words was first aroused by letters taken from the pockets of captive soldiers in an engagement against the whites in Indiana in 1791. These so-called "talking leaves" were much discussed and he was often ridiculed for his resolution to invent a similar scheme of communication for the Cherokees.

In 1809 he turned seriously to the task of his "talking leaves." Neglecting field and family, he spent most of twelve years on his unique alphabet. His original plan to create a character for each word in the language was abandoned to provide a symbol for every one of the eighty-five sounds in Cherokee. While he borrowed letters from the English and Greek alphabets, he knew no other written language than his own, and without a confusion of tongues, produced a syllabary so simple that it could be easily mastered.

His daughter Ahyoka, age six, was his first pupil. When they were tried under the Cherokee law for being filled with the evil spirit, they were separated by the warriors and forced to communicate by the use of their written signs. Amazed to find that they "could make the paper talk," the warriors became absorbed in the invention and within a week returned to their people reading and writing.

Old and young labored with the alphabet before their camp fires while they subdued their ancient superstitions and ushered in a renaissance of learning and culture. The Cherokees came rapidly and richly into their intellectual inheritance.

Sequoyah's achievement has no parallel in history. A primeval tongue, tuned to the song of birds and the sounds of night, was preserved for posterity in all its primitive and poetic power. A little lame, gray-eyed, sallow-faced man had fired bits of charcoal and scrolls of bark and skin with the spark of his genius.

Sequoyah took his syllabary to the western Cherokees in Arkansas where he ran a blacksmith shop and worked salt mines. He soon had the separated branches of the tribe corresponding.

In 1825 the Council declared his syllabary official and raised funds to establish a printing plant. Sequoyahan type was cast in Boston in 1827, and in 1828 the first issue of the *Cherokee Phoenix,* a weekly newspaper, was published at New Echota. The constitution of the Cherokees and the New Testament were printed in Cherokee.

Sequoyah was a member of the General Council of the western Cherokees in 1828 and a delegate to Washington to make the treaty by which the Cherokees exchanged their lands in Arkansas for lands in Oklahoma. Under this treaty he was given salt mines and made his home at Skin Bayou. In 1839 the eastern and western Cherokees were reunited and Sequoyah was chosen president of the western branch.

In planning the creation of an intertribal tongue and history of the Indian race, Sequoyah made many excursions among the western tribes. He left Oklahoma in 1842 on his last patriotic expedition. At least seventy-two, he set out with his son Tessy and a guide named Worm to locate the Cherokees who had fled the warring Osages into Old Mexico. The expedition was one of hardship and exposure, and Sequoyah, becoming too ill to travel, was left alone in the woods for weeks while his son and guide sought the lost colony. When the Cherokees were found, Sequoyah could not prevail upon them to move to the Territory. He died in Mexico in 1843. The location of his grave is unknown.

It is not surprising that so colorful and original a personality lives in both legend and history. Unlettered, Sequoyah invented an alphabet, untutored, he became a teacher; self-taught, he became the intellectual leader of a proud and patriotic people.

His spirit had hardly returned to his fathers when white men recognized his genius. Endlicher, the Austrian botanist, classified the giant Redwoods of California, *Sequoyah Gigantea.* In 1851 the Cherokee Council renamed Skin Bayou the Sequoyah District. In 1917, Oklahoma placed a bronze statue of him in Statuary Hall in the Capitol at Washington. The one-room log cabin in which he last lived, ten miles northeast of Sallisaw, has been preserved within the stone walls of a monumental structure as a perpetual shrine to the memory of the Cherokee seer and servant.

Samuel Dale

Born in Rockbridge County, Virginia, in 1772, of Scotch-Irish ancestry, Samuel Dale was a child of the frontier. His parents, natives of Pennsylvania, moved to Virginia soon after their marriage. Keeping pace with the expanding border, they settled in Green County, Georgia, where they both died in 1792, leaving to Samuel the responsibility of the eight younger children.

In 1793, at twenty-one, he was a federal scout in Georgia, running a wagon line for the transportation of homeseekers to the Mississippi Territory and carrying on trade with the Indians.

In 1803 he became a guide to mark out a highway through the Cherokee Nation to the Mississippi River. He set up a trading post, exchanging merchandise for tallow, hides, and pelts.

In 1812 he attended the Council of Took-a-batcha in Georgia and heard Tecumseh, the great Shawnee chief, stir the ire of five thousand braves as he urged them to drive the white invaders into the sea.

Engaged in the transportation of settlers into the Mississippi Territory while the Creeks went on the warpath and at the time the War of 1812 with Great Britain was declared, he volunteered.

The trail that led from Pensacola to Holy Ground, the Creeks' sacred city, was called Wolf-Path over which they received supplies. Where this trail crossed Burnt Corn Creek, Big Sam, as Dale was affectionately called by the Indians, was wounded in a skirmish.

Sam Dale occupied Fort Madison, a strategic outpost, and evolved a crude but effective system of night illumination with pine-knot faggots suspended on trace-chains between tall poles. He covered his block houses with plastered clay to resist the Indians' torches and flaming arrows, and he put the women of the fort into men's pants to fool the spies. Big Sam was the outstanding hero in a desperate conflict in canoes, in which he destroyed nine braves single handed in mid stream.

He was with the Mississippi Dragons and the Tennessee Volunteers in the destruction of the Holy City in which Andrew Jackson, General Claiborne, Sam Houston, and David Crockett took active part. In the course of that war Sam Dale and his men often lived on acorns, hickory nuts, rats, and horse meat.

When Andrew Jackson was in the midst of the Battle of New Orleans, Sam Dale made his record ride from Georgia to the Plain of Chalmette in eight days, seven hundred miles on his pony, Paddy, delivering important messages from the War Department.

In 1817 Sam Dale was elected as a delegate to the convention called to divide the Mississippi Territory, the eastern half to become Alabama. He was a delegate to the first Alabama general assembly and served two terms in the state legislature. He was made colonel of militia to suppress outlaws, and was memorialized by legislative enactment and made brigadier general for life with pay.

He was on the committee that received General Lafayette at Chattahoochee on his visit to Alabama, and he was appointed by the United States Secretary of War to remove the Choctaws of Mississippi to the Indian Territory after the Treaty of Dancing Rabbit.

In 1831 he settled on a farm in Lauderdale County and was the county's first representative in the legislature of Mississippi.

He was sumptuously entertained by President Andrew Jackson in Washington in 1832. On another occasion he visited Washington to seek compensation for corn and other supplies he had furnished federal troops during the War of 1812. Prominent men were cordial to him, but the "third auditor" to whom he was referred, proved, as Dale said "impracticable. . . . I would rather encounter half a dozen Indians . . . he worried me much and I left the matter unsettled." The claim was never paid.

Six feet two, rawboned, steel-spined, and fleet of foot, frontiersman, scout, guide, trader, patriot, Indian fighter, and farmer . . . few pioneers blazed wider trails through the American wilderness.

He was without book learning, but he had "the knowledge that passeth all understanding." He could fathom the character of a man by a careless gesture and had an uncanny sense of direction that guided him through trackless space.

He had the simple faith of a child and the strength of a giant. In his three score years and six, with all the tall tales current on a rough frontier, he was never credited with a dirty deed.

Like the Indians, for whom he had respect and a warm affection, he was a man of sentiment; he loved his country and had a deep reverence for the soil that enshrined his dead. As a lonely old man he sought the graves of his parents in Virginia which were covered with briars, and he wept unashamed "over their honest dust."

Loyal, kind, fierce, and fearless, he sleeps in a sequestered spot in a pine thicket near his home where he died in 1841, identified by a plain marker, his monument the forest and the everlasting hills.

William Harris Crawford

He was striking in appearance, of large, muscular build, well proportioned, and six feet three inches tall. Erect in carriage, affable in deportment, modest in dress, simple in his tastes, brilliant of mind, and free of penuriousness, William Harris Crawford was one of Georgia's most enlightened leaders.

He was descended from Thomas Crawford, who immigrated from Scotland to Virgina in 1643. The son of Joel Crawford and Fannie (Harris) Crawford, William, one of eleven children, was born in Amherst County, Virginia on February 24, 1772. During the Revolution, the family moved to South Carolina and then to what is now Columbia County, Georgia.

His father died when William was sixteen, and he struggled for an education while helping to support a large family. He attended the typical "field schools," much of the time learning by teaching. He attended Carmel Academy under the talented Reverend Moses Waddell who instilled within him, as he had in John C. Calhoun and others, a thirst for knowledge. He taught his way through Richmond Academy in Augusta as student and instructor, studied law, and began practice at Lexington, where he married Susanna Giradin in 1804, and near which he built Woodlawn. Crawford was engaged for seven years before he could afford to marry. As he prospered, he expanded Woodlawn into a plantation and at his death on September 15, 1834, was able to leave each of his eight children a generous division of his property and several slaves.

Crawford was elected to the state legislature in 1803. Not prone to pick quarrels but prompt to resist insults he became involved in a duel with Peter L. Van Allen, which was instigated by John Clarke, a political opponent. He killed his antagonist and was later challenged by Clarke who proposed that the combatants advance to a distance of five paces and continue to exchange shots until one of them could not stand, kneel, or sit. Crawford suffered a bullet-shattered wrist and became permanently crippled.

At thirty-five he was elected to fill a vacancy in the United States Senate, where his gigantic stature, open countenance, diligent endeavors, engaging affability, along with a fund of entertaining anecdotes, marked him for immediate success. He impressed his colleagues as having a mind of his own by opposing Henry Clay on the question of the renewal of the National Bank charter, and by his "Delphic Oracle" speech, in which he censored President Madison for ambiguities in his message on military preparation.

Honors crowded upon Crawford. He was elected president pro tempore of the Senate and declined the office of Secretary of War, only to accept appointment in 1813 as minister to France. During a homeward voyage, he was made Secretary of War, and then upon his arrival Secretary of the Treasury that his financial talents might be better utilized.

In 1816 Crawford was the choice of most of the Democratic-Republicans in Washington for the Presidency, but James Monroe was Madison's favorite. Monroe felt that as the last of the Revolutionary worthies he had a claim to the Presidency and that Crawford, being young, could wait. Crawford let it be known that his own feelings would not permit him to oppose Monroe, who won a second term. By 1823, the Federalist party had collapsed, and Crawford was easily the foremost presidential aspirant, being warmly supported by Randolph, Macon, Madison, and Van Buren. His group was often styled "the Radicals" because they clung to the rights of the states after most others had become nationalists.

But Crawford's old dueling enemy, John Clarke, then governor of Georgia, agitated opposition until the field was full of rivals, including Adams, Clay, Jackson, and Calhoun. However, Crawford's prospects continued good until the fall of 1823, when he was stricken with paralysis. For a year and a half he lay in seclusion, almost blind, incapacitated, but slowly improving. The election returned Crawford as a poor third among four surviving candidates. With no one elected, under the Constitutional provision, the choice was thrown into the House of Representatives, and Adams was elected.

Crawford was again offered the Treasury position which he declined because of ill health. He returned to Georgia, where he found little solace on the judge's bench of the state circuit court upon which his Georgia devotees placed him in 1827. Crippled in body and in mind, he nursed to the last a hopeless ambition for the White House, but his following had scattered to form new allegiances. He died on September 15, 1834.

Crawford was Secretary of the Treasury at a critical time. A sparsely settled, undeveloped country was struggling to overcome the losses of a severe and expensive war with England. A wide and exposed frontier had to be protected. Commerce at home and abroad was at a low ebb, the country's currency was depreciated, and national bankruptcy threatened. Under two presidents, for ten years, Crawford served as Secretary of the Treasury and had much to do with maintaining the solvency of the young republic. Napoleon said that he was one of the ablest men he ever met. Through the toils and turmoils and feuding animosities of thirty years of political strife, his bitterest foes found no stain upon his escutcheon, and posterity still proclaims the wisdom of his statesmanship.

Henry Clay

HENRY CLAY was born in Hanover County, Virginia, on April 12, 1777, the son of John Clay, a country Baptist preacher, and Elizabeth (Hudson) Clay. He was one of eight children and was four years old when his father died, leaving as a legacy a well-worn copy of the Holy Scriptures and a good name. A self-educated scholar, Clay's schooling was limited to three short terms in a community called The Slashes.

When he was fourteen, his mother remarried, and the family moved to Richmond where Henry was placed in a small retail store. He later secured work with the Clerk of the High Court of Chancery and then began the study of law with Attorney-General Robert Brooke. He obtained a license to practice and moved to Lexington, Kentucky, then the outstanding city of all the west in culture and influence.

Clay soon enjoyed a lucrative practice. His speeches advocating the gradual emancipation of the slaves in the state astonished his hearers by their boldness and force. He married Lucretia Hart in 1799, and they had eleven children. He was a member of the convention which revised the state constitution in 1803, and he was elected to the state legislature.

Clay was appointed to a seat in the Senate in 1806 to serve out an unexpired term, was returned to the state legislature, elected speaker, and in 1809 was elected to the Senate. When his Senate term expired, he was elected to the House and immediately on taking his seat was elected Speaker. His vigorous course against Britain's blockade policy did much to precipitate the War of 1812. In 1814, he was one of the commissioners Madison sent to negotiate a treaty of peace with Britain at Ghent. Upon his return, he was reëlected to the Congress, and was again made Speaker, and he held these offices until 1821, when he refused to stand for election.

Clay was offered and refused many official posts; Madison tendered him the ministry to Russia and the secretaryship of war; Monroe offered him the ministry to England and the secretaryship of war. Clay's loyal political and personal following stirred in him an ambition to become president, which he pursued to his dying day with unending heartaches. His impetuosity precipitated him into many conflicts, and he fought several duels, one with John Randolph of Virginia. He incurred the most momentous enmity of his life when he left the Speaker's chair to attack Andrew Jackson for his invasion of Florida. Jackson never forgave him.

Clay was a candidate for the Presidency in 1824, but John Quincy Adams was chosen, in an election that was thrown into the House. He served in Adams' cabinet as Secretary of State and then was reëlected to the Senate. He was unanimously nominated by the Whigs for president in 1832, but Jackson was elected. He then temporarily retired to his Ashland home, with its six hundred acres and fifty slaves, which for fifty years was a gathering place for political pilgrims.

Clay fully expected to be nominated by the Whigs in 1840, but Harrison was chosen and elected, and Clay rejected an offer of the secretaryship of state. He resigned his position in the Senate in 1842 and delivered a farewell address. His reception in Kentucky was so cordial that it constituted a mandate for the presidency in 1844. He was nominated, but the Democrats won with Polk. Never before nor since has the defeat of any presidential nominee in the country been so crushing to a candidate or to his constituency.

Polk's election brought on the annexation of Texas and war with Mexico, which Clay opposed. His favorite son, Henry, was killed at Buena Vista. Clay was received with such enthusiasm in appearances in the East that his nomination in 1848 on the Whig ticket was demanded by many, but Zachary Taylor was nominated and elected. When the problems growing out of the Mexican War and the sectional struggle had nearly driven the republic to disunion, Clay was returned to the Senate in 1849. There he made his final effort to save the Union, begging the radicals, both North and South, to abandon a course which could only lead to war. His series of resolutions known as the Compromise of 1850 definitely delayed the Civil War ten years and won for him the well-deserved sobriquet, The Great Pacificator.

Clay returned home by way of Cuba where he had gone to find relief from a cough. Back in Washington, determined to die in the service of his country, death closed his incomparable career in 1852.

In appearance Clay was unattractive . . . tall, homely, with a high forehead, gray eyes, and a big mouth. But he possessed to a high degree the personal magnetism to win and hold the intense devotion of men. When his home was in danger of being sold for his debts, unknown friends throughout the land raised fifty thousand dollars to satisfy his creditors.

He had a mellow speaking voice and in debate was the personification of grace and skill. By sheer eloquence and logic his grasp upon the imagination of others caused him to stand forth as the embodiment of national unity; he opposed all entangling European alliances.

Clay sat in the Senate at its meridian glory with Webster, Calhoun, and Sumner. He was not as profound as Webster, as philosophical as Calhoun, nor as classical as Sumner, but no man surpassed him in his understanding of human nature and fearlessness. For fifty active years he was the nation's most persistent advocate and logical candidate for president. It was said of him, "Had there been two Henry Clays, one would have made the other president."

John Caldwell Calhoun

CALHOUN, Clay, and Webster formed the famous triumvirate . . . Calhoun the thinker, Clay the leader, Webster the orator. Though they were political antagonists, when Calhoun died on March 31, 1850, Webster said of him, "He was a man of undoubted genius and of commanding talent." And Clay said of his worthy adversary, "He possessed an elevated genius of the highest order."

Secretary of War, Vice-president, Senator, Secretary of State, and political philosopher, South Carolina's most distinguished son, was born in the Abbeville district on March 18, 1782. His grandfather, James Calhoun, emigrated from Donegal, Ireland, to Pennsylvania in 1733. The Calhoun family, of Scotch-Irish, Presbyterian extraction, moved to South Carolina near the Cherokee frontier to establish the "Calhoun settlement," where John, the son of Patrick, was born March 18, 1782.

Brought up in a family prosperous enough to own a score of slaves, John became a pupil of his brother-in-law, Moses Waddell, in Columbia County, Georgia, and then went to Yale College. He was graduated in 1804, studied law in Tapping Reeve's school at Litchfield, Connecticut, was admitted to the bar in 1807, and opened an office near Abbeville.

In 1811 Calhoun married Floride Calhoun, the daughter of a cousin living on the "rice coast"; she brought him a modest fortune. He later enlarged his holdings to establish Fort Hill, a plantation in his native district, now the site of Clemson College.

His interest in public affairs began at his father's knee, his career with a speech denouncing British aggressions upon American maritime rights. He was elected to the state legislature in 1808 and to Congress in 1810; there he urged declaration of the War of 1812 and at its close assumed leadership in Congress on the questions of currency and internal improvements.

Calhoun's political rise was swift. As Secretary of War under President Monroe from 1817 until 1825, he demonstrated his pronounced genius at organization. He reduced the annual expenses of the army per man from 451 dollars to 287 dollars, with no loss in efficiency.

Calhoun was elected Vice-president in 1824 and again in 1828, serving with Adams, a Democratic-Republican, and then with Jackson, a Democrat. When the tariff of 1828 bore heavily upon his farming constituents, he issued a paper known as the South Carolina Exposition, setting forth his views on state sovereignty. In 1831, he issued a manifesto asserting the right of a state to nullify a federal law which it believed to be unconstitutional. When South Carolina passed an ordinance of nullification of the tariff act, Calhoun resigned the Vice-presidency and became Senator to defend its position.

President Jackson ordered troops to Charleston, but by a compromise negotiated by Clay armed conflict was averted; courageous and fearless of personal consequences, Calhoun had given up the nation's second highest office and surrendered all hope of the first. Thereafter, he became a bitter opponent of Jackson and strove to stifle the slavery controversy. As Secretary of State in the cabinet of President Tyler, a Whig, Calhoun was chiefly instrumental in securing the annexation of Texas and strove to avert war with Mexico.

He again entered the Senate and in 1849 proposed a southern convention to set forth the grievances of the slave states. His last speech on March 4, 1850, was read while he sat and listened. He died a few weeks later, believing it "difficult to see how two peoples so different and hostile can exist together in one common Union." His body was carried in state to Charleston and interred with an outpouring of praise and lamentation.

As a worthy political disciple of the nation's founding fathers, Calhoun appeared on the scene when the Democratic Party under Jackson and the Whig Party under Clay were contending for control. Devoted to history and dedicated to preserve the Constitution, he defined the American system with penetrating logic and an expansive imagination. In his "Disquisition" and "Discourse," he expounded the rights of the individual for whose benefit society and government exist . . . society to preserve the race and government to protect society.

In his speech on the Oregon question in 1846, he spoke of steam and electricity. As to the latter (when the telegraph was in its infancy) with impressive prevision he said: "Magic wires are stretching themselves in all directions over the earth, and, when their mystic meshes shall have been united and perfected, our globe itself will become endowed with sensitiveness, so that whatever touches on any one point will be instantly felt on every other."

In an "Address to the People of the South" in 1849, he wrote with startling precision on the results of abolition. He reviewed the history of slavery and foretold disaster. He called for unity in holding Southern rights paramount over party allegiance. The prophecy was corroborated within two decades: abolition by a dominant North against Southern resistance; hatred between the whites of the two sections; enfranchisement of the Negroes and a party union between them and the North to hold the Southern whites in subjection.

He foresaw the tragedy of 1861 more vividly than any man of his time and faced it frankly. Any just appraisal of the genius of John C. Calhoun places him high among America's major prophets.

John McDonogh

LOUISIANA'S four foremost philanthropists, Julien Poydras, Judah Touro, Paul Tulane, and John McDonogh, were all bachelors, and all were peddlers. Julien Poydras started out with a pack on his back. Judah Touro imported candles and codfish. Paul Tulane's career began with the purchase of an abandoned cargo of soap and blankets in New Orleans during a yellow fever epidemic. John McDonogh traded in molasses, sugar, hides, pig iron, and indigo. They all became planters and amassed sizable fortunes in cotton and real estate.

Of Scotch-Irish ancestry, John McDonogh was born at Baltimore on December 29, 1779. His father, a farmer, brick maker and Revolutionary soldier, reared a large family.

John began his career at an early age in the house of William Taylor, a Baltimore flour merchant, and was sometimes sent as supercargo with shipments of merchandise. He represented the firm in New Orleans in 1800 and soon went into business there for himself, handling miscellaneous merchandise. With faith in the future of mid America, he invested his increasing profits in real estate.

He made his real estate purchases with foresight, buying unimproved acreage near areas under development. His properties at one time completely circumscribed New Orleans. Though he could have turned his plantations over with profit, he kept them intact, putting thousands of acres into cultivation in the production of sugar and cotton. He sold his mercantile business in New Orleans in 1806, investing the money in acreage.

For many years John McDonogh was active in the business and social life of the city. He was an active member of the Episcopal Church and at one time was a director of the Louisiana State Bank. In 1814 he enrolled as a volunteer with Beal's Rifles in the defense of New Orleans.

John McDonogh moved to one of his plantations on the west bank of the Mississippi River in 1817. Here he lived the life of a hermit and concentrated on the accumulation of land and the management of his properties. Though he never married, it was rumored that his abrupt departure from the city was prompted by a disappointment in love; this was never substantiated. However, after he died a lady's slipper and a bit of faded ribbon were found among his private papers.

He educated four younger brothers and a sister, provided for a number of orphans, and when William Taylor, his former employer, was forced into bankruptcy, he made a home for him.

McDonogh initiated a novel scheme for the emancipation of his slaves. He was of the opinion that a slave could not appreciate his liberty unless he had earned it. Each slave was given some leisure, and if he consumed the time in toil, he was credited with it, and when his cash balance equalled his purchase price, he was emancipated. His first contingent of eighty slaves left for Liberia, Africa, on a ship furnished by the American Colonization Society in 1842.

In his later years McDonogh turned his attention to the use of his great fortune for the education of the boys and girls of Baltimore and New Orleans. At the time of his death, his estate was valued in excess of two million dollars, but litigation, inspired in cupidity, continued for twenty years. Finally a million and a half dollars was divided between the two cities, out of which New Orleans laid the foundation for its public school system by building thirty-six schools. Baltimore constructed an industrial training school.

In the consecration of his great wealth for the education of youth, McDonogh asked only "that it may be permitted annually to the children of the free schools to plant and water a few flowers around my grave." On McDonogh Day in New Orleans children strew flowers at the feet of his monument in Lafayette Square which was unveiled in 1898 and paid for by contributions of the city's school children. In Baltimore the covering of his grave with flowers is performed by the school children as a part of their commencement exercises.

McDonogh died at his plantation on October 26, 1850, and his remains temporarily rested in a tomb there upon which his code of conduct is inscribed. In accordance with his request, his body was removed to the Greenmount Cemetery at Baltimore in 1864, near a monument dedicated to his memory.

Tall, erect, clear-eyed, his features sternly etched into a countenance of strength, John McDonogh was striking in appearance. Dressed in black, his clothes cut to conform to the style of half a century before his time, he was as indifferent to men's changing whims as to their unkind words. Men said of him that he was penurious, eccentric, and visionary. They called him "McDonogh, the Miser," because he molded his life to his own peculiar pattern.

At the age of twenty-five John McDonogh set for himself an uncompromising challenge in the formation of "Rules for My Guidance in Life." "Remember," he wrote, "... labor is one of the conditions of our existence ... time is gold ... never think any matter so trivial as not to deserve notice ... never give out that which does not first come in ... without temperance there is no health; without virtue, no order; without religion, no happiness; and the sum of our being is to live wisely, soberly and righteously."

H.C.

William Wyatt Bibb

IN 1817 President James Monroe appointed William Wyatt Bibb first governor of the newly formed Territory of Alabama which was being swiftly transformed from a wilderness into a state through a period of internal upheaval. The Aaron Burr excitement had just subsided. Charged with conspiracy to create a republic in the west and with treason, the former Vice-president of the United States was arrested in what is now Alabama and sent to Richmond for trial.

War with England broke out in 1812 and gave the Americans the long awaited pretext for taking west Florida from Spain. A small army under General James Wilkinson occupied Mobile "without the effusion of a drop of blood."

With the outbreak of hostilities, the Indian situation became critical. The massacre at Fort Mims near Mobile in which 517 had been killed and only thirty-six escaped, along with the battles of Burnt Corn and Holy Ground, put the people on the frontier in a panic. On March 27, 1814, General Andrew Jackson, with militiamen from Tennessee, Georgia, and Alabama, conquered the Creeks in the battles of Talladega and Horseshoe Bend and then marched on to defeat the British in the Battle of New Orleans. The Creeks ceded to the United States nearly half of the present state of Alabama on September 14, 1816, and then the Chickasaw Nation relinquished all claim to its territory south of Tennessee.

The Mississippi Territory was divided at a convention near Sandy Hook in Marion County, Mississippi, in 1816. The eastern part of it was later organized as the Territory of Alabama by an act of Congress.

The governor had already carved out an enviable political career. He was born in Amelia County, Virginia on October 3, 1781, the son of William and Sally (Wyatt) Bibb. His father had been a captain in the American Revolution; his grandfather, John Bibb, a Huguenot, had come by way of Wales to Hanover County, Virginia, after the revocation of the Edict of Nantes. His mother was a descendant of Governor Frances Wyatt of Virginia, who was related to Martha Washington.

William was educated in medicine at the University of Pennsylvania. He was graduated in 1801 and located at Petersburg, Georgia, where he practiced his profession. He served in both the House and Senate of the state legislature and was elected on the Democratic ticket to the United States Congress at the age of twenty-four; he was repeatedly reëlected to serve until November 6, 1813, when he resigned.

Bibb was then elected to the United States Senate and served for three years, when he resigned before the expiration of his term. His second resignation was due to nation-wide disapproval of the congressional measure fixing the salaries of congressmen and senators at eighteen hundred dollar a year. The services of these officials prior to that time had been paid on a per diem basis during the sittings of the Congress and the action was looked upon by taxpayers as a raid on the public treasury.

Appointed governor of the Territory of Alabama, Bibb brought to his assignment a wide experience in statecraft. Having served in both branches of a state legislature and in both the national House and Senate, he was already a seasoned political leader. His knowledge of public affairs was considered of great value in the formative period of the organization of Alabama as a state, especially in the framing of its constitution. His public conduct met with such favor that when Alabama was admitted into the Union on December 14, 1819, Bibb was elected the first governor of the state. Bibb served, however, for a short time only. He died on July 10, 1820, from the effects of a fall from a horse frightened by a violent thunder storm. He was succeeded in office by his brother, Thomas Bibb, who was at the time serving as president of the Alabama Senate and who carried through on his brother's platform and program.

William Wyatt Bibb was survived by Mary Freeman Bibb, his widow, whom he had married in 1803. She was the daughter of Colonel Holman Freeman of Wilkes County, Georgia, a Revolutionary hero and Whig, a leader under Governor Elijah Clark. She was famed as "the beauty of Broad River."

These were exciting years in Alabama. The first cotton gin had been erected at Coosada in 1802. Jefferson College was founded in Autauga County in 1806, and St. Stephens Academy was chartered in 1818, a lottery being authorized to raise the money to erect academy buildings. The first pig iron was made near Russelville, Franklin County, and the first steamboat, the *Alabama,* was built to ply between St. Stephens, the Territory capital, and Mobile. The first newspapers in Alabama were established; the first Baptist church was erected on Flint River near Huntsville; a state bank was authorized; and an act was passed by the legislature to establish the University of Alabama at Tuscaloosa.

Alabama had growing pains in the early years of her emergence as a state, and William Wyatt Bibb is remembered as one whose youth, energy, and zeal helped give it needed momentum. He was only thirty-nine when he died, but he had enjoyed a full life of constructive achievement in the public service and had led a frontier people from troubled times into an era of peace and prosperity.

Zachary Taylor

BORN AT Montebello, Virginia, on November 24, 1784, Zachary Taylor was living in Baton Rouge, Louisiana, when he was elected President of the United States. A rugged soldier on the American frontier for forty years, he won from his fighting comrades the deserved sobriquet "Old Rough and Ready."

Zachary's formal education was limited to a little tutoring on a farm in Jefferson County, Kentucky, where his father, Richard, had migrated in 1785. He was a product of the soil and the school of experience, a curriculum from which men often graduate into great achievement.

Although Zachary Taylor saw brief service as a volunteer in 1806, his military career began with his appointment as first lieutenant in the United States Army two years later. He reported to General James Wilkinson at New Orleans during the Aaron Burr excitement and an epidemic of yellow fever. With intervening assignments, he was stationed again at New Orleans in 1819. He built Fort Jesup on the Louisiana border, was a recruiting officer at Louisville, helped perfect the United States Militia and in 1827 was located at Baton Rouge.

He was active in the Second Black Hawk War, and it was to him that Chief Black Hawk surrendered. In 1836, in the Seminole War, Zachary Taylor defeated the Indians in the decisive battle of Okeechobee. Frequently promoted, he received the brevet of brigadier general in 1838 and was put in command of Florida.

Ordered to Baton Rouge in 1840, he bought a residence and purchased a cotton plantation, Cypress Grove, forty miles above Natchez in Mississippi. He preferred farming to soldiering, and it was his purpose to retire from the army, but he was ordered to Fort Smith, Arkansas, in 1841 and back to Fort Jesup in 1844 in anticipation of the annexation of Texas.

In 1845 Taylor was assigned to serve on the new frontier. He collected an army at Corpus Christi, and when the Mexicans invaded Texas a year later, he was stationed at Point Isabel across the Rio Grande from Matamoras. He defeated a force three times the size of his own at Palo Alto and in a battle in which bayonet assault predominated sacked Monterrey. With four thousand men he defeated a Mexican army of twenty thousand at Buena Vista.

Colonel Jefferson Davis, who had eloped with one of Taylor's daughters much against her father's wishes, served under him in the Mexican conflict. The gallantry of Davis at Monterrey and Buena Vista moved Taylor deeply, and they became completely reconciled.

During the war, President Polk promoted Taylor to major general. His victories in the conflict climaxed a career that electrified the country, and he became the most popular candidate for president in 1848. He had no political aspirations. It was his desire to settle on his plantation Cypress Grove in Mississippi and raise cotton, corn, and cattle. His wife, whom he had married in 1810, had suffered many privations by his side, and she opposed his candidacy.

General Taylor had never voted for president. He saw the nation as an indivisible unit and without party affiliation or sectional bias. He embarrassed his supporters by writing his friends that he was not a candidate, that he even doubted his qualifications, but if the people spontaneously called him into service he was willing. He accepted the nomination on the Whig ticket in 1848, ran without any other platform than his promise to do his best, and was overwhelmingly elected.

When he retired to his cottage retreat at Baton Rouge during the campaign, his home became a political mecca for the masses. Unseeking, he was sought. "I am a Whig," he said, "but not an ultra Whig. If elected I would not be the mere President of a Party. I would endeavor to act independent of party domination. I should feel bound to administer the government untrammeled by party schemes."

With all the plaudits of the populace, President Taylor was unspoiled. The fortitude of the frontier had formed his character as definitely as time fashions a mighty oak, and he did not change his foilage when he became president. He had no friends to reward nor enemies to punish. He was built solid upon the ground, short and sturdy of limb; his eyes, shadowed by shaggy brows, were gray and sharp. He was the typical backwoodsman in tastes and manners, careless in dress and of speech. But he had the rare gift of common sense, a keen knowledge of men, faith in others, and self-confidence.

He was not in office long enough to stamp his term with his personality. He had been president less than a year and a half when, on July 4, 1850, he officiated in the laying of a cornerstone for the Washington Monument. The day was warm. He became overheated, ate cherries, drank iced milk, had an attack of cholera morbus, and died five days later.

The suddenness of his death shook a nation that sorely needed his stabilizing influence, for a new crisis was rising. With the slavery issue having been revived by the annexation of Texas and the addition of the territory of New Mexico and California, secession threatened. The Congress and the cabinet were opposed to each other and divided against themselves.

The Compromise of 1850, which only temporarily solved some of the prevailing problems, had not been passed, and the old soldier went to his last bivouac with the storm clouds of internal strife gathering about him. He had dreamed for years of living in peace on his broad acres, but when his final orders came "Old Rough and Ready" was in the thick of another fight.

H.C.

John James Audubon

JOHN JAMES AUDUBON was primarily a child of the woods. His life was birds and flowers. His father first tried to make a professional soldier of him and then a clerk, but his winged spirit could not be caged in an academy nor chained to a desk.

Born in Santo Domingo in 1785 of French parentage, Audubon moved to France and then in 1803 returned to the new world to become a merchant. Bankrupt and despondent, except for his fellowship with his birds and his wooing of and marriage to Lucy, he enjoyed little happiness. He lived in Kentucky in a log cabin with a dirt floor. He was in Natchez with holes in his shoes and penniless, doing a portrait for a cobbler in exchange for patches. He was in New Orleans in 1821, hungry, with Lucy and their children and unable to buy bread or paper upon which to make his sketches. There was the humiliation to his sensitive personality that he was painting birds while those around him were building an empire and Lucy was supporting him by teaching school.

Audubon probably inherited his artistic talent from his mother; all that is known of her is that she played a lute, loved flowers, and died young. He also owed much to his father's encouragement. It was Captain Audubon who first introduced him to birds and then criticized his sketches, which he worked at for months and annually destroyed. Of his father he said, "He was so kind to me that to have listened lightly to his words would have been ungrateful. I listened less to others and more to him, and his words became the law."

But Audubon must have observed some superior law that directed him to reduce to ashes the work of many months that he might try again to approach perfection. And the call that led him into the forest must have been one higher than the song of birds.

It was in Louisiana that his genius came to its fullest flower. He found here the French language. He found live oaks, Spanish moss, and tropical birds he had never seen before. It is little wonder that he stated freely that he was born in Louisiana and that the heart of the Pelican State went out to him and claimed him as its own.

When he found no publisher in the United States for his *Birds of America,* Lucy sent him abroad for months with the money she had saved through years of sacrifice. Outside of fiction, there has seldom been such conjugal devotion. She alone understood him, and through all the want and the woe of the years she never tried to divert him from the strange way he was to go.

To anyone who has felt the thrill of seeing Audubon's life-sized birds for the first time, it is little wonder that he found a publisher in London and that his exhibitions were a sensation in Edinburgh and Paris. The wild turkey, mocking bird, and redheaded woodpecker, Europeans had never seen before, and here was an artist who had dared to make birds realistic . . . who had painted them full of life, in their natural surroundings. Audubon returned home covered with fame. No other naturalist had ever suffered such privations in the pursuit of a dream and so fully realized it while living.

As his genius spread its wings to immortality, he could say in a spirit of justified pride, "I have made many mistakes in my life, but the one great mistake was listening to other people."

It is the lot of some men to fight battles, make machines, build cities, or create empires. Audubon's contribution to civilization lies in his influence upon the conservation of wild life. Every good sportsman and lover of the open spaces owes him a debt of gratitude for the inspiration he gave to the establishment of game preserves and societies for their promotion.

With a pencil and an observing eye he penetrated the wilderness to learn the hidden secrets of our feathered kingdom. He held a mirror up to nature that men and women might see and then help to make a better world.

Artist and ornithologist, Audubon wrote in *Birds of America* of "that favored land," Louisiana: "It is where the great magnolia shoots up its majestic trunk, crowned with evergreen leaves, and decorated with a thousand beautiful flowers that perfume the air around; where the forests and fields are adorned with blossoms of every hue; where the golden orange ornaments the gardens and the groves; where bignonias of various kinds interlace their climbing stems around the white-flowered stuartia, and mounting still higher, cover the summits of the lofty trees around, accompanied with innumerable vines that here and there festoon the dense foliage of the magnificent woods, lending to the veneral breeze a slight portion of the perfume of their clustered flowers; where a genial warmth seldom forsakes the atmosphere; where berries and fruits of all descriptions are met with at every step—in a word, it is where Nature seems to have paused as she passed over the earth, and opening her stores to have strewed with unsparing hands the diversified seeds from which have sprung all the beautiful and splendid forms which I should in vain attempt to describe . . . It is, reader, in Louisiana that these bounties of Nature are in the greatest perfection."

H. C.
'36

William E. Woodruff

"It has long been the wish of many citizens of this territory, that a press should be established here: their wish is now accomplished: we have established one entirely at our own expense, which we intend shall be permanent, and increase with the growth of the territory. . . . It is the duty of every man to be useful in whatever situation he is placed in life. We intend to keep this maxim. . . ."

On November 20, 1819, on the first election day in the Territory of Arkansas, William E. Woodruff made this editorial announcement in the initial issue of the Arkansas *Gazette,* the oldest surviving newspaper west of the Mississippi River. The first issue featured a story about American warships seizing the mouth of the Columbia River in the Pacific northwest, a letter denouncing the proposal of Tennessee's Governor McMinn to move Cherokee Indians from his state to Arkansas, and a list of unclaimed letters at Arkansas Post, including three for Stephen F. Austin, who had tarried there on his way to become the "Father of Texas."

William E. Woodruff was born at Fireplace, Long Island, New York, the son of Nathaniel and Hannah (Clark) Woodruff. At the age of thirteen, upon the death of his father, he became an apprentice printer at the Long Island *Star,* serving seven years to learn the trade.

With ink on his hands and an urge to go west to seek his fortune, he visited Wheeling, West Virginia, purchased a canoe, and journeyed to Louisville. He worked for a year as a printer at Russelville, Kentucky, and then went to Franklin, Tennessee. There William bought a second-hand primitive printing press and a "shirt-tail full of type," which he transported down the Cumberland River to the Ohio and over that river to the Mississippi. On the last stage of this budding journalist's journey he improvised a barge by lashing together a couple of pirogues and poled and punted his press up the Arkansas River to Arkansas Post, the territorial capital on the bank of the river.

There he built a log cabin of two rooms. In the larger room he cooked, slept, and kept his desk and type cases; his press occupied the other room. He began publishing the Arkansas *Gazette* on a sheet eighteen inches square and was editor, pressman, and his own printer's devil in a one-man shop. William started his newspaper in a village with a population of one hundred inhabitants, a collection of huts. He ran the newspaper for forty-four years and, except for the interruption of the Civil War and a short interval during which the press was being moved from Arkansas Post to Little Rock, the Arkansas *Gazette* has been in continuous operation, first as a weekly and later as a daily and weekly.

In 1821, Little Rock was made the capital of the Arkansas Territory, and Woodruff moved the Arkansas *Gazette* to that city, where he started with fewer than three hundred subscribers. As late as 1830, it was the only newspaper published in the territory and was consistently Democratic.

In 1838 Woodruff sold his newspaper property, but in 1841 it fell back into his hands and was resold in 1843. Three years later he established the Arkansas *Democrat,* an opposition newspaper, and in 1860 merged the two under the title Arkansas *Gazette and Democrat* though the latter name was soon dropped. The last issue under his personal management appeared in March, 1853, when he sold his interest and returned to private life. Called in his day the "grand old man of Arkansas," he died in Little Rock on September 2, 1898, survived by three sons and five daughters. On November 14, 1827, he had married Jane Eliza Mills.

A man of slight build, William Woodruff did not give the impression of one likely to cope with the lawless element on the American frontier. However, he must have had the courage of his convictions in what was at times a riotous community. One bully who took exception to something Woodruff had published threatened him in his shop. Cornered, Woodruff shot and killed the ruffian in self-defense. Exonorated before the bars of justice and public opinion, he retained the respect of his people.

In 1843, Woodruff founded the first lending library in the state. Inside each of the books he put in circulation was a printed label which read in part, "Please read and return in two weeks. Price $2.00 a year." During the Civil War most of these books were lost when a fire broke out next door to the building in which they were stored. The books were removed to the street and many of them were carried away during the occupation by book-hungry federal soldiers.

Editorials from Woodruff's pen, the testimony of his contemporaries, and the record of his useful life indicate that he was a man of integrity and sincerity. As a commentator on public affairs, he saw clearly, reasoned soundly, and judged calmly. He had a fluent and effective style. He had had little if any formal education, except what rubbed off on him at the type cases. Like most old-time printers who put words, sentences, and ideas together, as they set type by hand and who made the most of their calling, he was well-informed. The initial issue of the Arkansas *Gazette,* preserved in the state museum at Little Rock, is typographically neat and well-written.

As a young man, William E. Woodruff, self-educated, self-reliant and imbued with high purpose, pioneered with a hand printing press on the American frontier to spread the light of truth and understanding.

John Tyler

THE WHIG PARTY nominated William Henry Harrison for president and John Tyler for vice-president in 1840, both native Virginians. "Tippecanoe and Tyler Too" was the campaign slogan, which had reference to Harrison's victory over Tecumseh, the Shawnee chief, at Tippecanoe. The Whigs won, and President Harrison died exactly one month after his inauguration.

John Tyler was the first vice-president to reach the White House through the death of a president. When he learned of the President's death, he was shooting marbles with his grandchildren in Williamsburg and did not even know that the President was sick. Harrison died from an attack of pneumonia, along with the strain of the election and the pressure of office seekers.

The tenth president of the United States, John Tyler was born at Greenway the Tyler homestead in Charles City County on March 29, 1790. He was the second son of Judge John Tyler and Mary (Armistead) Tyler and the fifth John Tyler to be born in the ancestral home.

He attended the local school and at seventeen finished at the College of William and Mary, as had his father. He studied politics, read law under his father, relaxing from his studies in fiddling and poetry. He entered upon the practice of his profession and was elected to the House of Delegates where he served for five successive years, interrupted only by a brief enlistment in the War of 1812. "Honest John" was a tall, thin, cultured man with a high-bridged nose and blue eyes, of gracious manner, and with a gift for public speaking. He became increasingly popular with his constituents while he impressed his contemporaries in the House of Delegates.

He was elected to the federal House of Representatives in 1816 and served until ill health forced him to resign. He voted against Calhoun's "bonus" bill for internal improvements, against a protective tariff, for the censure of Andrew Jackson's conduct in the Florida campaign, and against the adoption of the Missouri Compromise measure of 1820. The Tylers, both father and son, were opposed to the slave trade and trusted to time and a more favorable climate for its ultimate abolition. They believed, however, that while slavery did exist, it should have the same protection as other property.

On his retirement from Congress, Tyler bought Greenway, which on the death of his father had descended to his older brother. He was again elected to the House of Delegates and in 1826 was elected governor and worked for the development of roads and schools. A year later he was elected to the United States Senate by the anti-Jackson element in the Assembly. He was reëlected to the Senate in 1833, and was again in the Assembly, taking an active part in political affairs. He was nominated for second place on the Harrison ticket and within a month of the inauguration became president. At the behest of Henry Clay all cabinet members resigned, with the exception of Daniel Webster.

It was not believed that his administration would result in much constructive work, but President Tyler's record was remarkable. He was amiable, efficient, and constructive. The government was conducted with a minimum of waste despite the fact that Congress had provided no system for keeping the public funds. The Seminole war was brought to an end, a treaty was negotiated with China opening the Orient to trade for the first time, and the Monroe Doctrine was strictly enforced. The greatest achievements were the negotiations of the Webster-Ashburton treaty and the annexation of Texas. He retired with the satisfaction that he had accomplished much for his country.

Tyler had married Letitia Christian, daughter of Robert Christian of New Kent County on March 29, 1813, and they had seven children. She died while he was in the White House. Two years later he narrowly escaped death when a large gun exploded during trials on board the warship *Princeton*. One of the victims of that accident was David Gardiner, a friend of New York. Gardiner's daughter Julia, encountering Tyler under these tragic circumstances, soon became his bride and presided as mistress of the White House during the closing days of his administration. Tyler was fifty-four; she was twenty-four. By this marriage there were seven children.

The Tylers were leading the quiet life of rural Virginia at Sherwood Forest, when the Confederate conflict recalled him to public service. An advocate of conciliation, he advised a convention of the border states to consider compromises which might save the Union. The Virginia Assembly proposed a convention of all the states, and when it met in Washington in February, 1861, Tyler acted as chairman. These efforts failing, Tyler was a member of the Virginia convention which met to consider the question of secession, and he declared for separation. He favored an offensive policy and urged the immediate occupation of Washington and the adoption of the name and flag of the Union.

These proposals rejected, Tyler served in the Provisional Congress of the Confederacy. He was elected to a seat in the Confederate House but died on January 18, 1862 before he could take office. Had it not been for Harrison's death, John Tyler might have filled a very small niche in history. But he appeared as the man of the hour, fully qualified to face the challenge and assume the responsibility.

John Anthony Quitman

AT THE time of his death in 1858 General John A. Quitman of Mississippi was the most popular man in all America.

Born of German parents in New York in 1798, his father, a Lutheran minister, directed his education toward the pulpit, but Quitman chose the bar.

At twenty he was a teacher of English in Pennsylvania; at twenty-one he was reading law in Ohio; at twenty-four he was a member of the bar of the thriving city of Natchez. Marrying into a Southern family of wealth he entered actively into the social and political life of the new and growing state of Mississippi.

Quitman became chancellor. He was elected a delegate to the constitutional convention of 1832. He became president of the state senate, was elected governor, and went to Congress.

While politically a Jeffersonian Democrat, he was in principle Mississippi's foremost independent. Again and again he was elected to office while on the "wrong side" of some issue, his personal popularity overcoming opposition. There was not an issue facing the people of Quitman's day that he failed to meet boldly with his convictions. He never bartered his beliefs for public favor.

A strong advocate of states' rights and the plantation system, he stated in his inaugural address as governor in 1850, "When the constitution, or the reserved right of the states or the people are threatened, upon the state governments especially devolves the duty of taking proper measures to defend the one and protect the other. . . . I deny the right of the federal government to supervise the manufactures or the agriculture of the country. . . ."

While jealous of the profession of law, Quitman was primarily the soldier. He was a student of military history, and military science and battle were his calling.

When Texas declared her independence and the Alamo fell, Quitman volunteered for service and went west with a small army which he personally financed to "lay out the promised land."

Later when the Mexican war broke out, Quitman was commissioned a brigadier general by President Polk and took command of a brigade of volunteers. He fought his way into Monterrey with heroism.

He was in Mexico City eight hours before any other soldier. In storming Chapultepec he seized a rifle, tied a handkerchief to it, and led his men through sheets of lead and fire over an open causeway to take the castle in one of the war's most daring attacks.

As a reward for his generalship and bravery he was made civil and military governor of the City of Mexico, the only American ever to rule where Montezuma once held sway and Cortez unfurled the flag of Spain.

As a military strategist, fearless soldier, and inspiring leader Quitman had few equals. The hotter the engagement the cooler he became. He emerged from the Mexican War a national hero.

Well-bred and well-educated, Quitman was a man of culture and refinement. Throughout his career he kept his name so spotless that it became an American byword for honor and patriotism. When arrested and charged with plotting the delivery of Cuba from Spain in violation of federal neutrality acts, he resigned from the governorship of Mississippi, that his arrest might cause the people of Mississippi less embarrassment.

The case against him dismissed, he was elected to Congress in 1855. Reëlected, he served until his death on July 17, 1858, at his home Monmouth Plantation near Natchez. His illness was ascribed to ptomaine poisoning.

Quitman was tremendously ambitious, both for himself and for his country. He had that inner urge that pushes men of heroic mold ahead. He sensed the ultimate separation of the states and believed in an expanding Southland. "By sternly standing by our principles," he said, "a time may come for us to strike with effect. We may succeed in securing an equality in the Union, or our independence out of it, or at least fall gloriously."

He wanted to see the political and territorial powers of North and South in balance. It was not enough that the United States should come out of the Mexican war with added territory embracing one-fourth of its great domain. Quitman thought we should annex all of Mexico and take Cuba and Nicaragua for good measure. He lit his patriotic torch by fires that burned with the dream of empire.

Had he lived until the Civil War it is easy to guess what might have been his part in it . . . his convictions on the issues underlying that controversy were so definite. He was toasted in Charleston, South Carolina, as early as 1851 as the first president of the Southern republic.

Princeton College gave him an honorary degree. Congress gave him a sword. The people gave him their hearts.

Teacher, lawyer, legislator, planter, soldier, and patriot, governor of Mexico and Mississippi, General John A. Quitman has an enviable reputation as one of the bravest and most loyal sons that ever carried the flag of Mississippi into the field of conflict.

H.C.

John Ross

AFTER THE American Revolution many Scots with Loyalist leanings who had served under their king went to live with the Cherokees. Among the Cherokees at the time of their removal to the Indian Territory, one-fifth were partially white.

John Ross, born near Lookout Mountain, Tennessee, on October 2, 1790, was the son of David and Mary (McDonald) Ross. His father was a Scot as was his mother, but she had one-fourth Cherokee blood. His mother called him Tsan-usdi, "Little John"; the Cherokees later named him Cooweescoowee, meaning "Big White Bird."

Though the Cherokees' expansive Nation had been reduced by treaty to fifty-three thousand square miles in the states of Georgia and Tennessee, they were coming richly into their own. Their standards of living and community life were not unlike those of the whites who settled among them. They built comfortable homes, even plantation dwellings with white columns and marble mantels, and the more prosperous ones owned slaves.

Within the Cherokee Nation in 1826 were thousands of cattle, sheep, hogs, and horses and well-tilled farms. The Nation possessed sixteen sawmills, thirty-one grist mills, and 762 looms.

Sequoyah invented the Cherokee alphabet in 1821, and reading and writing came into common use. Schools and churches multiplied, and the Nation adopted a constitution patterned after the federal document. The capital was at New Echota. Its people were promoting a seat of higher learning and a national museum when gold was discovered on their lands in 1829, and social justice gave way to greed.

The relentless pressure of the whites against their boundaries had already become a national scandal and a tribal issue when a removal treaty, gained by federal subterfuge, finally led to their expulsion. Corralled in stockades by soldiers of the republic, the Cherokees who had ignored the edicts of a trumped up treaty turned westward in an exodus called the "trail of tears." Some four thousand men, women, and children perished during the journey.

The life of Ross spanned that painful epoch in which the Cherokees were driven from their promised land into the Oklahoma wilderness. He had been taught by a tutor and later attended Kingston Academy in Tennessee. He was employed as a clerk at a trading post for a time. His first public assignment came when he was nineteen; he was sent on a mission to the western Cherokees in Arkansas.

At twenty-two John Ross served as adjutant of a Cherokee regiment in the army of Andrew Jackson and fought against the Creeks in the battle of Horseshoe Bend during the War of 1812. A member of the tribe's council in 1817, he was elected president in 1819 and helped draft its constitution. He was elected assistant chief of the eastern Cherokees in 1827 and principal chief in 1828, serving in that capacity until the migration.

Chief Ross became the leader of the faction opposed to the Cherokee removal, even defying the federal government until it used force to achieve its purpose. Only then did he reluctantly consent to lead his fourteen thousand followers over the western trail into what is now Oklahoma. In the Indian Territory he aided in framing the constitution of 1839, uniting the western and eastern Cherokees. Chosen chief, he continued in office until his death.

Chief John Ross's one dream in life was to establish the Cherokee Nation as a free and independent people, and through fifty-seven years of public service he consistently pursued that purpose. He rebelled against the injustice of might. The Scotch and Indian within him fused to form a tenacious temperament. He inherited a clannish love for his native heath and a nostalgic yen for tribal trails. At one time he was arrested and imprisoned by Georgia officials. His home in Tennessee was seized and his family evicted.

Ross was of medium height, had steel gray eyes and brown hair. Inured to the ways of the wilderness he was also something of the aristocrat. A man of tact and talent, character and culture, he was the stabilizing influence during the long travail.

In a political crisis that shook the republic and finally witnessed the assassination of Cherokee treaty leaders in a tribal feud, he kept the confidence of the great majority of his people. His integrity was such that millions of dollars of Cherokee funds passed through his honest hands. Resourceful and resolute, he led a life of service and sacrifice to improve the lot of a people in spiritual conflict with the sometimes savage forces of civilization.

He married Quatie, a full-blooded Cherokee, who was among the thousands who died during the weary march to Oklahoma in 1839. In 1845 he married Mary Bryan Staples of Wilmington, Delaware, a white woman of the Quaker faith, who was many years his junior. Their home near Park Hill which resembled an Old South mansion house was surrounded by fields cultivated by numerous slaves. At the outbreak of the Civil War he sought to keep the Cherokees neutral but later signed a treaty of alliance with the Confederacy which was repudiated in 1863. When Northern troops invaded the Indian Territory in 1862, he went to Philadelphia, which continued to be his home. He died in Washington, D.C., on August 1, 1866, while on an errand to assist in making a new treaty.

The days of his prosperity over, his slaves free and his acres idle, broken physically and financially, but steadfast in spirit, he died pleading the cause of racial righteousness.

Opothleyahola

ONE OF THE most heroic and tragic figures in the epic of Oklahoma, Opothleyahola was prominent in the affairs of the Creek Nation for fifty years. Born in what is now Georgia in 1790, he fought with the Creeks in the War of 1813–14.

The burning issue in Georgia and Alabama was the removal of the Creeks to the Indian Territory. Opothleyahola, an official spokesman for his chief, opposed the plan. Chief McIntosh, who favored the scheme, called a council and in violation of Creek law signed with others a treaty with the federal government.

McIntosh was tried for treason and shot. His death fanned the flames of controversy into a tribal feud that was to follow the Creeks even into the Indian Territory. The pressure of the white invaders finally forced Opothleyahola to face the inevitable, and he concluded a removal treaty in Washington in 1832. They were promised peace in their new home in the west "as long as the grass grows and rivers run." The spurious treaty signed by McIntosh was declared void, and the Creeks exchanged their possessions east of the Mississippi for lands in the Territory.

Having given his word of honor Opothleyahola remained loyal to the Union unto death. He even took up arms against rebellious Creeks in Alabama. Fearing, however, the old contention would continue in the Indian Territory where many McIntosh Creeks had gone, he negotiated for lands in Texas, but the Spanish and American governments intervened.

Taking advantage of dissensions in the tribe, United States authorities forced the first contingent of reluctant Creeks to travel west, ninety lesser chiefs being chained in pairs throughout the journey. The following year Opothleyahola led some eight thousand of his people from their ancient abodes to their new location north of the Canadian River in the Indian Territory. They had hardly recovered from the economic and political shock of their removal when the Civil War began.

Choctaws, Chickasaws, Cherokees, Seminoles, and even a number of the treaty Creeks, joined the Confederacy. Opothleyahola, favoring neutrality, opposed the alliance. He had no kindly feeling for the people of Georgia and Alabama, and to him the Civil War was no Indian quarrel. He had given his allegiance to the Union in 1832 and thought it folly to oppose a force that in the end he believed would triumph.

As the war flames spread into the Territory, Opothleyahola prevailed upon his followers to flee to Kansas. He mobilized two thousand ill-armed warriors in the valley of the Deep Fork near the present town of Eufaula, and it was a pathetic cavalcade that began its flight of sorrows. There were women, children, a band of Seminoles, and Negro slaves. Abandoning their prosperous farms they brought along their household goods and their herds and flocks.

Pursued by Confederate forces of his own race commanded by Colonel Daniel H. McIntosh, son of Chief William McIntosh, Opothleyahola was overtaken at Round Mountain. Escaping from an indecisive skirmish his warriors suffered heavy losses again in an attack by Colonel Douglas H. Cooper with a detachment of Texas cavalry at Chusto-Talasah (Caving Bank) on Bird Creek seven miles northeast of the present city of Tulsa. Here they would have been captured had Opothleyahola not convinced many Cherokees to desert the Confederates.

The fugitives were engaged again and met defeat in the Battle of Chustenalah near Hominy Falls west of Skiatook in Osage County.

Driven through the hills in a blinding blizzard in wild confusion, they crossed the Kansas boundary line near Walnut River and arrived in a state of destitution to pitch their tents in the Valley of the Verdigris in Montgomery County, Kansas. Many had been killed, others captured and their cattle and goods confiscated. Families which a month before had lived in comparative comfort were bereft of the necessities of life. Barefoot through the snow hundreds of them had died of exposure, famine, and pestilence; among them was the daughter of Opothleyahola. Two thousand of their ponies perished from starvation within a few days after their arrival.

For the Indians the white man's war had become one of self-extermination. Other refugees joined the Creeks until the number reached ten thousand, many of whom finally camped at the Sac & Fox Agency at Quenemo in Osage County. Broken in health but brave in spirit, Opothleyahola rode his lean pony miles over storm-swept prairies seeking aid from federal officials. He offered to lead a regiment back to the Territory, but in the spring of 1863 he, too, fell a victim to the great privation, died in exile, and was buried in an unknown grave near the Agency.

The most influential full-blood Creek of his generation, Opothleyahola's power lay in his loyalty, character, and eloquence. His devotion to the Creeks was constant. He assumed neither the white man's speech nor his raiment. Large of frame and clothed in blanket and shawl of brilliant colors he was impressive in appearance.

Chieftain of a noble race, champion of a righteous cause, Opothleyahola was a warrior worthy of the devotion of his people.

H.C.

John Gorrie

In the middle of the nineteenth century two personal friends were practicing their professions at Apalachicola, Florida, which before the Civil War was a thriving cotton port on the Gulf; they were Dr. Alvan Wentworth Chapman, physician-botanist, author of *Flora of the Southern United States* and Dr. John Gorrie, physician and inventor of an ice-making machine.

According to Dr. Chapman, "One day Gorrie came to me back of the prescription counter, where I was making bread pills . . . and his eyes danced as they always did when he jibed at his own profession. He said: 'Come on over to my workroom—I believe I've stumbled on it. . . .' "

Together the two physicians examined the cakes of ice, about the size of bricks. An iceship having failed to arrive in port as scheduled, artificial ice was served that evening at a dinner tendered by the city to visiting English cotton brokers.

Thus a mechanical miracle performed in the rustic laboratory of a country doctor in 1845 gave birth to a major industry and brought comfort to millions who enjoy the benefits of modern refrigeration and air conditioning.

Dr. John Gorrie was born in Charleston, South Carolina, October 3, 1803. He was probably of Spanish descent for his parents came from the West Indies and he was of dark complexion with black hair and eyes. He received his early education in the schools of Charleston and was graduated from the New York College of Physicians and Surgeons in 1833. After spending a few months in Abbeville, South Carolina, he settled permanently in Florida at Apalachicola.

There he soon became the community's leading physician and gave generously of his services to charity. Civic-minded, he took an active part in local and public affairs. The year following his arrival, he was appointed postmaster and held the office for four years. In 1835 he was a member of the city council and was its treasurer. In 1837 he was elected mayor and a year later married Mrs. Caroline (Myrick) Beeman. In 1839 he resigned from the office of chief magistrate to give full time to his practice.

In the course of his ministrations to the sick he had deep sympathy for those who were stricken with fever, particularly children. As early as 1839 he conceived the idea of artificially cooling the air of sickrooms and hospitals in the hope of curing and preventing malaria. The anopheles mosquito, intermediary host in spreading the dreaded disease, was then unknown, and the belief prevailed that malaria was a miasmic malady.

Under the nom de plume of Jenner, Dr. Gorrie published a series of eleven articles "On the Prevention of Malarial Diseases," in the *Commercial Advertiser,* the local paper, in 1844. Being mechanically minded and becoming more intrigued by the possibilities of a refrigeration machine, he abandoned the practice of medicine in 1845 to devote full time to his invention.

Having cooled rooms successfully, he began freezing water in 1845, succeeding on a small scale with machinery of his own design. The principle he used is still employed in many mechanical refrigerators in common use, freezing temperatures being produced through the absorption of heat and the simultaneous expansion of air.

Dr. Gorrie, who originated the first cold-air machine, applied for the first patents on mechanical refrigeration in this country and is generally credited with being the father of the ice industry. Having no capital, he had difficulty in financing his undertaking. A Bostonian in the city of New Orleans advanced him the funds to secure a patent, which was granted May 6, 1851.

Refrigeration was at the time a serious problem, especially during the summer. Natural ice, cut from northern lakes and streams, was being brought south by ships. The first ice cargo had arrived in Charleston, S. C., in 1799, and an ice warehouse was built in New Orleans in 1820. Methods practiced by the Indians and adapted to frontier life by the colonists included cold springs and caves.

Dr. Gorrie had great faith in the possibilities of his idea. Being a physician, he thought of ice in terms of the comfort and health of human beings, but he did not dream of the establishment of a great industry. Without funds, he traveled across the country unsuccessfully seeking financial assistance. Finally exhausting every hope and failing in his purpose, he returned to Apalachicola. In his melancholy, he suffered a nervous collapse from which he never recovered. He died in 1855 at the age of fifty-two without seeing the fulfillment of his ambitious plans, and realizing nothing from his invention.

The Southern Ice Exchange erected a monument to his memory at Apalachicola in 1899 with the inscription, "Pioneer who devoted his talents to the benefit of mankind," and the State of Florida placed a bronze statue of him in National Statuary Hall.

But mechanical refrigeration, cold storage, and air conditioning are the real monuments men have raised to his enterprise and genius. He pioneered in the making of ice and became the "Father of Refrigeration" and the founder of a great industry. Physician, inventor and humanitarian, he benefited millions and made an enduring contribution to the health, prosperity and livability of the whole world.

Alexandre Mouton

A DESCENDANT of Acadian exiles, Alexandre Mouton was born in the Attakapas country on the Bayou Carencro in Louisiana on November 19, 1804. Attending the district schools of Lafayette Parish where only French was spoken, he nevertheless acquired early in life a thorough knowledge of English which he used with fluency and effect. Graduating from Georgetown College in the District of Columbia, he read law, was admitted to the bar in 1825, and began practice at Vermilionville, now Lafayette, Louisiana.

In 1826 Mouton married Zelia Rousseau, granddaughter of Jacques Dupre, a wealthy cattleman of Opelousas. They had four children. His second wife was Emma K. Gardner, and they had six children. Soon after his first marriage he abandoned the law and settled on a plantation provided by his father to become one of the state's most successful sugar planters.

He began his long career in the state legislature in 1829, was twice speaker of the house, and in 1837 was chosen to complete the unexpired term of United States Senator Alexander Porter. Elected for a full term he served in the Senate until 1842 when he resigned to become a candidate for the office of governor.

Alexandre Mouton was the first Democrat to be elected governor of Louisiana. Under the leadership of Andrew Jackson, the Democratic Party was in the ascendant. Politically, Mouton was a pronounced Jeffersonian.

Inaugurated in 1843, he projected something of his political philosophy into his initial message: "We can justly attribute the evils we have suffered to no other cause than ourselves," he said. "Louisiana, under a good government, and poised in her own resources, will leave nothing to be wished by her sons. It is but too common to look abroad for causes which are to be found immediately among ourselves. It is too customary to look to the general government for relief in distress, whilst that relief should be sought at home."

The state was hopelessly in debt, its treasury depleted and its people heavily and sorely taxed when Alexandre Mouton admonished, "We must meet the exigencies of our own times, and not throw them upon our children; their days will have their evils, dangers and trials as ours have had. . . . The present generation received our state and metropolis without a stain and without debt. Let us, as far as depends upon us, transmit our heritage unimpaired to our successors."

The lamentable condition of state finances was so improved under his prudent leadership that he could say with justified pride in his next address to the legislature, "We have passed the deplorable crisis of immorality and distress, in which idleness, extravagance and reckless speculation . . . involved the whole country. Industry now animates all classes of society, and economy surrounds every fireside."

The constitution of 1845, framed under his guidance, was such a radical departure from the constitution of 1812 that it set the pace for later constitutional conventions. The state was precluded from partnership in any bank or corporation. Property qualifications as a requisite to office were eliminated and suffrage extended. The chief executive, heretofore chosen by the legislature, was elected by the people. The offices of lieutenant governor, state librarian, and state superintendent of education were created.

The constitution of 1812 had made no mention of nor provision for the establishment of public schools. That of 1845 provided for such a system and the location of a state university at New Orleans. The University of Louisiana, now Tulane, was founded.

During Mouton's administration the Medical College of Orleans, the Medico-Chirurgical Society, the French Society, the St. Charles Hotel Company, and a glass manufacturing plant received charters.

The new constitution having made changes in the length of the governor's term of office, Alexandre Mouton, though elected for four years, retired to his plantation in 1846.

Keenly interested in railroad development, he served as president of the Southwestern Railroad Convention held in New Orleans in 1852. Active in national politics, he was five times a presidential elector.

In 1858, southwest Louisiana was overrun by bandits, and Alexandre Mouton was chosen president of a vigilance committee organized for the purpose of establishing peace and order.

He was a delegate to the Louisiana Secession Convention in 1861, served as president, and voted to secede. Like many others, he lost heavily in both family and fortune during the war. Alfred, his son, a brigadier general in the Confederacy, fell in the battle of Mansfield while leading his men into action.

One of the most popular and picturesque personalities of his generation, Alexandre Mouton resided on his plantation until his death on February 12, 1885. Though he never recovered financially from the war, he never lost the confidence and affection of his people.

Frugal, courageous, and capable, Alexandre Mouton deserves a high place in political history among those worthy public servants who believe that a state should live within its income, pay its honest debts, and maintain its solvency as essential to its existence.

Seargent S. Prentiss

ORATOR AND congressman, Seargent S. Prentiss, the son of a sea captain, was born in Portland, Maine, on September 30, 1808. Crippled in infancy by a fever, he turned to his books and limped his way to achievement.

He graduated from Bowdoin College at sixteen and moved to Natchez where he tutored, read law, and was admitted to the bar. He moved to Vicksburg in 1832, was elected to the state legislature, and represented his district in the national Congress in 1837. He died on July 1, 1850, at Longwood, Natchez, the girlhood home of Mary Jane (Williams) Prentiss, his wife, and was buried at Gloucester.

In 1837, when Prentiss was elected to Congress, he was still in his twenties. His seat contested in a celebrated case that shook Washington and stirred the republic, he pleaded with Congress not to resolve against him:

"Upon all the States," he said, "do I most solemnly call for that justice to another which they would expect for themselves. Let this cup pass from Mississippi. . . . Rescind that resolution, which presses like a foul incubus upon the Constitution. You sit here, twenty-five sovereign states, in judgment upon the most sacred right of a sister State; that which is to a state what chastity is to a woman, or honor to a man. Should you decide against her, you tear from her brow the richest jewel which sparkles there, and forever bow her head in shame and dishonor. But if your determination is taken, if the blow must fall, if the Constitution must bleed; I have but one request, on her behalf, to make: When you decide that she cannot choose her own representation, at the same moment blot from the star-spangled banner of the Union the bright star that glitters to the name of Mississippi, but leave the stripe behind, a fit emblem of her degradation."

Is it any wonder that he was praised by Webster, Calhoun, and Clay, that famed triumvirate of eloquence, and that a nation responded while it rejoiced in the discovery of such surpassing talent? With the possible exception of Patrick Henry, America has produced no more natural orator. Political partisans defeated Prentiss, the consistent Whig, but he returned to Mississippi where he triumphed again and was reëlected to Congress.

Despite his youth, he was the most magnetic, the most fluent, and the most sought after speaker of his time. Sound and practical in his political and economic philosophy, he warned the South more than a hundred years ago not to lean too long on cotton but to look to the development of her natural resources and her native talent.

Had he been politically ambitious, which he was not, and had he lived a little longer, he might have applied his transcendent gifts to great purpose. He prophesied and feared a futile effort to split the Union. Though his genius flowered early, he could not have reached the fullness of his prowess when he died at forty-two. He fought two duels with Henry S. Foote. He indulged too freely in the convivial cup and squandered his substance at the gaming table. In a country inn at Woodville, Mississippi, he once defended a bedbug before a moot court organized by visiting judges and lawyers who had been aroused from their slumbers in the middle of the night by an infestation of nocturnal hemiptera.

As orator he excelled all others of his time. He had "a peculiar way of hurling out his words—a sort of hissing thunder. In speaking he was always energetic, often violent. . . . He could be pathetic and persuasive, and then his voice became as plaintive as a flute, his eyes humid, his face sad, and he seemed to cast himself, like a child, into one's arms. When he was in good humor his manner became playful, his eyes sparkled, his cheek dimpled, and there was no resisting him."

In the magic of his poetic prose, the newly formed state of Mississippi was "like a beautiful bride leaning upon the arm of her Father of Waters," and Portland, Maine, the city of his birth, was "the brightest jewel in the diadem that adorns ocean's brow."

Imbittered over the repudiation of the Union Bank bonds by Mississippi, Prentiss moved to New Orleans in 1945. In the change from the practice of the common to the civil law, he lost no prestige at bench or bar. He contracted cholera in Louisiana, from which he never fully recovered. Immediately following an eloquent defense of Lopez, the Cuban revolutionist, he returned to his room and collapsed; he was taken by steamer to Natchez where he died.

I bowed at the grave of Prentiss near Natchez at Gloucester and laid a rose, his favorite flower, on his silent tomb. It is the kind of sequestered resting place that he himself once described as fitting for the heroic Lafayette: "Let no cunning sculpture, no monumental marble deface with its mock dignity the patriot's grave, but rather let the unpruned vine, the wild-flower, and the free song of the uncaged bird, all that speaks of freedom and of peace, be gathered round."

Albert Pike

THE ARKANSAS TERRITORY was a wilderness of scattered villages when Albert Pike appeared at Fort Smith in 1833, wearing well-worn leather pantoloons and moccasins.

He was born in Boston on December 29, 1809, attended school in Massachusetts, but was primarily self-taught. Beginning in 1824, Pike spent seven years teaching at Newburyport.

In 1831 he went west. By stage and steamer he arrived in St. Louis, where he joined a party of traders bound for Santa Fe. His horse ran away in a storm, and he covered five hundred miles of the distance afoot. He joined a hunting expedition into the Comanche country and had completed a two-year trek when he arrived in Fort Smith with sore feet and no money.

Pike took a job teaching school in a log cabin near Van Buren at a salary of three dollars a month, one half in cash and half in pigs. Under the non de plume of Casca, he wrote a series of political articles for the Arkansas *Gazette* that attracted the attention of Robert Crittenden, a Whig, who prevailed upon Charles P. Bertrand, the editor, to invite Pike to become an associate.

Pike supplemented his meager income by serving as assistant clerk in the territorial legislature. In 1834 he married Mary Ann Hamilton and with her financial assistance purchased an interest in the Arkansas *Advocate*. In 1836 he became sole owner and editor and studied law on the side.

Pike's *Prose Sketches and Poems Written in the Western Country* was published in 1834. His "Hymns to the Gods," written when a teacher in Newburyport but first published in *Backwoods Magazine* in 1839, placed him among the American poets. An indefatigable student, he had a working knowledge of Latin, Greek, Sanscrit, Hebrew, and French.

Pike sold the *Advocate* in 1837, having in the meantime been licensed to practice law. He wrote in a sketch of himself, "I owned the *Advocate,* and was editor and typesetter, and generally useful in the office, for two years and three months and then sold it for $1,500. I tried for a year to collect the accounts due the office. Then one day, weary of it all, put the books in the stove, where they served for fuel, I had no further trouble with the accounts."

Albert Pike became one of the best informed and effective lawyers of the Southwest. Arkansas was admitted into the Union as a state in 1835, and he became its first supreme court reporter. In 1842 he published *The Arkansas Form Book* for the use of attorneys.

Pike took an active part in the Mexican war, commanding a cavalry of Arkansas volunteers at Buena Vista. His criticism of the conduct of a regiment under the command of Lieutenant Colonel John Selden Roane resulted in a bloodless duel in which they each shot twice.

He was a staunch Whig in a Democratic stronghold and was one of the promoters of the Know-Nothing Party. In 1853 he transferred his legal practice to New Orleans but returned to Little Rock four year later. During his residence in New Orleans, his feelings found frequent expression in published verse. Though Pike was not friendly to slavery and considered secession a last resort, he sided with the South and was appointed Confederate commissioner to negotiate treaties with the Indians.

He was later commissioned brigadier general. It was Pike's understanding that Indians recruited would be used for defense purposes in the Territory only, and when they were employed in the battle of Pea Ridge, he resigned and criticized his superiors. He was placed under arrest in 1862 but released. Near the close of hostilities he served as associate justice of the Arkansas Supreme Court.

With the surrender, Pike's property was confiscated. Looked upon with suspicion by both the North and South, he fled from Arkansas to New York and then to Canada. Through the intervention of friends, President Johnson issued an order permitting his return home on condition that he take the oath of allegiance. Indicted for treason, he pleaded the President's order and was restored to citizenship.

At fifty-eight he started life all over again. In 1867 he practiced law in Memphis and was editor of the Memphis *Appeal* until 1868 when he moved to Washington. There he continued his practice and edited *The Patriot* until 1870. He then turned his talents almost exclusively to the philosophy of Freemasonry.

Pike was secretary-general of the Scottish Rite Masonic Body for the Southern Jurisdiction for thirty-two years. He contributed many volumes to the literature of the order and was highly revered in Masonic circles at home and abroad. When he died on April 2, 1891, in the Scottish Rite Temple in Washington, in his eighty-second year, he was the most exalted Freemason in the world. He was survived by two sons and a daughter. A third son had drowned in the Arkansas, and another had died fighting for the Confederacy.

Albert Pike was impressive in appearance. He was more than six feet tall, well-proportioned. His flowing locks and long beard framed a strong and striking countenance.

His unbounded energy was reflected in the lusty vigor of his speech and poetry. He was a man of imagination and skill, nimble of mind and limb, adventurous, independent, and determined.

Crawford Williamson Long

TWO NATIVE sons of Georgia, Crawford W. Long and Alexander H. Stephens, were once roommates at the state university; Stephens became a well-known statesman, and Long, the discoverer of anesthesia. The legislature of Georgia has placed the statues of both in the nation's Capitol as the state's two most worthy citizens.

Crawford W. Long was the son of James Long by his wife Elizabeth Ware and was born in Danielsville, Georgia, on November 1, 1815. His grandfather, Captain Samuel Long, was a Scotch-Irish Presbyterian born in the province of Ulster, who settled at Carlisle, Pennsylvania, about 1761. He fought in the American Revolution in the Army of Lafayette, taking part in the siege of Yorktown. After the close of the war he moved to Georgia.

Crawford Long, the son of a cultivated father, entered Franklin College (now the University of Georgia) at the early age of fourteen and graduated in 1835, second in his class. After a year of teaching in the academy which his father had founded at Danielsville, he began studying medicine first under a preceptor, later at Transylvania University, Lexington, Kentucky, and finally at the University of Pennsylvania, where he received his medical degree in 1839. The succeeding eighteen months he spent in a New York hospital where he gained a reputation for being a skillful surgeon.

In 1841 Dr. Crawford Long began a general practice of medicine in the village of Jefferson, Jackson County, Georgia, where he inherited the clientele of his old preceptor, Dr. Grant, and enjoyed an excellent rural practice. Studiously inclined, he read widely in general literature on his calls and became a scholar. On August 11, 1842, he married Caroline Swain, the niece of Governor David Lowry Swain of North Carolina.

In the early forties laughing gas parties became something of the rage in rural America. Traveling charlatans popularized the fad by putting on public demonstrations in which volunteers inhaled nitrous oxide to produce exhilaration. Under the influence of the gas they provided entertainment, as hypnotists sometimes do. Some of the young blades of the countryside prevailed upon Dr. Long to stage a "nitrous oxide frolic" of his own, and not having any of the gas available he offered a substitute. Telling of the incident later, he said: "I informed them . . . that I had medicine (sulphuric ether) which would produce equally exhilarating effects; that I had inhaled it myself, and considered it as safe as the nitrous oxide gas."

The young men inhaled the gas and became hilarious. Several of them suffered severe bruises but under their intoxication felt no pain. One dislocated an ankle and did not suffer when it was set.

From his observations Long inferred that ether must have the power of producing insensibility, and he decided to test it in his surgical practice. On March 30, 1842, he administered sulphuric ether to James Venable, who when completely anesthetized had removed from the back of his neck a cystic tumor. The patient testified that he experienced no pain during the operation. In all, Dr. Long used ether in eight operations before he made his experiments public. In fact his experience with ether was not published until 1849, when, as a result of the controversy that had risen over the claims of W. T. G. Morton that he had discovered anesthesia, Long described his first five operations in a short paper contributed to the *Southern and Surgical Journal,* under the title "An Account of the First Use of Sulphuric Ether by Inhalation as an Anesthetic in Surgical Operations."

Other claims followed, naturally. Dr. Long was ever modest in urging his priority to the discovery, but in the year before his death, Dr. J. Marion Sims, world-famed gynecologist of South Carolina and Alabama, investigated Long's claim fully and presented them in an able paper published in the Virginia *Medical Monthly,* declaring Long to be the "first discoverer of anesthesia."

Dr. Sims, who came to the loyal aid of a fellow physician, realized that Long's transcendent discovery had made possible major operations theretofore intolerable. Dr. Ephraim McDowell of Danville, Kentucky, had performed the first successful ovariotomy in 1809 by removing a twenty-pound ovarian tumor from courageous Jane Todd Crawford without the use of any anesthetic, but such torturing operations were rare before Dr. Long made his signal contribution to surgical science.

Long moved to Athens, Georgia, in 1850, where he acquired a large surgical practice and where he died on June 16, 1878. There in 1910 an obelisk was credited to his memory. The French have also dedicated a statue in Paris in appreciation of the ingenuity of a country doctor who by virtue of his discovery linked his name to immortality.

Prior to the Civil War, Dr. Long had, by inheritance and hard work, amassed a fortune. Although successful in his practice up to the day of his death, he never succeeded in rebuilding his fortune. As he served the suffering, he had often expressed the wish that he might die in harness. While performing the professional duties incident to his last case, he suffered a stroke of apoplexy from which death came in a few hours. He was a physician who blessed the lives of millions by converting laughing gas into a miracle drug.

H.C.

Samuel Houston

LEADER, PATRIOT, soldier, statesman, empire builder, no other man has had such a penetrating and far-reaching influence upon the character, spirit, and political destinies of the southwest. The Lone Star that shines so brilliantly to the name of Texas in the diadem of states wears its brightest luster in memory of Sam Houston whose strong hands did so much to put it there and whose great soul kindled its patriotic fires.

He was born in Rockbridge County, Virginia, seven miles from Lexington on March 2, 1793, the son of Major Sam Houston, a veteran of the Revolution, who died in 1807 while on a tour of inspection of frontier army posts. The widow, Elizabeth (Paxton) Houston, moved her large family of six sons and three daughters to the vicinity of Maryville, Tennessee.

For a time her son Sam lived with the Cherokees among whom he found peace, learned poise and into the tribe of which he was formally adopted as "The Raven." He enlisted in the army at twenty, was wounded in the war with the Creeks, and won the praise and confidence of Andrew Jackson.

He studied law, was admitted to the bar, went to Congress, was elected governor, and was frequently mentioned as a presidential possibility. In the midst of a heated campaign for reëlection Sam Houston's bride of a few weeks abandoned him for reasons that are still their secret. The political gossip mongers made the most of it, and Sam Houston resigned his office, joined the Cherokees, married a squaw, and drowned his sorrows in strong drink.

Broken in health, sunken in spirit, and wounded in pride, this man of iron will arose from the depths of such despair to take command of himself again.

The acquisition of Texas by the United States had become a lively issue on both sides of the Rio Grande, and there was in this cause a challenge sufficient to satisfy the restless spirit of this gigantic personality. The boundless leagues of Texas fit well into Sam Houston's expansive heart and mind, and in such a vast environment his genius quickly came to its full fruition.

As a delegate he attended the memorable convention at Washington-on-the-Brazos that declared the independence of Texas on March 2, 1836, on his forty-third birthday, and he was chosen commander in chief of the armies of the republic.

At the same time the Alamo fell, to write in patriot's blood one of the saddest chapters in the annals of history. Sounding the battlecry of "Remember the Alamo" Sam Houston surprised the forces of Santa Anna to win an amazing victory in the face of enormous odds. With a shattered leg he emerged from the battle of San Jacinto America's new idol. His heroism became a byword, and in the elections that followed he was chosen president of the Republic of Texas.

Like some inspired Hercules, Sam Houston turned to his labors. Within a year he had stabilized the currency of the new republic, set up the machinery for the collection of customs, paid salaries, put the constitution in operation, and given Texas standing in the neighboring family of states.

Defeated for reëlection, he returned to a lucrative law practice, married again, and settled down for one of the few periods of his hectic career in which he found real happiness. Again elevated to the presidency he directed his uncanny cunning to the annexation of Texas by the United States until public sentiment in both republics crystallized for such a union.

Sam Houston became the first United States senator from the state of Texas, and in the bitter fight in Washington on the issue of secession he alone among all the Democratic senators voted against it. Returning to the political arena of Texas, he became governor, but his pleadings against secession all in vain, he was deposed. Accepting the verdict in good grace he retired with his convictions intact to his farm at Huntsville. There he died on July 26, 1863, three weeks after the fall of Vicksburg, surrounded by all his family except his eldest son, who was then wounded and a prisoner in a northern camp. Before he died his popularity was already on the rise again.

Six feet three, dynamic, a commanding personality, Sam Houston bestrode the chaotic times in which he lived like a colossus. In body and soul he was big enough even for Texas. Man of steel, he was of that rare and super-physical stuff that could fall again and again to arise each time to new heights in personal and political achievement.

He was more than Texas' man of the hour . . . he is her man of the ages. It was upon the strong arm of Sam Houston that Texas leaned until it could walk alone.

When he went to his reward it had been fifty years since he had departed from his mother with her admonition, "My son, take this musket and never disgrace it; and remember, I would rather all my sons should find one honorable grave than that one of them turn his back to save his life."

With her blessings she placed upon his finger a band of gold, his talisman. When he died the ring was removed, and engraved on its inner side was the single word "honor." Her Samuel had not betrayed her.

Stephen Fuller Austin

FOR NEARLY three hundred years Spain, France, and Mexico made intermittent, feeble, futile efforts to colonize Texas, but the restless home seekers from the United States occupied its open spaces within the span of a generation.

Moses Austin agreed with the Mexican government to introduce three hundred families in 1820. His son Stephen and others contracted to settle ten thousand families. The Texas revolution was partially financed with land bounties to soldiers. One development company distributed free land at the measure of one section to each head of a household and one-half section (320 acres) to each unmarried man. The company furnished 2,100 log cabins; 1,800 rifles and muskets; and 162,000 rounds of live ammunition, retaining alternate sections of land for its own benefit.

Stephen F. Austin, founder of Texas, was born at the lead mines (now in Wythe County) on the southwestern frontier of Virginia, on November 3, 1793.

At the age of ten he went east to an academy in Connecticut and at fourteen attended college in Kentucky. At seventeen he worked in his father's store. He became a member of the legislature of the Missouri Territory. He farmed in Arkansas, studied law and French, and edited a newspaper in New Orleans.

In 1821 Stephen's father died in the midst of his Texas colonization project and charged his son to carry on with it. Austin, at twenty-eight, moved to Texas to lift the family debt and recoup its fortunes.

He blazed a trail for millions. His colonization project logically led to the Texas revolution and the establishment of the republic. The annexation of Texas by the United States inspired the Mexican war which brought to the United States a vast territory now embracing one-fourth of its great domain. By legislative enactment Austin has been proclaimed the Father of Texas.

But Austin's path was no royal road to great achievement. Mexico had won her independence from Spain. When the new rulers revoked his colonization contract, he went to Mexico City to regain the government's consent. In the political confusion of the times it took a year. Austin was forced to pawn his watch to get home, but he returned with his contract, a knowledge of the Spanish language, and an understanding of the Mexican people.

He was the most persistent man of his generation, and his genius for leadership had few parallels. With the confidence of Mexican officials he exercised for a time a colonizing monopoly in Texas and during these early years Stephen Fuller Austin was the absolute ruler of this self-made kingdom.

He dealt with the most delicate and dangerous situations with a diplomacy rarely excelled. The Protestant faith and slavery were generally prohibited, and Mexican officials, beginning to fear the loss of Texas to an aggressive people with a record for expansion, closed its borders. With patience and loyalty, Austin returned to Mexico City pleading his cause and suing for political peace. Arrested and imprisoned, he was confined to his cell for months in a cholera-ridden city. Discouraged, he returned to his settlements to find Texas in revolt.

All other means for reform having failed, he, too, took up arms against Mexico, his adopted country. He went on a mission to the States to borrow money and buy supplies for the struggling Texas republic that had declared its independence.

The Alamo had fallen and General Sam Houston's little army had defeated Santa Anna at San Jacinto when Austin returned to become secretary of state in his president's cabinet for a few weeks only. Weakened from overwork and exposure, Austin contracted a cold and died of pneumonia at the age of forty-three.

For fifteen years he had poured his energy and enthusiasm into the colonization of Texas. "My ambition," he said, "was to redeem this fine country—our glorious Texas. . . . I had read of the withering march of the bloodhounds of war over the fairest portions of the Old World, spreading fire and famine and desolation and death. . . . I could not understand it, but I could understand how that happiness might be promoted by conquering a wilderness by the axe, the plough and the hoe."

Elsewhere he wrote, "I have no house. I make my home where the business of the country calls me. . . . I have spent the prime of my life and worn out my constitution in trying to colonize the country. . . . I am not ashamed of my poverty."

Austin never married. Texas was his only love. A lonely man, he dreamed of a league of land at the foot of the mountains on the Colorado, a suitable site for building an academy where he could spend his last years with his books. He died in a cabin, but he lies buried in the soil that he had chosen for a home and where stands today the University of Texas in the capital city that bears his name. There in perpetuity is a shrine to his patience, character, and courage, a monument to his loyalty, his leadership, his industry.

Explorer, pioneer, colonizer, empire-builder, impresario, and patriot . . . seldom does it lie within the scope of one man's life to so change the course of empire.

William Barrett Travis

William Barrett Travis was only twenty-seven when he died in the Alamo on March 6, 1836, leading 188 fellow compatriots in the cause of Texan independence and into the pages of imperishable history.

Except for this one herculean feat there was nothing extraordinary in the brief career of this courageous young man. He was born near Red Banks, Edgefield County, South Carolina, on August 9, 1809, the oldest of the ten children of Mark Travis and Jemima (Stallworth) Travis.

In 1818 the Travis family moved to Alabama and settled in Conecuh County where William had such schooling as the limited means of his father and the frontier afforded. He studied law in the office of Judge James Dellet at Claiborne and before his twentieth birthday was admitted to the bar. While reading law and awaiting clients he earned his living teaching school. At nineteen, he married Rosanna Cato, one of his own pupils, and to them were born two children.

The marriage was an unhappy one, and being financially embarrassed, Travis abandoned his family and went to Texas in 1831. A reconciliation was never effected, and they were divorced four years later. Travis settled at Anahuac, the legal port of Galveston Bay and the headquarters of a military garrison commanded by Colonel Bradburn, a Kentuckian in the Mexican service who was having trouble with the Americans.

These were unsettled times in Texas. Mexico had gained her freedom from Spain in 1821 to become an independent state. After the Louisiana Purchase in 1803, American settlers invaded Texas, many under the impression that it really belonged to the United States or would one day. The issue was settled by the Treaty of 1819 with Spain, but the Americans continued to come in increasing numbers, even after a Mexican decree was passed in 1830 checking further immigration. At the time Travis arrived the estimated population of Texas was twenty thousand, most of whom were from the United States.

In 1832, Travis moved to San Felipe, where he set up a law office, was appointed secretary of the ayuntamiento, and became an ardent leader in local politics and of the "war party."

The Americans were agitating for Texas independence from Mexico when Antonio López de Santa Anna, seized power in Mexico and became a political and military dictator under the title of *El Presidente*. In 1835 Santa Anna decided to drive the Americans out of Texas and colonize the country with Mexicans.

When Santa Anna sent troops to regarrison the fort at Anahuac, abandoned since 1832, Travis raised a company of volunteers and captured and disarmed the Mexican soldiers. Though this action was repudiated by many of the Americans seeking to avoid trouble with Mexico, public opinion soon crystallized in favor of Travis' action, and the Texas revolution began.

American settlers won the Battle of Gonzales; Texans captured Goliad; they won the Battle of Concepción; San Antonio was captured, and the Mexican general Cos surrendered. Free of Mexicans, the Texas Declaration of Independence was issued at Washington-on-the-Brazos on March 2, 1836, and Texans with the exception of Sam Houston and a few others believed the war was over. Sam Houston thought Santa Anna would send reënforcements.

Travis having performed valuable service in commanding a scouting company during the siege of San Antonio was appointed major of artillery, and shortly afterward was transferred to the cavalry with the rank of lieutenant colonel. He was ordered to occupy and reënforce the Alamo, which the Texans had taken in December, 1835, in joint command with Colonel James Bowie.

When Santa Anna appeared with as many as six thousand troops, Travis answered a demand for surrender with cannon shot. Bowie was stricken with typhoid-pneumonia during the siege in which all of the 188 men under the command of Travis were killed. They fought bravely, asking no quarter in a desperate struggle, hand to hand, muzzle to muzzle, musket and rifle, bayonet and bowie knife. The "gallant Travis" died beside his gun. Near his side fell James Butler Bonham, another of the ragged little garrison, a lifelong friend of Travis, who had borrowed the money to come to Texas that he might fight for its freedom. Between six and eight hundred Mexicans died in this fierce encounter that lasted an hour and a half.

Travis was six feet tall, weighed about 175 pounds, and from all reports was as charming and congenial as he was courageous. At the early age of twenty-seven, he had scaled that loftiest of peaks where the famed reside, to take his enviable place among that exclusive company of patriots willing to die that others might live.

No male defender survived. Santa Anna ordered the bodies burned. The fifteen or more who were spared were women, children, slaves, and servants. Upon the cenotaph erected at Austin in memory of the defenders of the Alamo is inscribed this worthy tribute: "Thermopylae had its messenger of defeat, but the Alamo had none."

CJ NAAR

James Bowie

In the days when men in the Deep South settled their personal disputes by duel, the bowie knife was a popular weapon. The bowie knife was a nine-inch blade equipped with a guard at the base of the hilt to protect the hand. It was designed by either James Bowie or his brother Rezin. One legend is that James had injured himself in an Indian fight by letting his hand slip from the hilt to the blade of a butcher knife and that he employed an Arkansas silversmith and blacksmith by the name of James Black, to design the knife which bears his name.

In origin and use the bowie knife has inspired much folklore; it achieved fame—if it was not first employed by James Bowie of Rapides Parish—in the sandbar duel at Vidalia, Louisiana, in 1827. A duel had been arranged between Thomas H. Maddox and Samuel Levi of Natchez on a sandbar across the Mississippi. After the difficulty had been adjusted by the exchange of two shots without effect, the duelists were joined by friends in a deadly free-for-all in which fifteen of the number were wounded and six killed. Bowie, who had been shot early in the engagement, drew his famed knife and killed Major Norris Wright.

After that the bowie knife became regular equipment of frontiersmen and backwoodsmen from Florida to California for four decades. It was made in large quantities by a firm in Sheffield, England, and shipped to New Orleans. Texas Rangers rode with it. Pirates along the Mississippi used it to disembowel their victims. Its handle and blade were so well balanced that it could be thrown as well as wielded; it was as practical for skinning animals, cutting meat, and eating as it was useful in close combat. It was said of the bowie knife, "It is more trustworthy in the hands of a strong man than a pistol, for it will not snap."

The Bowie family moved to Lecompte, Catahoula Parish, Louisiana, in 1802 from Burke County, Georgia, where James was born about 1799. He was the son of Rezin and Alvina (Jones) Bowie and had three brothers.

Of James Bowie's youth little is actually known, except that he reached maturity in Louisiana. He was six feet tall, of sinewy build and erect carriage and well-proportioned. He was of fair complexion and had blue eyes, was quiet and reserved in temperament. Of his physical courage, strength, and agility many tales were told. It was said of him in Louisiana that he roped and rode alligators on the Bayou Boeuf.

He is reported as having made large sums of money through the sale of Negro slaves smuggled into Louisiana and Texas by Lafitte the pirate. Soon after the sandbar duel, Bowie moved to San Antonio, Texas, prospecting for the location of the lost San Saba mine, legendary with the Spaniards. A rumor prevailed that he had found it, but the search went on in Texas.

Bowie became a Mexican citizen in 1830 and acquired extensive tracts of land by inducing Mexicans to apply for Texas grants from their government and then purchasing these grants at nominal prices. Land speculation was rife at the time, and the millions of leagues of public domain which lay unclaimed were a temptation.

Bowie wooed and won Ursula Veramendi, daughter of the Mexican Vice-governor Juan Martin de Veramendi of San Antonio. They were married in the governor's palace, the massive doors of which are preserved in the Alamo Museum in San Antonio.

There was growing tension between the Americans in Texas and the Mexican government, and separation was inevitable. The people of Louisiana were vitally interested in Texas independence. New Orleans became a recruiting center for volunteers, and the New Orleans Grays went forth to participate in the revolution.

James Bowie joined the War Party. He was chosen a member of the first committee of safety organized at Mina (now Bastrop) on the Colorado in 1835. He fought in the engagement with the Mexicans near San Saba in 1831 and at Nagodoches in 1835. He was made a colonel of volunteers in October, 1835, and with James W. Fannin led ninety men to select a camp site near San Antonio. Surrounded by about four hundred Mexican troops near the Mission of Concepción, the enemy was almost annihilated. Never in command of more than a handful of men, Colonel James Bowie was an important factor in the campaign which captured San Antonio and cleared Texas of the Mexican army by the end of 1835.

But under the dictator Santa Anna, the Mexicans returned in 1836 with an army of six thousand men. Colonel James Bowie and Colonel William B. Travis were in joint command of a small detachment at San Antonio, most of whom were volunteers and Bowie was of that small band of immortals who perished in the Alamo on March 6, 1836.

In the darkest hour of the siege of the Alamo, William Travis is said to have taken his saber and drawn a line on the floor of the Mission, calling upon those willing to die for Texas to cross over. Bowie, ill on a cot, asked to be moved across the line. When the bodies were being identified and gathered by the enemy the day after the battle to form a funeral pyre, Bowie's body was found on his cot surrounded by twenty foes, his trusty blade near at hand.

David Crockett

THE AMERICAN frontier produced a type of individual peculiar to that environment, and no other part of the world could have created David Crockett.

Davy was born on August 17, 1786 near the present Rogersville in Hawkins County, Tennessee, the son of John and Rebecca (Hawkins) Crockett. His father was either born in Ireland or at sea on the voyage over, and his mother was born in Maryland. His father fought in the American Revolution at the Battle of King's Mountain and, when the war was over, moved with his family from Lincoln County, North Carolina, to Tennessee, about three years before David was born.

David's father kept a tavern where the boy lived until he was thirteen when he ran away to Baltimore to escape a thrashing by his father. On his fourth day at school he had quarreled with another pupil and had given him a sound beating. After wandering about for three years, he returned home where he worked for a year for each of two neighbors to pay off two notes of his father amounting to thirty-six and forty dollars, respectively. At this juncture he attended school for the second and last time, and for less than six months, to learn the alphabet and to cipher. This completed his formal schooling. Throughout his life he prided himself on his lack of education; to him correct spelling appeared as something "contrary to nature" and grammar "nothing at all" despite "the fuss that is made of it."

As a child David helped around the tavern, hitching and feeding the teams of the travelers, and ground corn at his father's mill. He had five brothers and three sisters, and the log house he lived in was without windows. His father turned him over to a cattleman, and the first money he ever earned was six dollars paid to him for four weeks' work driving a herd four hundred miles on foot. He took the money, quit, and upon his return home was bound to a Virginia hatter for eighteen months.

At eighteen this intrepid pioneer married Polly Findley. On rented land, with a horse, his bride's dowry of two cows with calves, and fifteen dollars borrowed from a family friend, he cleared a patch in the wilderness and built a one-room log cabin. Though Davy won fame as a mighty hunter, he was a poor farmer; indolent and shiftless, he did not prosper. A couple of years later, with his wife and two babies, he moved to Lincoln County near the Alabama line. Here he enlisted in the Creek war of 1813 under the command of General Andrew Jackson and served as a scout.

David's wife Polly died in 1815, leaving him three children, and he acquired two more children by his marriage some years later to the widow of a fellow soldier.

Crockett's political career began as a magistrate in a sparsely settled region on Shoal Creek where he moved after his short stint in the Creek war. He was made colonel of the militia and in 1821 was elected to the state legislature. He boasted that he had never read a newspaper and though ignorant of public speaking he won popular favor with his homespun wit and was highly respected for his skill with a rifle. When he lost all his property by fire, he moved to the Obion River to occupy himself hunting and living on venison and bear meat until reëlected to the state legislature.

Crockett's decision to seek the office of congressman sprang from a jocular proposal, and his humor, along with ridicule of his two opponents, swept him into office. He served for three terms, in the Twentieth and Twenty-first Congresses (1827–31), was defeated for the Twenty-second, and was elected to the Twenty-third (1833–35). Because of his eccentricities and earthy stories, the backwoodsman was naturally popular in Washington, where he also won a reputation for his common sense and shrewdness. His fame spread until his coonskin cap and marksmanship became legendary while he was still living; when he died his prowess was put to song.

Politically independent, he dared to oppose President Andrew Jackson on a number of measures. He said of his political philosophy, "I am at liberty to vote as my conscience and judgment dictate to be right, without the yoke of party on me, or the driver at my heels, with his whip in hand, commanding me to ge-wo-haw, just at his pleasure."

In April, 1834, David Crockett commenced his celebrated "tour of the north," making public appearances in Baltimore, Philadelphia, New York, and Boston. After returning to Washington, he left for home to prepare for a new campaign. A revival of Jackson's popularity in his congressional district caused his defeat. Disheartened by this reverse, he resolved to leave Tennessee.

A product of the wild frontier, unlettered and unprepared for any special calling, Crockett at fifty years of age was out of a job. Generous, openhanded, frank, upright, and endowed with a bubbling good nature and overflowing self-confidence, he turned his eyes toward Texas. The movement for independence there appealed to him, and he was soon on his way.

He arrived at the Alamo in February, 1836, just in time to take part in its heroic defense. And there he fell, one of many heroes.

Mirabeau Buonaparte Lamar

MIRABEAU LAMAR came from Warren County, Georgia. He was a cousin of Gazaway Bugg Lamar, shipowner, banker, cotton merchant, Confederate agent, and philanthropist. He was the uncle of Lucius Quintus Cincinnatus Lamar, Mississippi statesman, senator, and associate justice of the United States Supreme Court. The unusual names of members of this family were due to the eccentricity of an uncle who named them.

Mirabeau was born on August 16, 1798. His parents, John and Rebecca (Lamar) Lamar, were cousins descended from Thomas Lamar who emigrated from France to Virginia and then settled in Maryland before 1663. Mirabeau was the second of a family of nine children, several of whom achieved distinction. The father, a thrifty farmer, gave them all a sound common school education.

After an unsuccessful venture as a merchant in Alabama, Lamar became the private secretary of Governor George M. Troup, of Georgia in 1813 and took an active part in the movement to secure the expulsion of the Creeks and Cherokees from Georgia against the opposion of the national government. After his marriage, on January 1, 1826, to Tobitha B. Jordan of Perry, Alabama, he became the editor of the Columbus *Enquirer* of Columbus, Georgia, the official organ of the states' rights party.

Lamar's wife died in 1833, and defeated for Congress he became interested in the trek to Texas, which was gathering momentum. After a short trip there in 1835, he returned in 1836, borrowed a horse, and was soon on his way to join Houston's army at Groce's Ferry. In the battle of San Jacinto he so distinguished himself as the commander of the cavalry that he was appointed secretary of war in the provisional cabinet of President David G. Burnet.

He advocated the execution of Santa Anna, who survived San Jacinto to wage war against the United States, and was bitterly opposed to the more lenient policy of Austin and Houston. An excellent horseman and ready orator, he rode the hustings as a candidate for vice-president and was elected in 1836. Two years later, after a curious campaign marked by the suicides of two leading opponents, he became the second president of the Republic of Texas.

Lamar's habit of writing verse, which he later brought together in a volume entitled *Verse Memorials,* strengthened the belief of his political opponents that he was more dreamer than statesman.

His administration, however, was punctured by a number of constructive measures. After the United States first rejected the offer of annexation, Lamar launched a positive foreign policy with the view of laying a basis for permanent independence. He established diplomatic relations with France and England and attempted in vain to negotiate with Mexico for recognition. He undertook a program for the commercial development of the natural resources of the country, formulated a new land policy, initiated a system of public education, and strengthened the Texas Army and Navy. He became the founder of the new city of Austin on the Colorado.

Lamar sought to expand the boundaries of the Texas republic to include the important trading post of Santa Fe, New Mexico. His ill-fated expedition of three hundred volunteers and traders were captured, and those not killed were placed under guard, marched to Mexico, and imprisoned; the survivors finally were released.

In his plan to extend the sovereignty of Texas to the whole region north and east of the Rio Grande, he secured the expulsion of the Cherokees from eastern Texas and sent a successful punitive expedition against the Comanches and Kiowas in the west. He was as ruthless and effective in dealing with the Indians in Texas as he had been adamant earlier in driving the Creeks and Cherokees from Georgia.

Successful in many things, Lamar was unable to solve the growing financial difficulties of Texas, and when Houston was reëlected president in 1841, the value of the paper currency of Texas had almost reached the vanishing point.

Lamar's closing years were relatively uneventful. In 1844 he reversed his former position and became an advocate of Texas annexation on the ground that it was necessary to the preservation of slavery and the security of the South. After services during the Mexican war at Monterey and Laredo under General Zachary Taylor, he returned to his Texas plantation at Richmond. After remaining a widower for eighteen years, he married Marietta Moffitt of Galveston.

Suffering financial reverses, Lamar accepted an appointment as minister to Nicaragua in 1857, but finding it impossible to gain ratification of a proposed treaty which would have given the United States a virtual protectorate over the isthmus, he was recalled in July, 1859, and died at his home in Richmond on December 19, 1859.

He was simple in manner, honest in purpose, generous in money matters, and famed for his hospitality, and his devotion to the welfare of Texas and his faith in its future were generally recognized and praised by a pioneering community that was naturally suspicious of red-blooded men who wrote poetry. Dedicated to the cause of Texas, Lamar lived a more moving epic than he ever penned in his poetic *Memorials.*

James Sevier Conway

THOMAS AND ANN (Rector) Conway of Tennessee had seven sons and three daughters. James Sevier and his brother Elias Nelson each served as governor of Arkansas. Another brother, Henry, was elected territorial delegate to the national Congress and was killed by Robert Crittenden in a deul that grew out of a political dispute in 1827.

Their grandfather Henry was a soldier in the American Revolution. To preserve his slaves and other property from possible capture by the British, he put them into the care of his son Thomas and John Sevier, the son of a companion in arms, and sent them from Virginia into what became Green County, Tennessee. Here Thomas settled and reared his large family. All the sons who reached maturity attained some distinction. The daughters each married into the Sevier family. Thomas became a member of the Senate in the lost State of Franklin, that ill-starred commonwealth that was carved out of North Carolina to enjoy a precarious existence of four years and, eventually, to be embraced by Tennessee.

James Sevier, the second son of Thomas, was born on December 9, 1798. Along with his six brothers, he was given every educational advantage the frontier offered. When he was sixteen, the Conway clan moved to St. Louis and later lived in Saline County, Missouri. At twenty-one James went to the Arkansas Territory with his brother Henry under a federal contract to survey land. President Andrew Jackson, a friend of the family, appointed James to the office of public surveyor, a position he held until Arkansas was admitted into the Union in 1836.

James Sevier Conway made his home in Lafayette County, and while marking the state's boundaries he developed a cotton plantation on the Red River with a hundred slaves.

On December 21, 1826, he married Mary J. Bradley, formerly of Nashville. His great ambition to become the first governor of Arkansas was realized in 1836. Though political parties did not exist in the Territory, James Conway ran for the office on a "Democratic-Republican" ticket and polled 5,338 votes against his opponent's 3,222. He was inaugurated with much pomp, with Albert Pike administering the oath of office.

Arkansas, a typical frontier state, was sparsely populated and financially impoverished. Pioneers were trailing in with covered wagons, and there was the usual lawless element. Conway set about to establish order, organize the state government, and raise public revenue.

The most notable event of his administration was the passage of acts chartering the State Bank and the Real Estate Bank and the issuance of state bonds to support the two banks. This enterprise began badly; the speaker of the House of Representatives was also president of the Real Estate Bank, and in the course of a quarrel on the floor of the House he killed a fellow representative. Not long after the opening of these banks specie payments were suspended, and the banks became a continuing political issue. Depositors and stockholders lost heavily in a disaster of local magnitude.

Though Governor Conway had been severely criticized for permitting a "piratical crew of fortune seekers" to "scuttle the financial fame of the state," he was absolved from any guilt. No one has ever questioned his integrity. New capital was needed, and Arkansas was not alone in her state banking venture. Other states were making the same sad experiment.

Governor Conway had the misfortune of experiencing another financial disappointment during his incumbency. Federal funds to the amount of twenty-five thousand dollars were turned over to him to pay Arkansas volunteers called into the service. Because of an illness he turned this money over to an army officer who proved careless in his accounts, and judgment was taken against Conway for a considerable sum. Congress, however, on the recommendation of its committee of investigation, canceled the debt.

Arkansas had growing pains during Governor Conway's administration. The population of the state doubled in four years to reach nearly one hundred thousand. Land speculation was the foremost business activity. Little progress was made in higher education, though Batesville Academy (Arkansas College) was incorporated. However, a number of rough one-room log schools were established where children were taught "readin', 'ritin', and 'rithmetic," and little else except occasionally geography. Yet, from such schools some of our best educated men emerged. Probably with his banking fiasco in mind, Conway retired to Walnut Grove, his Red River plantation, when his term expired in 1840, and he never again aspired to public office. There he cultivated his broad acres in peace until he died on March 3, 1855.

James Sevier Conway, with a brother, surveyed the boundaries of Arkansas. He organized the government and initiated her into the sisterhood of states. His brother Elias Nelson came after him to fill the office of chief executive in 1852, and where James may have failed financially, Elias signally succeeded. The defaulted banks were still unliquidated, and Elias assumed official responsibility for the debts without fear or favor, as he restored the credit and honor of the state. At the end of his second term, after eight years in office, he left a substantial surplus in the state treasury in gold and silver.

Individually, neither of the Conways achieved national distinction, but together they had a permanent influence upon the destinies of a great state.

Isaac Shelby

THE FIRST governor of Kentucky, Isaac Shelby, the son of Evan and Laetitia (Cox) Shelby, was born near North Mountain, Maryland, on December 11, 1750. His father, a soldier and pioneer, born in Wales, had come to America with Isaac's grandparents at the age of fifteen.

Isaac learned early the use of arms and became inured to the hardships of the American frontier. He acquired a fair education, worked on his father's plantation, was occasionally employed as a surveyor, and, before he was of age, served as deputy sheriff of Frederick County. In 1771 he moved with his father to the present site of Bristol, Tennessee.

Isaac served as a lieutenant in his father's Fincastle Company at the winning battle of Point Pleasant. His report of this action is one of the best contemporary descriptions of that encounter. Shelby remained second in command of the garrison of Fort Blair until July, 1775, when he visited Kentucky and surveyed lands for the Transylvania Company. Because of his health, he returned home in July, 1776, just in time to participate in the battle of Long Island flats.

Shelby was appointed captain of a company of minutemen by the Virginia committee of safety, and a year later Governor Patrick Henry made him commissary of supplies for a body of militia detailed to garrison frontier posts. In the spring of 1779, he was chosen a member of the Virginia legislature, representing Washington County, and soon afterward Governor Thomas Jefferson made him a major in the escort for the commissioners appointed to run the western boundary line between Virginia and North Carolina. When the line was determined, Shelby's residence was found to be in North Carolina, so he resigned his commission, but was at once appointed colonel in the North Carolina militia. He was in Kentucky, perfecting title to lands he had selected on a previous visit when he heard of the fall of Charleston and the desperate situation in the southern colonies.

Shelby organized a force, joined McDowell at Cherokee Ford, South Carolina, and at the head of a detachment captured a formidable Loyalist stronghold, Thicketty Fort, on the headwaters of the Pacolet River. He also won victories at Cedar Springs, and Musgrove's Mill, but the report of General Gates's defeat at Camden forced Shelby to retreat. In concert with John Sevier and others, Shelby organized an expedition against Ferguson, whose combined Provincial and Loyalist force was overwhelmingly defeated in the decisive battle of Kings Mountain on October 7, 1780, which marked the turning of the tide of the American Revolution. Shelby and Sevier each received the thanks of the North Carolina legislature, and a sword and a pair of pistols. Shelby was also accorded credit for the scheme of attack which led to the battle of the Cowpens on January 17, 1781. And the Continental Congress joined the North Carolina legislature in resolutions of appreciation.

Accompanied by Colonel John Sevier, Shelby joined others and captured the British post at Fair Lawn, South Carolina. He then removed to Boonesborough, Kentucky, where he married Susannah Hart, daughter of Captain Nathaniel Hart on April 19, 1783. For his years of service to his country, he received a liquidation certificate, which his agent sold for "six yards of middling broadcloth, and I gave one coat of it to the person who brought it out to me!"

In 1783 Shelby was appointed a trustee to Transylvania Seminary. He helped organize the Kentucky Society for Promoting Useful Knowledge, and for several years served as high sheriff of his county. He was a member of the convention which framed the first constitution of Kentucky, and was elected the state's first governor. At the close of his term he declined reëlection, and spent the next fifteen years giving attention to the cultivation of his farm. Shelby prospered as a horse trader and mule dealer; supplying the Cotton Kingdom was a flourishing business. South Carolinians once boycotted Shelby in an effort to force Henry Clay to reconsider his stand on the Tariff of Abominations.

However, when war with Great Britain became imminent, in 1812, Shelby was called out of retirement to be elected governor for the second time. At the age of sixty-three, he led four thousand Kentucky volunteers to join General William Henry Harrison in the invasion of Canada, an expedition which resulted in the decisive defeat of the British at the battle of the Thames.

For his patriotic services he was awarded a gold medal by Congress, and was tendered the portfolio of War by President Monroe, which he declined. He was commissioned, with General Andrew Jackson, to negotiate a treaty with the Chickasaw Indians for the purchase of their lands west of the Tennessee River, and was president of the first Kentucky Agricultural Society, and chairman of the first board of trustees of Centre College. At his death he was buried at his historic home, Traveller's Rest.

As a soldier and administrator, Shelby evidenced a high degree of political wisdom and executive ability. Above medium height, sturdy, and well proportioned, he was capable of enduring protracted labor, privation, and fatigue. When Kentucky was passing through its formative stage, he gave that state his experience and strength.

3

The Rise and Fall of the Confederacy

Jefferson Davis
Albert Sidney Johnston
Matthew Fontaine Maury
Leonidas Polk
Raphael Semmes
Robert Augustus Toombs
John Slidell
Judah Philip Benjamin
Alexander Hamilton Stephens
Howell Cobb
Braxton Bragg
Pierre Gustav Toutant Beauregard
Henry Watkins Allen
James Longstreet
Nathan Bedford Forrest
John Cabell Breckinridge
Thomas Jonathan Jackson
Edmund Kirby-Smith
William Lowndes Yancey
Richard Taylor
Patrick Ronayne Cleburne
Zebulon Baird Vance
Augustus Hill Garland
James Ewell Brown Stuart
Joseph Wheeler
Robert E. Lee

Jefferson Davis

THE TENTH child of Samuel and Jane (Cook) Davis, Jefferson Davis was born in a log cabin, in Christian (now Todd) County, Kentucky, on June 3, 1808. The Davises later migrated to Louisiana, and from there to a plantation near Woodville, Mississippi. Joseph, the eldest of the sons, moved to Natchez to practice law and grow cotton, and soon amassed a fortune to lift the family from obscurity.

At seven, Jeff took a thousand-mile journey on horseback with Colonel Thomas Hinds to enter St. Thomas College, a seminary in Kentucky. At nine, he attended Jefferson Academy at Port Gibson, Mississippi, and at thirteen, was back in Kentucky, attending Transylvania University. At sixteen, he entered West Point, where he first met Robert E. Lee. With a commission of second lieutenant, Davis participated in the Black Hawk War. He married Sarah Knox, a daughter of Colonel Zachary Taylor, against Taylor's wishes, resigned from the army, and returned to Mississippi where his bride of three months died of malarial fever.

From 1835 to 1845 Davis was a planter in seclusion. He cleared Briarfield plantation from the rough, sharing the work with his slaves. An omnivorous reader, he concentrated on the study of history, economics, and constitutional law. With firm convictions on slavery, he became a strong advocate of state sovereignty, and was elected to Congress in 1845. In the same year he was married to Varina Howell, daughter of a planter.

Davis supported the policy of war with Mexico and, when war came, returned to Wilkinson County to organize the Mississippi Rifles. Joining General Taylor, with whom he had become reconciled, he won the praise of the General for his gallantry at Monterrey and Buena Vista and national fame for his V-formation attack. On his return home, he was elected to the United States Senate. Though still on crutches, he took an active part in its deliberations. Regarding the organization of the Oregon Territory, he consistently denied that there was any power in Congress or in the people of the Territory to interrupt the slave system by denying a slaveholder the right to take his personal property with him. In 1850 he was reëlected, but resigned the following year.

On the election of Franklin Pierce in 1853, Davis was appointed Secretary of War. He enlarged the army, revised its tactics, strengthened the nation's defense, and introduced improvements at West Point. In 1857 he resigned to reënter the United States Senate, where he pursued a consistent course on the subject of states' rights. When Abraham Lincoln was elected, Davis believed that war was inevitable. And when Mississippi seceded, he resigned from the Senate.

Mississippi had appointed him major general of state troops at the time he became the compromise candidate for president of the Confederacy. He was in his garden at Briarfield, supervising rose-cutting when notified. He was made president of the provisional government, and was inaugurated at Richmond on February 22, 1862.

President Davis was unable to win Europe over to the side of the Confederacy. The federal blockade of ports cut off supplies and precluded the exportation of cotton which was the backbone of the Confederacy's economy. Suffering from neuralgia and nervous indigestion, he carried on with determination, contending for a cause that was lost before it began, ultimately becoming the scapegoat for the sins of the South.

When Richmond fell, Davis and his cabinet fled. With a reward of one hundred thousand dollars offered by President Andrew Jackson for his capture, he was overtaken at Irwinville, Georgia, by federal cavalry on May 10, 1865. Charged with conspiracy in the assassination of Lincoln and later indicted for treason, he was taken to Fortress Monroe, Virginia, and shackled by a half-literate blacksmith, but not without a struggle. Though his irons were removed within a week, he languished in prison for two years, before he was released on one hundred thousand dollar bail.

Even though he pleaded for a trial for years, Davis never came before the bar of justice and it was not until 1869 that his case was finally dismissed. His fortune wrecked, his home ruined, and his health impaired, he lived many of his last days in poverty, except for the charity of admirers. He spent his declining years at Beauvoir on the Mississippi Gulf Coast, a home willed to him by Sarah A. Dorsey, a friend of Mrs. Davis. Here he spent three years writing *The Rise and Fall of the Confederate Government.* When he died in New Orleans on December 6, 1889, his body was taken to Richmond.

Davis had never regained his citizenship. Mississippians would have returned him to the United States Senate, but he refused to ask the federal government for a pardon without which he was denied the right to hold public office. By the invitation of the Mississippi State Legislature, he visited Jackson in 1884 Seventy-six years old, feeble but firm, he restated his political convictions. Addressing the legislature, he said he had never repented: "If it were to do all over again, I would do just as I did in sixty-one."

Davis had been loath to leave the Union in 1861 and was as loath to return to it in 1884. The most maligned of American leaders, willful and unreconstructable, he was a man of great integrity. In defeat, the acid test of greatness, he demonstrated an amazing spirit of defiance. And as long as men cherish their individual freedom and revere the Constitution, and are willing to fight for their convictions, he will be remembered as statesman, soldier, patriot.

Albert Sidney Johnston

When Albert Sidney Johnston was mortally wounded in the battle of Shiloh in the Civil War, his death was temporarily concealed from his loyal rank and file.

President Jefferson Davis spoke for the whole south when he said: "It may safely be asserted that our loss is irreparable and that among the shining hosts of the great and good who cluster about the banner of our country, there exists no purer spirit, no more heroic soul. . . ."

Johnston was born in Washington, Mason County, Kentucky, on February 3, 1803, the youngest son of John Johnston, a country doctor.

Sidney studied under private tutors in western Virginia and at Transylvania University where he excelled in mathematics and Latin. He was graduated from West Point in 1826, eighth in his class, and was breveted second lieutenant.

He was later commissioned, joined the 6th Infantry at Jefferson Barracks, Missouri, and distinguished himself in the Black Hawk War. On January 20, 1829 he married Henrietta Preston and because of her illness resigned from the service. After her death, he tried farming near St. Louis but soon gave it up and went to Texas where he enlisted as a private in its revolutionary army.

His appointment by General Thomas J. Rusk as adjutant general aroused the jealousy of General Felix Huston who challened Johnston to a duel in which Johnston was seriously wounded. He recovered to assume command, and he and Huston became fast friends.

In 1838, President Lamar made him secretary of war, and he successfully defended the Texas border against Mexican invasion and Indian raids. He resigned from the cabinet and returned to Kentucky where he married Eliza Griffin, his first wife's cousin. He then bought China Grove, a plantation in Brazoria County, Texas, which for three years caused him much financial grief. The soldier was no farmer.

When the Mexican war started, Johnston was commissioned colonel, 1st Texas Rifle Volunteers, by General Zachary Taylor and served at Monterey under General Butler as inspector general. He was appointed paymaster in the United States Army in 1849, serving for five years. In 1855, President Pierce appointed him colonel of cavalry. He assumed command of the Department of Texas from 1858 to 1860 as brevet brigadier general and led an expedition to quell the Mormons of Utah who were in revolt against the national government.

Johnston was in California in charge of the Department of the Pacific when Texas seceded from the Union. Despite flattering offers from the federal government, he committed his family to Dr. John S. Griffin, his brother-in-law, and marched across the country to offer his services to President Davis at Richmond. He was immediately appointed general and assigned to command the department of the west.

Resolved on a bold course, Johnston occupied Bowling Green, Kentucky. He called for troops and began to organize an army. His problem then, and thereafter, was the need for manpower. In every engagement with the enemy he was outnumbered two to one.

At Mill Spring on January 19, 1862, through the disobedience of part of his command, he was defeated by General George H. Thomas. He suffered defeats at Fort Henry and Fort Donelson and withdrew to Nashville. When General Buell captured that city, he retreated to Murfreesboro and thence to Corinth. When President Davis was implored to replace him, he replied: "If Sidney Johnston is not a general, I have none."

The federal forces held a strong position at Shiloh Church near Pittsburg Landing. With Johnson's concentration of forty thousand men at Corinth complete, he moved against General U. S. Grant on April 6, 1862. When Generals Bragg, Hardee, Polk, and Breckinridge as corps commanders, he drove everything before him, pressing the federals back to the Tennessee River in a complete rout. At this moment of triumph, tragedy struck. While leading his men in a final charge, he was shot from his horse and with an artery severed, bled to death.

General Johnson's body was carried to New Orleans and temporarily entombed. In 1867, Texas claimed him, and his remains were removed to Austin. Stops were made at Galveston and Houston where his friends, denied a military funeral procession by General Philip H. Sheridan, Military Reconstruction governor, demonstrated their devotion by following his body silently as it passed through the streets.

Heroic Sidney Johnston was every bit the dauntless soldier. Over six feet tall, straight as an arrow, broad-shouldered, with massive chest and square jaws, he looked the part. He was admired for his fine horsemanship on the frontier, and he once clubbed a puma to death. Of unimpeachable character, he had the respect of soldiers and officers. General Zachary Taylor said he was the best soldier he ever commanded.

Matthew Fontaine Maury

AT NINETEEN, Matthew Fontaine Maury left Franklin, Tennessee, for Washington, to become a midshipman in the United States Navy. America's seafaring scientist was born near Fredericksburg, Virginia, on January 14, 1806, the fourth son in a family of five sons and four daughters. He sprang from a family founded by a Dutch sea captain who settled in the colony in the days of Charles II.

In Matthew's fifth year his father took the family to Tennessee, settling on a farm near the village of Franklin. Matthew attended rural schools until he was nearly killed in a fall from a tree at the age of twelve. No longer able to do hard work, he was sent to Harpeth Academy where the apt pupil soon became assistant teacher.

Without his father's knowledge or consent, young Maury talked Congressman Sam Houston of Tennessee into getting him an appointment as midshipman in the United States Navy. Since there was no naval academy then, he was immediately assigned to sea duty. His first trip was to Europe on the war vessel that took Lafayette back to France after his memorable visit. He then went around the world, followed by a voyage to South America. Returning in 1834, he married Ann Hull Herndon of Fredericksburg, Virginia. Establishing his residence there, he used his leisure in the publication of a work on navigation which he had begun during his sea duty.

In 1836 Maury was promoted to the grade of lieutenant. In 1839 he suffered a fall from a carriage that left him lamed for life. Unable to perform active duties, he devoted his time to study and the improvement of the navy. His forcibly stated views, published over the pen name of Harry Bluff, produced much needed reforms.

In the interest of commerce, Maury advocated the warehousing system. In 1842 he was appointed superintendent of the depots of charts and instruments at Washington, afterward the hydrographic office. As naval observatory astronomer he added the task of determining the direction of ocean winds and currents. In 1855 he published *The Physical Geography of the Sea,* the first textbook of modern oceanography, which went through numerous editions and translations. In the early 1850's the idea of a trans-Atlantic cable was being discussed, and Maury prepared a chart representing in profile the bottom of the Atlantic, called "the telegraphic plateau." The citizens of New York presented him with a silver service and a purse of five thousand dollars in appreciation of his contributions to commerce.

Maury cherished as a favorite project the opening of the Amazon Valley to free trade, hoping that the project would draw slaves from the United States to Brazil. In the growing antagonism between the North and South, his sympathies were naturally with his section, but he favored conciliation. Three days after the secession of Virginia, he tendered his resignation and proceeded to Richmond, where he was commissioned a commander in the Confederate States Navy.

He established the naval submarine service at Richmond and experimented with electric mines. Before the bureau was far advanced, Commander Maury was sent to England as a special agent. Here his international reputation made him an effective spokesman for the Southern Cause. He was instrumental in securing needed ships and continued his experiments with electric mines. With the purpose of using these mines, he set out for America, but when he reached the West Indies the Confederacy had collapsed.

Confederates serving abroad were excluded from pardon under the amnesty proclamations; so Maury offered his services to the Emperor of Mexico in a scheme for the colonization of confederates. When the revolution there intervened, he returned to England where he busied himself with perfecting his electric mines and where he wrote a series of geographies for school use. He was presented with a purse of three thousand guineas raised by popular subscription in gratitude for his services to the maritime world, and Cambridge University honored him with the degree of doctor of laws.

Maury returned to the United States in 1868 to accept the professorship of meteorology at the Virginia Military Institute at Lexington, where he stressed the importance of weather forecasting. While on a lecture tour in the fall of 1872 in promotion of this idea, he was taken ill at St. Louis and died on February 1, 1873.

A self-educated scientist, Maury led his biographer, John W. Wayland, to write in 1930, "The thing . . . that made Maury a great man was his ability to see the invisible. . . . He saw the cable before it was laid. He saw a railroad across the continent before it was built. He saw a ship canal from the Mississippi to the Great Lakes before it was dug. . . . He saw a great training school for our Naval officers . . . and weather reports for our farmers, long before either was a reality. He saw a ship canal across the Isthmus of Panama more than a century before it was constructed. He was a seer and a pathfinder not only on the seas, but under the seas, across the lands, and among the stars."

Leonidas Polk

THOMAS POLK, a soldier of the American Revolution, was of Scotch-Irish stock; he founded the University of North Carolina. Colonel William Polk, his son, also fought in the War for Independence. He had twelve children, the second of whom was Leonidas. Thomas Polk's grandnephew, James K. Polk, was the eleventh president of the United States.

Leonidas, Louisiana's "Fighting Bishop," was born at Raleigh, North Carolina, on April 10, 1806. He attended preparatory schools and then entered the state university. His military-minded father prevailed upon him to accept an appointment to West Point where he was graduated in 1827 and breveted a lieutenant of cavalry.

While studying at the academy, Leonidas was baptized by Charles P. McIlvaine, the eloquent chaplain, who easily persuaded him to enter the ministry. Lieutenant Polk resigned his commission and entered the Virginia Theological Seminary. He was ordained deacon in the Protestant Episcopal Church in 1830 and a year later advanced to priesthood. In 1830 he married Frances Devereaux, his childhood sweetheart.

Reverend Leonidas Polk served the Monumental Church in Richmond, Virginia, as assistant for a year and then traveled in Europe. Upon his return he became rector of St. Peter's Church at Columbia, Tennessee.

In 1838 Polk was appointed missionary Bishop of the Southwest, a sparsely populated diocese that embraced Louisiana, Alabama, Mississippi, Arkansas, and the Indian Territory. In 1841 he became the first Protestant Episcopal Bishop of Louisiana. Under his evangelical leadership Episcopal churches were established at Shreveport, Plaquemine, Opelousas, Thibodaux, Napoleonville, and Donaldsonville. During his episcopate at New Orleans he ordained sixteen deacons and nineteen priests, and the number of churches grew from three to thirty-three.

Mrs. Polk having inherited four hundred slaves, the Bishop bought a sugar plantation with the idea of setting up a more enlightened system for master and servant, but the altruistic experiment did not prosper. Polk believed in the gradual emancipation of slaves.

He took the initiative in a movement to establish an Episcopal University in the South, where its aristocratic youth might be better taught and trained for responsibility as masters of a subject race. As his grandfather had founded a university before him, Bishop Polk laid the cornerstone for the University of the South at Sewanee, Tennessee in 1860, the reality of his dreams and labors "for a home of all the arts and sciences and of literary culture in the Southern States."

When the Civil War broke out a year later, the Bishop felt that the South was fighting for a sacred cause. Jefferson Davis, his fellow cadet at West Point, offered him a major generalship. Just as the lieutenant had removed his uniform to wear the cloth when he was called to preach at the age of twenty-one, the Bishop at fifty-one put by his robes to wear the gray and fight with the Confederacy.

His familiarity with the Mississippi Valley prompted him to urge its importance upon Jefferson Davis, and he was assigned the responsibility of fortifying it.

General Polk defeated General Grant in an engagement at Belmont, Missouri. At Shiloh he commanded the Confederate right wing, four times personally leading charges. He was in the operations around Corinth, conducted the Confederate retreat from Kentucky, and was promoted to lieutenant general. At Chickamauga he held the right wing, was later in command of the department of Alabama, and then joined Joseph E. Johnston for the Atlanta campaign.

Oblivious to danger, Polk risked his life unnecessarily, and while reconnoitering on Pine Mountain, near Marietta, on June 14, 1864, he was killed by a cannon ball.

General Polk had had only limited military training, and his appointment as a Confederate general was partly made for its moral and psychological effect. He was so constituted that he could not follow the orders of his superiors. Braxton Bragg cited him to be court-martialed for dilatory tactics at Chickamauga. He was removed from command during the controversy but was reinstated.

With the Holy Bible in one hand and his sword in the other, he was a good influence on the rank and file throughout the conflict. While other generals waged war to preserve the Constitution, the "Fighting Bishop" was engaged in a holy crusade.

Polk was of good stature and erect in his carriage. Perry said of him in his *History of the American Episcopal Church* that Polk was "a man whom noble men might love and meaner men might fear." His son, William M. Polk, followed his father into the Civil War at the age of seventeen. Of him it was said that no soldier in the conflict took part in more battles and skirmishes. William later studied medicine at Tulane University, became dean of the Medical School at Cornell, and wrote a biography of his father.

Polk was a product of that peculiar and sometimes inconsistent aristocracy of the South, which will probably fight until the end of time for its beliefs. In the pulpit and on the battlefield, he lived up to the tradition of a family that offered itself again and again for the cause of freedom.

Raphael Semmes

As COMMANDER of the C.S.S. *Alabama* during the Civil War, he captured eighty-two merchant ships and sank a man-of-war.

Of French Catholic ancestry, Raphael Semmes was born in Charles County, Maryland, on September 27, 1809, the elder son of Richard Thompson Semmes and Catherine (Middleton) Semmes. Both parents dying during his early childhood, Raphael was brought up in Georgetown, near Washington, by an uncle. At sixteen he was appointed midshipman in the navy, his active career beginning on a sloop-of-war, and he waited five years for a vacancy in the commissioned ranks. During this probation period he served in Mediterranean, Caribbean, and South Atlantic waters and during his leaves of absence studied and practiced law in Maryland and Ohio. In Ohio he fell in love with Anne Elizabeth Spencer, whom he married on May 5, 1837.

From 1837 to the outbreak of the Mexican war, Semmes spent most of his time on survey duty on the southern coast and commanded the "Somers" in 1846 in the blockade of Mexico. While chasing a runner, his brig encountered a tropical squall and sank in ten minutes with the loss of more than half of his crew. After the disaster he participated in the bombardment of Vera Cruz, took part in the expedition against Tuxpan, and accompanied Scott's army to Mexico.

In November, 1847, he returned to his home at Prospect Hill, Baldwin County, Alabama, and wrote his memoirs, practiced law, and filled lighthouse inspection assignments. He became a commander, but resigned on February 15, 1861, to offer his services to the Confederacy.

On a tour of northern cities he bought large quantities of percussion caps and gun powder, which he was able to ship south before the commencement of hostilities. Upon his return to Montgomery he was made chief of the Lighthouse Bureau and was given the first highseas command in the new navy, the C.S.S. "Sumter," under orders to "do the enemy's commerce the greatest injury in the shortest time."

The "Sumter" was still only the packet steamer "Havana" lying in her berth at New Orleans. But Semmes soon had her reconditioned as a man-of-war with a crew of 114 officers and men. On the third day at sea Semmes took and burned the "Golden Rocket." He captured nine other vessels in Caribbean waters, two on a cruise to Brazil, and then crossing the Atlantic to Gibraltar, he took six prizes en route. Here he was blockaded by the enemy, and since the "Sumter's" hull and boilers were in much need of repair, he laid her up.

For his "gallant and meritorious conduct in capturing and destroying the enemy's commerce on the high seas," Semmes was promoted to captain and voted the thanks of the Confederate Congress. His passage homeward was interrupted at Nassau by orders to take command of the "Alabama," then nearing completion in Liverpool. To observe neutrality the British launched the ship as the "Enrica," and she was transferred to Semmes in the Azores, commissioned as a man-of-war, and under his command became the terror of the seas. Semmes seemed to be everywhere, the Newfoundland Banks, the Caribbean, the coast of Africa, South Pacific, Indian Ocean, up the Atlantic to Cherbourg, France.

There for an overhauling, awaiting the emperor's permission to dock, the U.S.S. "Kearsarge" appeared over the horizon. With all of Cherbourg and half of Paris gathered on the cliffs to bear witness, the "Alabama" steamed out and opened fire. They fought it out until the "Alabama" went down trying to make the French shore. Semmes hauled down his colors and gave orders to abandon ship. She sank in about fifteen minutes. Semmes wrote long afterwards that she went down, "like a living thing in real pain—she threw her bow high out of the water, then went down stern first to her last resting place." Semmes, the last to abandon ship, was in the water half an hour before being rescued by the French.

After a rest in Switzerland, Semmes, who had been promoted to rear admiral, returned by way of Mexico. He arrived at Richmond in January, 1865, to command the James River Squadron. He surrendered at Greensboro, North Carolina, was paroled, and returned to Mobile, where he was arrested and imprisoned by order of the United States Secretary of the Navy despite the protection which his parole should have afforded him. Held on the absurd charge of having violated the usages of war by escaping from the "Alabama" after her colors were struck, he was brought for trial before a military commission. The Supreme Court denied the commission's jurisdiction, and he was released.

Upon his return home Semmes was elected probate judge of Mobile County but was driven out of office under orders from the United States Secretary of War. He accepted the chair of philosophy and English literature at Louisiana Seminary, now Louisiana State University, but was forced to quit. He became editor of the Memphis *Daily Bulletin* and was soon hounded out of that position. After a number of lecture tours, he returned to Mobile and engaged in the practice of law until his death at his home on Point Clear, Mobile Bay, on August 30, 1877.

Robert Augustus Toombs

A SMALL AREA IN Georgia, a corner of the state's cotton belt, produced three of the South's ablest leaders, Alexander Stephens, Robert Toombs, and Howell Cobb. The lives of Stephens and Toombs, who were intimate friends, paralleled each other. Toombs, talented and forthright, became United States senator, Confederate secretary of state, and brigadier general in the Confederate Army.

Unlike Stephens, who was born in humble circumstances, Toombs was reared in comparative luxury. He was born in Wilkes County on July 2, 1810, the fifth child of Robert Toombs, who had been a major in the Revolution and was a well-to-do cotton planter, and the latter's third wife, Catherine Huling. His father died when he was five, and he was reared by his guardian, Thomas W. Cobb.

Robert was expelled from the University of Georgia for card playing and then entered Union College, Schenectady, New York, graduating in 1828. He later studied law at the University of Virginia and was admitted to the bar in Elbert County. Eight months after his admission, he married Julia Du Bose.

After several years as a member of the state legislature, Toombs was elected to Congress as a states' rights Whig in 1845. He was reëlected for three terms, and beginning on March 4, 1853, he served as United States senator. He had been reëlected for a second term at the outbreak of the war.

The reputation of Toombs had preceded him. He was already a legendary character, recognized for his political prowess. He was one of the most magnetic personalities of his epoch. Like Lincoln, he was a genial comrade of courthouse squares, taverns, and stage coaches. Stories of his eloquence on the hustings, his anecdotes, his fearlessness in the face of injustice, his tenderness to the underdog, and witty speech were common knowledge. The report that Toombs was to speak quickly filled the galleries.

Toombs's speeches rolled out with resonant ease. On a second's notice his bulky frame would rise, and his deep voice would fill the chamber, never pausing for lack of a word. He was at his best in fiscal matters. The most obtuse financial problems yielded their secrets as he dissected them. He opposed measures appropriating federal money for local projects and declared, "I do not want a dollar of public money expended in the state of Georgia."

Like Lincoln and Stephens, Toombs opposed President Polk in his Mexican war project. He felt that the acquisition of territory would precipitate a disastrous sectional controversy. Though a thorough going proslavery man, he was still a worshiper of the Union and the Constitution. The Toombs-Stephens coalition stood for the federated system and against those who attempted to undermine it. Both Whigs, they joined with Howell Cobb, a Democrat, to organize a Constitutional-Union Party hoping to preserve the federal government.

When the forces of fanaticism, North and South, could not be contained by his energy and eloquence, Toombs became a torrent of rebellious vituperation. As he walked out of the United States Senate, he defied the North to keep the South in the Union. "Come on and do it!" he shouted. And to the Georgia legislature he flung the challenge, "Make another war of independence; fight its battles over again; reconquer liberty and independence." The legislature joined the Confederacy.

When the provisional government was formed to adopt a constitution, Toombs had reason to believe he might be made president. When Davis was chosen, Toombs, whose rare ability as a financier marked him as the logical man for Secretary of the Treasury, was made Secretary of State.

Alone in Davis' cabinet, Toombs opposed the attack on Fort Sumter. He resisted the president's method of relying on credit instead of taxation to finance the war. He liked to call the Southern cause a "revolution" and cried out for a "counter-revolution" against Davis' despotism. He applied for a military commission and, in July, 1861, was given command of a Georgia brigade on the Virginia front, still retaining membership in the Confederate Congress. Though without military experience, his contingent held the stone bridge on the field of Antietam, where an enemy bullet shattered his left hand.

At the close of the war, Toombs was marked as one of the men to be seized and punished. When the Union troops rushed into Toombs's house he was waiting to be called to dinner. Escaping through a back door while his wife stalled the intruders, he mounted a horse and rode away. He hid for a time and finally reached Havana and Paris, where he was joined by Mrs. Toombs. After returning to the United States in 1867, he called on President Andrew Johnson, an old friend, but his citizenship was never restored because he refused to ask Congress for a pardon.

He resumed his practice of law with such success that his fees were reported to have brought in more than a million dollars. And he became an influential factor in the overthrow of Reconstruction government in Georgia with its plundering carpetbaggers. Cataracts dimmed his vision in his last days. Despondent over the passing of his wife, he indulged in strong drink and died on December 15, 1885.

Toombs would have prevented the conflict if he had had his way. A true Southern gentleman, he was magnanimous to his enemies, generous with his friends, scornful of hypocrisy, and devoted to his state and to the Constitution.

H.C.

John Slidell

FURIOUS BATTLES on many fields during the Civil War have pushed into the background the less spectacular contests on the diplomatic front waged between the Union and the Confederacy.

In London, Paris, and Mexico City, Unionists and Confederates matched their cunning against each other and the seasoned wisdom of representatives of older states. President Jefferson Davis sent William L. Yancey of Alabama and George W. Randolph of Virginia to England, John T. Pickett of Kentucky to Mexico, and John Slidell to France, all seeking recognition for the Confederacy.

As state legislator, district attorney, congressman, or senator, John Slidell was the political boss of Louisiana through three decades. During James Buchanan's administration Slidell was the power behind the president.

John was born in New York City about 1793. After graduating from Columbia College in 1810 he went to work in a mercantile establishment. When the business failed as a result of the embargo during the War of 1812, Slidell studied law. Ruined financially and ostracized because of a duel over the affections of an actress, he went to New Orleans to recoup his fortunes. His knowledge of commercial law was sound, and his practice was soon yielding him an annual income of ten thousand dollars. In 1835, at the age of forty-two, he married Mathilde Deslonde, a beautiful Creole of twenty.

Slidell did yeoman's service in the state legislature, was an unsuccessful candidate for Congress in 1828, and was appointed district attorney for New Orleans in 1829. In 1834 and again in 1836 he was defeated for the United States Senate. In 1842, however, he was elected to the Congress where he advocated use of the civil law in the federal courts of Louisiana and worked for a reduction of the tariff on everything except sugar.

He served in Congress until 1845 when President Polk appointed him commissioner to Mexico to settle the Texas boundary dispute, to adjust Mexican claims, and to negotiate the purchase of New Mexico and California. Though he failed on his mission, his activities publicized the Mexican matter, preparing the American conscience for a war to secure by arms what could not be gained through diplomacy.

Soon after his inauguration, President Pierce offered Slidell a diplomatic post in Central America, but he accepted instead a commission to sell New Orleans & Nashville Railroad bonds in London.

He was ambitious to attain a seat in the Senate and was defeated for the third time in 1848. His opponent, Pierre Soulé, an extremist on Southern issues, contrasted with Slidell who held more moderate views. Five years later, however, Soulé was appointed minister to Spain, opening the way for Slidell's advancement to the Senate.

As senator, he favored repeal of the Missouri Compromise, introduced a bill to appropriate thirty million dollars for the purchase of Cuba from Spain, and labored for the nomination of Buchanan. He was Buchanan's campaign manager in 1865 and was largely responsible for his election.

Although Slidell was a Union Democrat, when Lincoln was elected president and Louisiana seceded, he resigned from the Senate, stating in his final address that he was retiring to defend the new Confederacy which "if it may want at first the grand proportions and vast resources of the old, will still possess the essential elements of greatness . . . the capacity and will to govern . . . in the spirit of the constitution. . . ."

In the autumn of 1861 President Davis appointed Slidell commissioner to France to procure recognition of the Confederacy and obtain a loan. In company with James M. Mason of Virginia, who was on a like mission to England, he reached Nassau safely and embarked on the British mail steamer "Trent." Their capture and removal to the U.S.S. "San Jacinto" and detention at Fort Warren in Boston created an international furore. Threatened by a British declaration of war, the United States government released Slidell who arrived in Paris in 1862 where he was enthusiastically received.

Politically wise, trained in intrigue, fluent in French and Spanish, John Slidell was well qualified for his diplomatic post. He made friends easily at the Court of Napoleon III and won the respect of his colleagues. But his was a lost cause on the diplomatic front. Though England's real sympathies were for a weakened, divided republic, she refused to support the confederacy in the face of a threat of war by the Union. Many federals believed that a major war might reunite the country against a common foe.

Though friendly to the Confederacy, France refused recognition until England first yielded. France had dreams of extending her empire to embrace Mexico and Texas. Though cotton was the key to the world's economy, neither nation could be tempted to forego neutrality to enrich its coffers. So the South collapsed on the diplomatic and financial fronts before her armed forces met defeat at Appomattox.

With the armies of the Union everywhere on the ascendant, Slidell's prestige in Paris declined. He went into exile in bitterness and disappointment and never returned to the United States. He applied to President Andrew Johnson for permission to return to Louisiana, but the letter was never answered. After the surrender his family resided in Paris, where his children married. He died at Cowes in 1871.

Judah Philip Benjamin

JUDAH PHILIP BENJAMIN, Louisiana's most illustrious lawyer, was born a British subject of Jewish descent on the Island of St. Thomas, West Indies, on August 6, 1811. As a child he moved with his parents to Charleston, South Carolina, and was educated at Fayette Academy, North Carolina, with two years at Yale. He left Yale at seventeen to accept a position with a commercial house in New Orleans. Poor but resolute, he supplemented his wages as a tutor of English.

Later employed as a clerk in a notary's office Benjamin prepared for the law and passed the state bar examinations in 1832, just as he came of age. He gained something of a local reputation because of a published digest of decisions of the Supreme Court and rose rapidly at the bar. His part in the celebrated Creole case, involving delicate questions of international law, gave him national standing. In his prosperity he purchased a plantation and made a study of sugar chemistry and new refining processes.

Benjamin's endorsement of a sixty-thousand-dollar note for a friend cost him his plantation, and he was forced again into active practice. With political interruptions he henceforth pursued his chosen profession. He was elected to the state legislature as a Whig in 1842, and ten years later to the United States Senate, serving two consecutive terms. He was the leading spirit in drafting the state constitution of 1852.

Active in the commercial development of New Orleans, Benjamin was one of the organizers of the Jackson Railway, now the Illinois Central. He projected a railroad across the Isthmus of Tehuantepec, Mexico, and was of the opinion that the Compromise of 1850 placed the South at a national disadvantage that only an outlet to the trade of the Pacific could overcome. Believing a solid South was essential to the situation, he switched his political allegiance to the Democratic Party. When Lincoln was elected president, Benjamin advocated secession, and shortly after the withdrawal of Louisiana, he made a brilliant speech of resignation in the Senate.

Three weeks later Jefferson Davis called him to the Confederacy's cabinet as attorney general. Once in the course of a debate with Davis, hard words passed, and Benjamin challenged him to a duel. There followed immediate apologies and a reconciliation which developed into the closest friendship of the Confederacy. Phlegmatic in temperament, Benjamin's personality was a complement to the president's high-strung spirit. Davis made him secretary of war in 1861, just when the problem of obtaining munitions from Europe had become acute. The loss of Roanoke Island in 1862, along with other defeats, centered blame on Benjamin for the Confederacy's failure to equip its soldiers. Under the concentrated fire of Congress, Davis appointed him secretary of state.

In 1864–65 Benjamin believed the cause of the Confederacy so acute that only an enrollment of slaves as volunteers, with the promise of freedom, could stem the tide. Davis and Lee finally agreed reluctantly, and an agent was sent to London, promising general emancipation in return for British aid in lifting the federal blockade. He was told he had come too late.

When Richmond fell, Benjamin fled with the president's party. Before the capture of Davis by federal cavalry, Benjamin, unable to travel farther on a horse, left his chief and escaped from the coast of Florida in an open boat. After many vicissitudes he made his way to the West Indies and to England.

At fifty-five he started life all over as a student of English law at Lincoln's Inn in London. With a little money he eked out a livelihood as a writer for the *Daily Telegraph*. In recognition of his talents, the Benchers of his Inn of Court waived the usual three-years' rule, calling him to the bar after less than five months.

Liverpool was the market for Southern cotton, and its business leaders had many connections with the merchants and shippers of New Orleans. Benjamin located in that circuit just as the last of his little fortune was swept away by the failure of his bank in New Orleans. He had been engaged in the preparation of a *Treatise on the Law of Sale of Personal Property* which he published in 1868. Retainers immediately poured in upon him. He was made Queen's Counsel, qualified to practice in all courts of common law and equity, and established himself as without a superior in cases on appeal. His annual fees reached seventy-five thousand dollars, and his practice increased until he was forced to confine his talents to cases before the House of Lords and the Privy Council. Between 1872 and 1882, he appeared as counsel in no less than 136 important cases which came from every part of the British Empire.

He divided his time between London and Paris, where he had maintained a home for his wife and daughter before the war. Stepping off a moving street car in Paris in May, 1880, he was thrown to the ground with serious injuries. His right arm was torn from its socket. Contrary to the advice of his physician, he resumed his practice but was forced to retire in 1883. The bar of England gave him a farewell banquet. He died ten months later in Paris.

Lawyer and statesman, known as the "Brains of the Confederacy," Judah P. Benjamin was one of the legal giants of his age. His source of power lay in his profound knowledge of the law, his keen capacity for analysis, and his faculty for succinct statement. Dynamic in determination, he arose again and again from defeat and poverty to success and fortune.

H.C.

Alexander Hamilton Stephens

A MERE wisp of a man, Stephens throughout his life never weighed one hundred pounds and he could not remember a day free from pain. Yet, Alexander Hamilton Stephens became one of the intellectual giants of his generation, the peer of any statesman of that tragic era.

The future congressman and Confederate vice-president was born on his father's farm in Taliaferro County, Georgia, on February 11, 1812. At six he followed the plow as a "corn dropper" and, despite his fragile frame, became a field hand doing menial tasks to help feed a large family on a few acres.

His father, Andrew Boskins Stephens, had three children by his first wife, Margaret Grier, and five by his second wife, Matilda Lindsey. His father and stepmother both died within a week when he was fourteen. "Little Ellick," as he was affectionately called by his constituents, went to live with an uncle. Impressed by the lad's eagerness to learn, a patron advanced him the money to attend school in Washington, and a Presbyterian society lent him the funds for a course at the University of Georgia. Stephens finished first in his class, taught school until he paid back his debts, and at twenty-two moved into the court house at Crawfordsville as legal aid to the sheriff, while he read law and was admitted to the bar.

Rapidly becoming a leading advocate, he won a seat in the state legislature as a Whig, and after serving four years was elected to Congress where he remained until he retired in 1859. The scholar in politics, dedicated to strict adherence to the federal Constitution, states' rights, and the preservation of the Union, he became a political power on the national scene. His size was a joke, but his stature transcendent. When a political opponent offered to grease his ears and swallow him whole, Little Ellick replied that his adversary would then have more brains in his stomach than he had in his head.

Stephens bitterly opposed secession. Though he believed the states had the right to secede, he thought it was the wrong strategy. He fought for the independent Whig ticket with Daniel Webster as its candidate; both stood for moderation. When Webster died before the 1852 campaign was over, he voted for him anyway.

His slight figure and thin voice contrasted with the potency of his prose, the copiousness of his knowledge and the persuasiveness of his logic. Yet, he could not quell the emotional upheaval. As late as January, 1861, he stood by the Constitution and insisted that secession would be a mistake. In facing the Georgia legislature in his last attempt to save the Union he praised the "government of our fathers, with all its defects," as the best form of government on earth.

Finally Stephens reluctantly surrendered to the cause with deep misgivings and was elected vice-president of the Confederacy. He had no faith in its leadership and less in the outcome. He resisted the centralized government of President Davis just as he had the federal government. He opposed the president's suspension of habeas corpus and the introduction of martial law . . . designed to facilitate the conscription of soldiers and to maintain order . . . as a violation of the Confederate constitution Stephens had drafted. Before the war was over Stephens and Davis were not on speaking terms. Davis, resolute and headstrong, was determined to fight it out to the last soldier; Stephens, equally resolute, wanted to talk it out. One of the three commissioners sent North to meet with Lincoln and make peace, Stephens met with an order for unconditional surrender.

He repaired to Liberty Hall, his home, to await the inevitable end. He surrendered quietly to Yankee troops when they arrived and was placed in an underground cell at Fort Warren, Boston. Because of his ill health, he was moved to a better room. He applied to President Johnson for a pardon; hearing nothing, he requested but was refused an audience. A parole was finally granted, and he went back to Georgia, a gray-haired old man at fifty-three. His slaves, who had run his places for him, stood by even as the Confederacy fell, and they continued as his loyal servants.

That he could survive two decades more through Reconstruction and live to become governor of Georgia is something of a miracle. He was elected to Congress in 1866 by Democrats and Republicans and made a speech on peace, prosperity, and internal harmony that won praise the world over, but he was denied his seat. He spent his declining years writing a school history and his account of the Civil War. He was inaugurated governor on November 5, 1882. After that he just withered away and died in office on March 4, 1883.

Stephens never married. The Constitution was his love, and he spent fifty active years in a herculean effort to preserve it. When the war was over, he warned if "passion and prejudice" should prevail and the "embers of the late war shall be kept a-glowing until with new fuel they shall flame again," the fate of the republic would be calamitous. Born in poverty, cradled in adversity, and disciplined early in privation and self-denial, he rose to a position of prominence at the bar, and by his sheer will he overcame all obstacles to achieve an eminent place in history. "I am," he said, "afraid of nothing on the earth, or above the earth, or under the earth—except to do wrong."

Howell Cobb

SELDOM, IF EVER, has it been a state's good fortune to have three such able sons as Howell Cobb, Robert Toombs, and Alexander Stephens serving it simultaneously.

Howell Cobb was solicitor general of Georgia at the age of twenty-two, a member of Congress at twenty-five, speaker of the House of Representatives at thirty-four, then governor, United States secretary of the treasury, president of the Provisional Congress of the Confederate States, and major general in the Confederate Army.

The son of John A. and Sarah (Rootes) Cobb, he was born at Cherry Hill, Jefferson County, Georgia, on September 7, 1815. To give his children better educational advantages, Colonel Cobb moved to Athens where Howell entered the university and was graduated in 1834. Before he was twenty, he married Mary Ann Lamar, the daughter of a prominent planter of Georgia. He was born into a family which, by reason of its wealth, social position, and the reputation of its members, logically marked him for a political career.

He was admitted to the bar in 1836, where he gained an immediate reputation because of the vigor and the maturity of his arguments before juries, and he was elected solicitor general of the western circuit by the state legislature. In Congress where he served for six terms, his energy, courage, tact, judgment, and eloquence inspired the devotion of his followers and won the respect of political opponents, who together elected him Speaker of the House of Representatives in 1849 at a time when ability in public life stood high.

When the Compromise of 1850 was a major issue, Cobb was so severely criticized for supporting the measure that he declined to be a candidate for reëlection to the House and returned to Georgia where he ran for the office of governor to vindicate his position.

When Cobb and Daniel Webster agreed on the compromise, the wrath of Massachusetts was aimed at Webster because he had abandoned the position of the North and at Cobb in Georgia who was charged with having surrendered the rights of the South. Cobb was joined by Stephens and Toombs who up to this time had been his political opponents. In the climax of this exciting campaign, Cobb was elected governor, Toombs senator, and Stephens was returned to Congress. All three were triumphantly vindicated.

Three years after a successful term, Cobb was reëlected to Congress, serving on the Ways and Means Committee where he put forth all his energies and influence in an effort to avert the threatened conflict. Because of his support of James Buchanan, his personal friend, in 1856 Cobb was appointed Secretary of the Treasury, in the Buchanan administration.

On December 8, 1860, after President Buchanan's denial of the right of secession, Cobb resigned, and after the election of Lincoln, Cobb advocated immediate secession. He became one of the most active supporters of separation in the campaign preceding the secession convention which met in Montgomery in January, 1861, to dissolve the Union. He was made chairman of the convention to organize the Southern Confederacy, and many thought he would have been a better choice for the presidency than Jefferson Davis. Lack of military training and his earlier espousal of Unionist principles stood in the way of his election.

Howell Cobb raised a regiment, was elected colonel, and was assigned to duty in the Virginia peninsula under General Magruder. At the same time he continued to act as president of the Provisional Congress until ratification of the Confederate constitution and the permanent organization of the government. He took part in the battles of Seven Pines, the second battle of Manassas, the Seven Days' fight, the capture of Harper's Ferry and Sharpsburg and was cited in general orders for gallant service and later made major general.

At the termination of hostilities, following his release on parole, Cobb returned to his family in Macon and, after an interlude of twenty-five years in the public service, continued in the practice of law. He was an uncompromising foe of Congressional Reconstruction policies. While north on a business trip he was suddenly stricken with apoplexy and died on October 9, 1868.

Howell Cobb was of massive mold. With a large head, a heavy shock of hair, gray, well-spaced eyes, broad shoulders, and a double chin, he stood out in any company. To the manor born, he married well, owned plantations and a thousand slaves. Endowed with a sound heart and mind, he was neither enervated nor spoiled by his prosperity but stimulated instead to make the best use of his assets and talents.

He could be caustic when necessary. In Georgia no public man had ever aroused as much animosity as its states' rights governor Joe Brown, who was a thorn in the side of the Confederacy in 1863. Cobb railed against this "cracker" from the hills. He said he had never attended a hanging but if Brown should be the chief performer in such a ceremony, he would gladly join the spectators.

Joseph R. Lamar, associate justice of the United States Supreme Court, said of him that "the native strength of his intellect was aided by a quickness of mind, natural eloquence and a knowledge of human nature." It was his good fortune to be universally respected. He was truly a prophet not without honor in his own country.

H.C.

Braxton Bragg

HE WAS BORN in the village of Warrenton, North Carolina on March 22, 1817. His father, Thomas Bragg, was a contractor and builder, his mother, Margaret Crossland, a woman of animation and refinement. Braxton Bragg received his early education in the public schools of his county, was appointed a cadet in the United States Military Academy at sixteen, and was graduated fourth in the class of 1837.

Bragg entered the army as a second lieutenant, 3rd artillery, participated in the Seminole war in Florida, was stationed for a time at Fort Moultrie, South Carolina, and was a fearless fighter in the Mexican war under General Zachary Taylor. He took part in the battles at Fort Brown and Monterrey, for both of which actions he was breveted to a captainship. His conspicuous courage at Buena Vista on February 23, 1847, during which his men faced and routed a superior Mexican force, led to his promotion to lieutenant colonel.

After the Mexican war was over, in 1849, Bragg married Elisa Brooks Ellis of Louisiana. In 1856 he resigned from the army and purchased a plantation in Lafourche Parish, Louisiana. He also became commissioner of public works for Louisiana and designed the drainage and levee system of his adopted state.

When Louisiana passed its ordinance of secession, Bragg was appointed a colonel and soon thereafter a major general in the Louisiana militia. On March 7, 1861, Bragg was appointed and confirmed brigadier general in the provisional army of the Confederate States and assigned to command the Gulf Coast from Pensacola to Mobile. He was promoted major general a few months later and assumed command of A. S. Johnston's 2nd corps, which he led at Shiloh. With great energy he assaulted the federal lines and captured thousands of prisoners and many guns. A month later, the federals were reënforced by General D. C. Buell's fresh army, with only exhausted Confederates to resist them. Fighting bravely, the Confederates slowly retreated until the order was given to withdraw to Corinth, Mississippi.

On April 12, 1862, Bragg was promoted to general, and on June 27 he relieved Beauregard of the command of the Army of Tennessee.

In the Kentucky campaign Bragg captured Munfordville, hoping his activity would win Kentucky over to the Confederacy. He repelled the federal forces under Buell at Perryville in a drawn battle, but unwilling to fight to a decision Bragg withdrew to Tennessee. Kentucky had shown no desire to join the South, and the campaign was a failure. With only thirty-eight thousand men Bragg faced Rosecrans with forty-seven thousand men at Stone River and made great gains, but Bragg, with his men exhausted, refused to exploit his victory and withdrew to Tullahoma. Bragg invited his subordinates to express their opinion of him and received frank statements that his presence was a liability. President Davis, however, decided to keep him in command.

Later Rosecrans maneuvered Bragg out of Tullahoma and then out of Chattanooga. Forced into the mountains he attacked Rosecrans at Chickamauga to win a notable victory. Had he continued his offensive he might have captured large forces. This was a repetition of Shiloh, Perryville, and Stone River, and Bragg was censured for his failure to follow through to victory.

With Grant assigned to the command at Chattanooga, Bragg was forced to retreat to Dalton, Georgia, where he turned his army over to Johnston. Though deprived of active command, Bragg retained the confidence of President Davis, who made him his military adviser. During 1864 he was at Richmond, nominally the army's commander in chief. His last battle was on March 8, 1865, when he opposed a part of Sherman's forces at Kingston, North Carolina. After the surrender, he accompanied President Jefferson Davis in his flight to Georgia, was captured, and paroled.

Bragg's plantation was lost during the war. To recoup his fortunes, he practiced as a civil engineer in New Orleans. As commissioner of public works in Alabama for four years, he supervised the harbor improvements at Mobile. He later moved to Texas and died at Galveston on September 27, 1876.

General U. S. Grant, who knew him well, said of him, "Bragg was a remarkably intelligent and well informed man, professionally and otherwise. He was also thoroughly upright. But he was possessed of an irascible temper, and was naturally disputatious."

One characteristic anecdote was to the effect that Bragg once temporarily commanded a company while also serving as post quartermaster. In the capacity of captain of his company he requisitioned the post for some item. As quartermaster he declined to honor the requisition and on the back of it wrote his reasons. As captain he replied and then referred the whole matter to a superior officer who exclaimed, "Heavens, Mr. Bragg, you have quarrelled with every officer in the army and now you are quarrelling with yourself!"

The record of every soldier of the Confederacy suffers by comparison with the matchless Robert E. Lee. Though Bragg's tactics are moot questions among military strategists, no man ever questioned his vigor, valor, or integrity. Irritable, he had his faults, but fear was not one of them. He was a dauntless warrior, a strict disciplinarian, and thorough organizer. Tall, bearded, and clumsy, he was endowed with superior strength. A veteran of three wars, his life was spent in heroic service in the cause of country.

Pierre Gustav Toutant Beauregard

THE FOREBEARS of Gustav Beauregard walked with kings. Scion of ancient and honorable French and Welsh families, he traced his ancestry to the year 1290. His grandfather visited the Louisiana colony in the service of Louis XIV and settled there. Gustave, born in the parish of St. Bernard on May 28, 1818, was the son of Jacques Toutant de Beauregard. His mother was Hélène Judith de Reggio.

Beauregard attended private school in New Orleans until he was eleven when he was placed under the tutelage of the Messieurs Pougnet, officers of the French Army under Napoleon, exiled in New York. At sixteen he entered the United States Military Academy at West Point, from which he was graduated second in a class of forty-five in 1838.

Beauregard served for eight years in fort construction work in Louisiana, advancing from second to first lieutenant of engineers. In 1846 he served in the Mexican war as an engineer on the staff of General Winfield Scott, that fighting Virginian. He directed the fortification of Tampico and saw active service during the siege of Vera Cruz and the battles of Cerro Gordo and Contreras, winning the brevet of captain for bravery. During the brilliant assault on the Garita de Belen in the capture of Mexico City, Beauregard was twice wounded and for gallant and meritorious conduct was made a major.

After the Mexican war he was put in charge of the Mississippi and lake defenses in Louisiana. He also superintended the erection of the New Orleans custom house, supervised the building of the fortifications of Mobile, and was chief engineer in charge of constructing the drainage system of the city of New Orleans.

Beauregard was promoted to captain in 1853 and in 1860 was appointed superintendent of West Point. Having openly avowed his purpose to offer his services to Louisiana should she secede from the Union, he had no more than reported for duty than the Secretary of War directed his transfer to New Orleans. With the secession of Louisiana, Beauregard resigned from the United States army and joined, as a private, the battalion of Orleans Guards, composed of the elite of the Creole population of the city. Immediately commissioned brigadier general in the Confederate army, he was put in command of the forces at Charleston, South Carolina. Acting on instructions from the Confederate government he demanded the surrender of Fort Sumter on April 11, and the following day ordered fired the first gun that formally began the Civil War.

Beauregard's victory created a wave of popular enthusiasm upon the crest of which he rode to command one of the two armies of the Confederacy being assembled near the Potomac. Later these were merged under General J. E. Johnston to form the historic army of northern Virginia.

He was second in command to General Albert Sidney Johnston at Shiloh and assumed command when Johnston was killed. Falling back upon Corinth, Mississippi, he had to abandon that place to a larger force under General Halleck, suffering his first defeat. While on sick leave for a throat operation in Richmond, he was compelled to turn his command over to General Braxton Bragg.

Upon Beauregard's recovery his relations with President Jefferson Davis rapidly deteriorated until they were hardly more cordial than those existing between the president and Joseph E. Johnston. Beauregard was placed in charge of the defense of the South Carolina and Georgia coasts and performed ably, especially in defending Charleston in 1863 and 1864. In May, 1864, he supported Lee in Virginia and probably saved Richmond for a time by discerning Grant's intention against Petersburg before General Lee could be made aware of it.

The closing months of the war found him once more second in command as at Shiloh to General Joseph E. Johnston with whom he served throughout the campaign of the Carolinas until the surrender.

With other Louisianans Beauregard bought a wagon, a supply of tobacco, nails, twine, and household goods and bartered his way back to Louisiana. For five years he was president of the New Orleans, Jackson & Mississippi Railway. He declined flattering offers to command the armies of Roumania and those of Egypt. He was for a time manager of the Louisiana lottery, a lucrative position, but one in which he was subjected to much criticism. In 1888 he became commissioner of public works of the city of New Orleans and was for many years adjutant general of Louisiana.

Beauregard was twice married, in 1841 to Laure, daughter of Jules Villère, a sugar planter of Plaquemines Parish, and in 1860 to Caroline, daughter of André Deslonde, a sugar planter of St. James Parish.

He wrote *Principles and Maxims of the Art of War* in 1863, *Report of the Defense of Charleston* in 1864, and *A Commentary on the Campaign and Battle of Manassas* in 1891. He died in New Orleans on February 20, 1893.

Small in stature, soldierly in bearing, animated, modest, courteous, and courageous, he was the product of a long line of fighting, cultured ancestors. Typically French, he knew no other language until he left his native heath in Louisiana.

Love of liberty and loyalty to Louisiana were Beauregard's predominating passions, and throughout his long and useful life he held an enviable place in the affections of the people of his state.

Henry Watkins Allen

LOUISIANA'S soldier, patriot, and statesman, Henry Watkins Allen occupies a heroic niche in the hall of fame that enshrines her great immortals. Born in Virginia in 1820, he moved to Missouri at thirteen upon the death of his mother. He clerked in a store and attended Marion College. At seventeen, following a dispute with his father, he ran away from home and sought employment at Grand Gulf, once an important port on the Mississippi in Claiborne County, Mississippi. He became a teacher on a plantation and read law at night.

He had begun the practice of his profession at twenty-two when Sam Houston called for volunteers to wage war against Mexico for the independence of the "new republic." Henry Allen organized his own company and went to Texas.

Upon his return he eloped with a planter's daughter and fought a duel with her father, in which he was severely injured. The families were reconciled, and he settled on a plantation and lived the only few years in which he was completely happy. Upon the death of his wife he moved to Tensas Parish, Louisiana, and then to West Baton Rouge.

He served in the Mississippi legislature in 1846 and was elected to the Louisiana legislature in 1853. In the following year, at thirty-four, he entered Harvard to continue his legal studies. Sympathetic with the cause of the Italians in their struggle for freedom, he went abroad to offer his services to Garibaldi. Arriving in Europe too late to join the conflict, he toured the continent and in 1861 published a book entitled *The Travels of a Sugar Planter.*

While away he was reëlected to the legislature and was engaged in various pursuits when the Civil War began. Henry Allen enlisted as a private but was elected lieutenant colonel and quartered at Ship Island. There he suppressed a mutiny, trained his troops, and in 1862 was promoted to colonel and ordered to join Beauregard in Tennessee. In leading his regiment at Shiloh, he was wounded in action.

Repairing to Vicksburg he helped rebuild its fortifications while under fire. He accompanied Breckinridge in an attack against the Unionists at Baton Rouge where his right leg was shattered by a shell. Incapacitated for field duty, he was appointed brigadier general in 1863 and was transferred to the Trans-Mississippi Department at Shreveport, making the perilous journey through the enemy's lines on crutches. Upon his arrival he was elected governor of West Louisiana, New Orleans, and the West Florida Parishes being occupied by federal forces.

Cut off from the port of New Orleans and separated from the rest of the Confederacy, he was surrounded by poverty and starvation. In his message to his legislature he said, "Start the hammer and the loom. Let the furnace smoke and the anvil ring. . . . We have immense resources. We can save the currency and the country."

Governor Allen went out among his people in an ambulance. What was done within six months through his aggressive leadership is an example of almost superhuman achievement. Louisiana cotton had been confiscated by the Confederate government and sold in Mexico. He diverted this revenue to Louisiana and the armies under his command. He operated mule wagon trains to the Mexican border where he exchanged cotton for life's necessities.

He established a system of state stores. He purchased a foundry in Texas and manufactured kettles, pots, and tools. He established a laboratory at Mount Lebanon and extracted castor oil from palm Christi plants. He set up a turpentine still in Sabine Parish. He made carbonate of soda and installed a dispensary at Shreveport for the distribution of medicine.

He turned out cordage at Minden and cloth in Claiborne Parish. He manufactured and provided the women of the state with carding sets for weaving homespun out of wool and cotton. He imported newsprint from Mexico and published school books at Shreveport. He set up a distillery, restricting the use of alcohol to medicinal purposes.

In the midst of a growing prosperity that was transforming the state into a veritable workshop came the tragic news of Appomattox and Lee's surrender.

It was difficult for the Confederate armies in Texas, Louisiana, and Arkansas to quit the conflict. They had not been defeated and could have held out longer. But the back of the Confederacy was broken, and Governor Allen sued for peace that Louisiana might be spared an armed invasion.

In his farewell address to the people of the state he admonished them to accept the inevitable. "I am one of the proscribed," he said, "I must go into exile. I have stood by you, fought for you, and stayed with you up to the very last moment. . . . I go to seek repose for my shattered limbs."

Financially crushed, Governor Allen borrowed three hundred dollars from friends and moved to Mexico City, where he was cordially received by Emperor Maximilian. There he established *The Mexican Times,* a successful newspaper published in English.

But there was no repose for his shattered limbs. Within a year, at forty-six, he died from his wounds. His remains were brought to Baton Rouge and placed beneath a monument erected in his memory in front of the State House.

Such is the heroism of a man who laid down his life for his country. He was the Confederacy's most able administrator and Louisiana's resourceful defender. His name is written high upon the roll of her immortals.

H.C.

James Longstreet

KNOWN as "General Lee's Warhorse," James Longstreet was one of the Confederacy's most distinguished soldiers. Though his generalship throughout the Civil War is a subject of recurrent controversy and his postbellum political conduct in Louisiana was questioned, his heroic reputation as a warrior grows more resplendent with the years.

James was born in the Edgewood District of South Carolina on January 8, 1821, the son of James and Mary Anna (Dent) Longstreet. His grandfather, William Longstreet, pioneered in the building of steam engines for the operation of cotton gins and sawmills and was one of the earliest to apply steam to the navigation of boats. Augustus Baldwin Longstreet, an uncle, served successively as ante bellum president of Centenary College of Louisiana, the University of Mississippi, and the University of South Carolina. The wife of L. Q. C. Lamar of Mississippi was James first cousin.

While James was in his early childhood his parents moved to Augusta, Georgia, where his father farmed until his death. His mother then resided at Somerville, Alabama, from which state James was admitted to West Point. He attended the academy with Sherman and Grant and was graduated in the class of 1842.

Longstreet was breveted a second lieutenant of the 4th Infantry and was stationed at Natchitoches. In 1844, he was in the army in Louisiana under General Zachary Taylor, served under him in the Mexican war until after the battle of Monterrey, and was then with Scott during the expedition to Mexico City. Severely wounded at Chapultepec and breveted major, he continued in the paymaster's department. Following his resignation from the army to join the Confederacy in 1861, he sought a similar commission; he said he had abandoned his aspirations for military glory. He had already won two brevets for gallantry, however, and because of his brilliant military record was commissioned brigadier general in the Confederate army.

Longstreet participated in the first battle of Manassas and subsequently was at the head of a division in the Peninsular campaign and the Battle of Seven Days. His division became the nucleus of the famed "I Crops" in the army of Virginia, which was commanded by him throughout the conflict. His corps saw action in the second battle of Manassas, Sharpsburg and held the left of Lee's front at Fredericksburg. As lieutenant general he took part in the campaign of Gettysburg.

Longstreet's splendid performance during the Seven Days' battles around Richmond won Lee's entire confidence, and Lee placed under his command more than half his infantry.

In the Battle of the Wilderness, Longstreet arrived upon the field as the Confederate right had been turned and routed. He drove the enemy back until its entire flank was in confusion. At this critical moment, when he was leading fresh troops into action through the forest, he was fired upon by his own men by mistake and seriously wounded. This unfortunate episode stayed the Confederate assault for two hours and enabled the enemy to bring up effective reinforcements.

After the death of "Stonewall" Jackson in 1863, Longstreet was Lee's most able lieutenant and assumed the role of his mentor. At the head of his corps in the Battle of Gettysburg, he was full of misgivings. The story is one of Longstreet's reluctant and despairing acquiescence in obeying orders he believed would bring disaster. He delayed action until it was too late for Lee to turn the tide. He was vigorous and effective when he approved the plans of his superior but slow to move when he questioned his commander's course.

Gettysburg virtually concluded Longstreet's service with the army of northern Virginia. He was dispatched to Georgia, did admirably at Chickamauga, was unsuccessful at Knoxville, and on the second day of the Battle of the Wilderness in April, 1864, was again wounded in action. He returned to duty in time to take part in the futile defense of Richmond and surrendered his corps with the Confederate army at Appomattox.

After the war Longstreet became head of an insurance company in New Orleans and prospered for a time as a cotton factor, but he joined the Republican Party and consequently was ostracized. He was appointed postmaster and collector of internal revenue by his old friend President Grant. He was later postmaster of Gainesville, United States Marshal for Georgia, and when he died on January 2, 1904, was United States Commissioner of Pacific Railroads. Even in his eighties Longstreet carried himself, as he did the scars of four battles, with justified dignity. He was slightly below medium height, broad-shouldered, solidly built, and striking in appearance.

He was twice married, first, on March 8, 1848, to Maria Louise Garland of Lynchburg, Virginia, who died in 1889; second, on September 8, 1897, to Helen Dortch, who survived him.

Longstreet's espousal of the Republican cause during the riotous Reconstruction times made him unpopular in the south and may have influenced its writers to do his career less than full justice. Claims he made in his military autobiography further aggravated the feeling against him. No one, however, can deny Lee's fighting lieutenant his place in military history. He was essentially a combat officer, and though he did not possess the peculiar qualities necessary to a successful independent command, his great skill in handling men made him a well-nigh perfect corps commander.

C J NAAR

Nathan Bedford Forrest

IT IS not surprising that General Robert E. Lee considered Nathan Bedford Forrest the greatest soldier under his command. Several times wounded, Forrest had twenty-nine horses shot from under him. He was born in Bedford County, Tennessee, on July 13, 1821, the eldest son of William and Marian (Beck) Forrest. About 1730, his great-grandfather, Shadrach Forrest, of English birth, moved from Virginia to North Carolina, then dubbed by Virginians the "Valley of Humiliation." Bedford's father first moved to Tennessee in 1806, where he was a blacksmith, and then to Hernando, Mississippi, where his death left Bedford at sixteen the sole support of a large family.

With little schooling young Forrest became a farm laborer and then a horse trader, real estate broker, and dealer in slaves. He accumulated the capital to purchase cotton plantations in Mississippi and Arkansas. In 1845, he won the hand of Mary Ann Montgomery, a lady of the plantation set. Her foster father, a Cumberland Presbyterian parson, disapproved of the marriage. He told Forrest, "You cuss and gamble . . . and Mary Ann is a church girl."

However by 1861, Forrest, a full-fledged Mississippi Delta planter, was worth "a million and a half dollars," and when he enlisted as a private in the 7th Tennessee Cavalry he raised and equipped a battalion of mounted troops at his own expense. Taking part in the defense of Fort Donelson, he led his command to safety through a gap in the encircling line of Union troops. Promoted from lieutenant colonel to colonel, he fought at Shiloh where he was severely wounded. Appointed brigadier general in July, 1862, he was until the end of the war engaged in bold raids against Union communications, fortified posts deep within the lines, or superior forces in the open field. Fighting generally on foot and using horses as a means of rapid transportation, he covered ground with great speed to deliver surprise attacks. His simple strategy was to get there "fustest with the mostest."

Forrest severed Grant's communications in west Tennessee in December, 1862, and in 1863 saved the railroad between Chattanooga and Atlanta. Following a quarrel with General Bragg, President Davis gave Forrest an independent command in north Mississippi and west Tennessee, and he was promoted to major general. In April, 1864, he captured Fort Pillow, later routed a superior force at Brice's Cross Roads, and then stood off General A. J. Smith at Tupelo. In command of all cavalry and promoted to lieutenant general, as of February 28, 1865, he was finally overwhelmed by superior forces at Selma, Alabama, in April, 1865, and was forced to surrender.

Tall, bearded, of commanding mien, Forrest was mild of manner and quiet in speech. In the excitement of battle, however, he was fierce, savage, and profane. His aggressive spirit led him sometimes to ride in the thick of the fight in personal combat. When wounded at Tupelo, he retained his command, leading his cavalry in a buggy until he was able to ride again. His courage was such that his horse, King Philip, left unattended, once charged a company of blue-coated federal soldiers who visited Forrest's plantation after the war was over. With no other weapon than a knife, Forrest once overawed and dispersed a mob bent on lynching. Knowing himself to be wrong when challenged to a duel, he dared to apologize to his challenger.

When the war was over, Forrest returned to his plantation, reëmployed his freed slaves, and set out to recover his lost fortune. In 1867 he sold out at a substantial price and returned to Memphis. An attempt at the insurance business ended in bankruptcy. He then served as president of a railroad, but after the panic of 1873 and the yellow fever epidemic had ravaged Memphis, Forrest was again bankrupt. He gave up his Memphis home and moved to President's Island on the Mississippi where he operated a sort of "penal plantation," employing convict labor from Shelby county at ten cents a day. He was then able to compensate his creditors and made his peace with his maker by joining the Presbyterian Church.

Reconciled to the inevitable, Forrest was fully reconstructed until the scalawags and carpetbaggers took over. During the Reconstruction many secret political societies sprang up to encourage organized violence among the Negroes. The Ku Klux Klan was the Southern white man's answer, one of a number of organizations with similar objectives. The Klan became the supreme agency of resistance to such radical governments as that of Parson Brownlow in Tennessee and Forrest became the Grand Wizard of the Ku Klux Klan. When order and peace were restored Forrest resigned.

Historians make much of Forrest's grammatical shortcomings; his habitual use of quaint dialectal expressions live in his reports to intrigue the biographer. He used *fit* for *fought* and *cotch* for *caught.* With no formal education he never learned to spell. But when he died in Memphis on October 29, 1877, twenty thousand people attended his funeral procession. He alone was in uniform. Jefferson Davis was one of his pallbearers.

In many respects he was a typical Southerner of his time, a rugged individualist, shrewd trader, and indefatigable fighter, a self-made, successful man. And the military instinct within him approached genius. As a leader of men, he had few equals.

John Cabell Breckinridge

He was a member of the state legislature of Kentucky at the age of twenty-eight, was elected to Congress at thirty, became vice-president of the United States at thirty-six, and was a candidate for president of the United States on the Southern Democratic ticket at thirty-nine. Elected to the United States Senate from Kentucky while vice-president, he was already in the Confederate army when the Senate declared him a traitor and expelled him.

John C. Breckinridge, the only son of Joseph Cabell and Mary Clay (Smith) Breckinridge, was born in Lexington, Kentucky, on January 15, 1821. His father, who died at thirty-four, was an eminent member of the Kentucky bar. His grandfather, who was born in Virginia, came to Kentucky in 1792 and subsequently became United States senator and attorney general under President Thomas Jefferson. John attended Centre College, a Presbyterian school at Danville, was graduated in 1839, and after pursuing the study of law at the College of New Jersey (later Princeton) and Transylvania College, he went to Frankfort and then Burlington, Iowa, finally settling in Lexington which was his home until he died on May 17, 1875. In December, 1843, he married Mary C. Burch of Scott County.

Breckinridge was commissioned a major of the 3rd Kentucky Volunteers, whom he led into Mexico in 1847, but he arrived too late to reap any military glory. He entered politics as a Democrat, a candidate for Congress in a Henry Clay Whig stronghold, was victorious, and rose rapidly as a successor to that popular leader. The legislature chose him to deliver the address of welcome when Clay returned after guiding through Congress the Compromise of 1850 which was expected to produce "peace in our time" between the North and South.

Breckinridge was described as "tall, well-formed, with fair complexion, regular face of great mental power, large blue eyes, and auburn hair; intellectual, composed, and full of conscious genius and future prowess." Though of dignified bearing and serene nature, he did get involved in a rough and tumble Congressional debate in 1854 and barely escaped a duel with New York's Frank B. Cutting.

At the end of his second term Breckinridge resigned to resume his law practice and to replenish his fortunes. He led the Kentucky delegation to the Democratic national convention in Cincinnati where he was nominated vice-president. Elected and inaugurated with James Buchanan in 1857, he became the nation's youngest vice-president. Two years later, when the Democratic Party split into two factions, he became one of the three candidates for president but carried only the states of the Deep South in an election in which Lincoln became president.

Like Missouri, Kentucky did not secede. She first declared her neutrality, but when the armies of both sides invaded the state, Kentucky embraced the Union troops, ordered the Confederates out, and a Federal military régime took over. Breckinridge fled Washington to escape arrest and helped to organize the provisional Confederate government of Kentucky. In November he was appointed a brigadier general.

With his son Cabell by his side as his aide, he fought from Kentucky to Vicksburg to Virginia and was promoted to major general as of April 14, 1862. He was in the battle of Shiloh, in the attack on Baton Rouge, and in the thickest of the fight at Murfreesboro. He commanded the department of southwest Virginia in 1864, was with General Lee in the Shenandoah Valley, and with General Jubal Early in the raid on the outskirts of Washington. In 1865 President Davis called him to Richmond to become secretary of war. Although Breckinridge had little military training, his innate ability as a leader of men, his resourcefulness, and impressive personality made him one of the war's outstanding commanders.

After Appomattox Breckinridge fled southward with the Confederate cabinet, was present as an adviser to General J. E. Johnston in his surrender to General Sherman, and after the cabinet disbanded at Washington, Georgia, he made his way by horseback to the Florida coast in a hazardous flight. There he insisted that his son Cabell accept a parole and return to Kentucky. The general, an aide, Colonel James Wilson, and his Negro servant, Tom, set out in an open lifeboat in rough waters and finally arrived in the harbor at Gardenas, Cuba. He embarked for Europe where he remained until 1869 when he went to Toronto, Canada. In March of the following year he was given permission by the federal government to return to Lexington where he was warmly welcomed, second only to Henry Clay in the affections of Kentuckians. Had his disabilities of citizenship been removed he could have had any office within the gift of the people.

Determined to take no further part in politics, Breckinridge devoted himself to law and private business until he died following operations on his liver on May 17, 1875, at the age of fifty-four. Memorial services were held for him in the Kentucky legislature, his friends "feeling no apprehension that posterity will deprecate or underestimate the exalted virtues we know him to possess." Republicans and Democrats joined in praising one who struggled to maintain the Union as a confederacy of states under the Constitution, and, when that failed, fought just as bravely to create a southern nation of independent states.

Thomas Jonathan Jackson

THOMAS JONATHAN JACKSON, who won the nom de guerre of "Stonewall" in his initial engagement at First Manassas in 1861, was born in Clarksburg, West Virginia, on January 21, 1824. His great-grandfather emigrated from London to Maryland in 1748, married, and moved to West Virginia, where he founded a large family. Jackson's father and mother both died in poverty during his early childhood, and he was brought up by a bachelor uncle. Of frail physique, he grew in strength on his uncle's farm, and when appointed a cadet at the United States Military Academy at eighteen, he was holding the office of county constable.

Jackson was graduated from West Point in 1846 in a class which was to furnish twenty-four general officers to the United States and Confederate armies. Having received the brevets of captain and major during the war with Mexico for courageous conduct at Churubusco and Chapultepec, he was for a time on duty at Fort Hamilton, New York harbor, and at Fort Meade, Florida.

Jackson retired from the army in 1851 and became an instructor of artillery tactics and natural philosophy at the Virginia Military Institute. Deeply religious, he conducted a Sunday school for slaves. Both his wives were daughters of Presbyterian ministers; his first wife, Eleanor Junkin, died fourteen months after their wedding; he married Mary Anna Morrison in 1857. He traveled at home and abroad and was enjoying active fellowship in the Presbyterian Church, when the Civil War interrupted his domestic, educational, and religious activities.

Jackson deplored the prospect of war, which he described as the "sum of all evils." Before he was ordered to Richmond, he had been on the inactive list, except for commanding the cadet corps at the hanging of John Brown on December 2, 1859. He was soon sent to Harper's Ferry as colonel of infantry. In June he was made brigadier general and moved with the rest of General Joseph E. Johnston's army to the battlefield of First Manassas, where he steadfastly sustained the federal onslaught at a critical moment. "There is Jackson standing like a stonewall," cried Brigadier General Barnard E. Bee, as his own troops retreated.

He was promoted to major general on August 7, 1861, and in the campaign of the Shenandoah Valley out-generaled McDowell, Banks, and Fremont and eventually drove back upon the Lower Shenandoah three federal armies, two of them of strength superior to his own. He subsequently joined Lee against McClellan in the Seven Days' battles.

This consecrated fighter won new laurels at every succeeding engagement. His lightning-like turning movement against Pope in August, 1862, was a crucial factor in the victory that followed at Second Manassas. A few weeks later he captured Harper's Ferry with some twelve thousand men. He saved Lee at Sharpsburg when he learned that his chief had been surprised by a large Union force. Thereafter Lee reorganized his army, and Jackson was promoted to lieutenant general as of October 10, 1862, and made commander of the 2nd Corps.

In December, 1862, Stonewall Jackson commanded the right wing in the victory at Fredericksburg. His military prowess reached its peak, however, in his famous flank march at Chancellorsville where his savage assault threatened at one time to roll up Hooker's entire line against the fords of the Ripidary. It was the last of Stonewall Jackson's famous marches and one of the most effective operations of its kind in the history of the war. Leaving fourteen thousand men on Hooker's front, Jackson struck the rear of the Union right, completely routing the corps. Returning from the front in the twilight, Jackson was severely wounded by his own men.

He died on May 10 at Guiney's Station from pneumonia after his left arm was amputated. General Lee wrote with deep feeling, "He has lost his left arm; but I have lost my right arm." Lee gave Jackson full credit for what was, perhaps, the most spectacular victory of his career and said of him, "I know not how to replace him." The army of northern Virginia was never the same after Jackson's death. He was so loyal to Lee that he once professed he was willing to follow him blindfolded. Though Lee conducted some of his most brilliant maneuvers in 1864, he did not find another lieutenant who so well understood him or could execute his orders with such powerful coördination. In any list of half-dozen greatest American soldiers, Stonewall Jackson is included by all critics.

At thirty-nine, tall and spare, Stonewall Jackson was called "Old Jack" by his adoring soldiers, who cheered him where-ever he went. He wore a weather-beaten cap and gigantic boots, with the plainest uniform. He rode an ugly horse at the head of his column and was often mud-spattered. His religious convictions and piety were well-known throughout the army. His favorite company was one composed of Presbyterian preachers. On the eve of battle, he would rise several times during the night to pray. In action he fought with such fanaticism that his most trusted lieutenant was convinced that he was temporarily insane. His fame as a fighter spread afar. A bronze statue of him was unveiled in Richmond in 1875, paid for by popular subscription among admiring Englishmen.

Edmund Kirby-Smith

SOLDIER AND EDUCATOR, Edmund Kirby-Smith was born at St. Augustine, Florida, on March 28, 1824. His father, Joseph Lee Smith, a Revolutionary soldier, was born in Connecticut where he married Frances Marion Kirby, adding her surname to his own to form the name of Kirby-Smith for their children.

In 1821 Edmund's parents moved to St. Augustine where his father was a territorial judge for ten years. He attended the local schools, his instruction supplemented by the tutoring of cultured parents. St. Augustine was frequented at the time by William Cullen Bryant and Ralph Waldo Emerson, and Edmund's home became a gathering place for visiting celebrities.

Of a family of warriors on both sides, it was not surprising that Edmund chose a military career. At twelve he was sent to school at Alexandria, Virginia, where he prepared for the United States Military Academy. He entered West Point in 1841 and was graduated four years later. He attended with a number of cadets who later distinguished themselves on both sides of the Civil War.

Upon graduation he was assigned to the 5th Infantry and saw service in the Mexican war under Taylor and Scott. Participating in all the major engagements, he was breveted for gallantry in the battles of Cerro Gordo and Contreras. At the close of the war, when he was twenty-five, he became assistant professor of mathematics at West Point. Three years later, in 1852, he was in command of the military escort for the Mexican Boundary Commission. As botanist for the expedition, his scientific observations were published by the Smithsonian Institution.

Promoted to captain in 1855, Kirby-Smith was transferred to the 2nd Cavalry and sent to Texas to subdue hostile Indians. He toured Europe in 1858 on leave of absence and upon his return rejoined his regiment. During the Wichita expedition in New Mexico, he was wounded in the battle of Nescatunga. Following his recovery, he commanded that contingent and a year later was promoted to major.

When Florida seceded from the Union, Kirby-Smith resigned from the army, returned to his native state, and offered his services to the Confederacy. Commissioned colonel of cavalry, he was ordered to Lynchburg, Virginia, where he mustered in arriving regiments.

As one of the Confederacy's most active and resourceful soldiers, he fought on every front in the thickest of the fight. He was chief of staff to General Joseph E. Johnston at Harper's Ferry and organized the army of the Shenandoah. He was severely wounded at Manassas, where he helped turn the tide of battle for a time in the Confederacy's favor.

While recuperating at Lynchburg he met Cassie Seldon; they were married on September 24, 1861. Returning to the field a month later he led a division under Beauregard. In 1862 he was in command of the department of east Tennessee, Kentucky, North Carolina, north Georgia and western North Carolina. He invaded Kentucky, fought and won the battle of Richmond, cleared Cumberland Gap of federal troops, occupied Lexington, and threatened Cincinnati. He was congratulated by the Confederate Congress and successively promoted to brigadier general, major general and lieutenant general.

In 1863 Kirby-Smith was ordered to Richmond where he reorganized the army, and was given command of the Trans-Mississippi department. Cut off from the East after the fall of Vicksburg, he became the virtual ruler of a region embracing Texas, Louisiana, Arkansas, and the Indian Territory, called "Kirby-Smithdom." Such communication as he had with Richmond was through the federal blockade. Utilizing the resources of the country, he exported cotton at premium prices and imported machinery for manufactories. Texas produced grain and beef in abundance for his troops. He repulsed the federal expedition under Banks at Mansfield, Louisiana, and was commissioned general.

His amazing career as a soldier ended with the fall of the Confederacy, and when his force surrendered on June 2, 1865, he went to Mexico where he planned to settle. Returning to the United States, however, he was for a time president of an insurance company and then president of the Atlantic & Pacific Telegraph Company. An active layman in the Protestant Episcopal Church, he considered the ministry but abandoned the idea because of his age and established a short-lived military academy in Kentucky.

In 1870 he became president of the University of Nashville, resigning in 1875 to accept the professorship of mathematics at the University of the South, a chair which he occupied with distinction until he died on March 28, 1893.

Kirby-Smith was the last of the Confederate generals to surrender and the last surviving full general of either army before his death. His service to the Confederacy was circumscribed only by the voice of conscience and the call to duty. As one of her favorite sons, Florida unveiled a bronze statue of him in the nation's capital on August 24, 1918. As soldier and scholar, patriot and teacher, his achievements are recorded in the pages of history and his name enshrined in the hearts of those who revere the memory of their fighting compatriots.

William Lowndes Yancey

INITIALLY the greater number of statesmen and military leaders of the lost cause wanted neither secession nor war. They preferred to live in peace within the Union. Among the extreme secessionists, however, was William Lowndes Yancey of Alabama.

He was born in his grandfather's home, The Aviary, Warren County, Georgia, on August 10, 1814, the son of Benjamin Cudworth and Caroline (Bird) Yancey. His father was a midshipman in the colonial navy in the War for Independence and was later an associate of John C. Calhoun in the practice of law at Abbeville, South Carolina.

When William was three his father died, and his mother returned to her father's house. Later she went to live in Hancock County, Georgia, near Mount Zion Academy. There she married Nathan Sidney Smith Beman, head of the academy, who took her and her two children to Troy, New York.

Young Yancey attended the schools of Troy and Williams College but left college before graduating to enter the law office of an old friend of his father's, Benjamin F. Perry at Greenville, South Carolina.

Yancey plunged into the nullification controversy as a public speaker and editor of the Greenville *Mountaineer.* On August 13, 1835, he married Sarah Caroline Earle, the daughter of a wealthy planter. They lived for a time on a farm near Greenville but moved to Dallas County, Alabama, in the winter of 1836-37. Two years later, while visiting in Greenville, Yancey killed his wife's uncle in self-defense and was sentenced to a fine and a year's imprisonment, which was commuted. In Alabama he rented a plantation, and he and a brother bought the *Commercial Advertiser* and the Wetumpka *Argus.* He then bought a farm but was forced to resume the practice of law when his stock of slaves was almost wiped out by poison.

Yancey rose rapidly in the profession and was soon regarded as the leading advocate and most eloquent orator in the state. He was elected to the lower house of the state legislature in 1841, to the upper house in 1843, to the Congress in 1844, and was reëlected, serving until his resignation on September 1, 1846.

His first debate in Congress with Thomas L. Clingman was so violent that a duel was fought in which neither was injured. He was relieved of all political disabilities arising from fighting the duel by a special act of the Alabama legislature, passed over the governor's veto.

Yancey became the recognized leader of the movement for southern independence. From the time he resigned from Congress until the inauguration of Lincoln, he wielded a powerful influence; he believed in secession, was for a southern republic, and even advocated reopening the African slave trade.

The Alabama platform of principles written by him in 1848 in answer to the Wilmot proviso was his confession of faith, and he never deviated from it, even when the temptation of the vice-presidency was offered him on the Democratic ticket in 1860. Yancey spent twelve years arousing the South to the impending danger to their institutions. States' rights associations were formed, and a League of United Southerners was organized. By 1860 he dominated Alabama politically, as old-line Whigs and Democrats adhered to the principles expressed in Yancey's platform. The platform presented by Yancey stated that the Constitution is a compact between sovereign states, that citizens are entitled to enter into territories with their personal property intact, and without interference.

When Yancey went to the state Democratic convention at Montgomery on January 11, 1860, the legislature had already appropriated two hundred thousand dollars to arm the state against attack. The issue was not pressed to a conclusion in the Charleston national Democratic convention, and a majority of Southern delegates walked out. At an adjourned convention at Baltimore, Douglas adherents completed the destruction begun at Charleston by refusing to seat the Yancey delegation from Alabama. So the Constitutional Democratic Party was organized under Yancey's guidance, and Breckinridge was nominated for the presidency.

Following Lincoln's election, Yancey directed the proceedings of the Alabama convention and penned the ordinance of secession. In March, 1861, he was sent by Provisional President Jefferson Davis as the Confederacy's first Commissioner to England and France, seeking recognition. It was a hopeless situation with which the outspoken, undiplomatic Yancey could not cope, and when Queen Victoria proclaimed English neutrality, his brilliant but futile career came to a climactic close.

He returned to Alabama in 1862, was elected to the Senate of the Confederacy, and served until his death on July 27, 1863. When he died, at forty-nine, he was resisting centralized government in the Confederacy as he had fought it in the Union.

William Lowndes Yancey was an independent, dedicated spirit. He paid no homage to power or position, scorned condescending acclaim, and obeyed only the dictates of his own conscience and judgment. He spoke the truth as he saw it.

H.C.

Richard Taylor

THE SON of a famous father always has a reputation to live up to, and Richard Taylor, only son of Zachary Taylor, measured up well to the nobility of a distinguished father.

Richard was born near Louisville, Kentucky, on the family farm on January 27, 1826. His boyhood was spent in frontier camps with his father. He was tutored at Edinburgh and in France, attended Harvard, and in 1845 was graduated from Yale.

When Richard was twenty he served as secretary to his father who was on duty at Matamoras, Mexico, but an attack of rheumatism forced him to seek relief at Hot Springs, Arkansas, and in Virginia. After managing his father's cotton plantation near Natchez, he established a sugar plantation in St. Charles Parish. While developing the property he collected a magnificent library; an omnivorous reader, he concentrated on military history.

Taylor was a delegate to the controversial Democratic conventions of 1860 and strove to prevent the party's disruption. As a member of the Louisiana Senate, he reported the bill to call a state convention, was elected a delegate, and voted for secession. As chairman of the committee on military and naval affairs he urged immediate preparation for war, and with the beginning of the war it was only natural that he join the Confederate forces. His father had been a soldier; his three sisters all married army men, one being the wife of Jefferson Davis.

Taylor was appointed colonel of the 9th Louisiana Infantry and was mustered in on July 6, 1861. A month later, in Virginia, he was appointed brigadier general and served in the Valley campaign. As a part of Stonewall Jackson's command, he joined Lee at Richmond and, although prostrated by illness, directed his troops from an ambulance during the Seven Days' battles.

Taylor was promoted to the rank of major general on Jackson's recommendation and assigned to the command of the district of Louisiana, which included all the states west of the Mississippi. After the capture of New Orleans, Confederate authority in Louisiana ceased to exist, and Taylor set about the difficult task of restoring confidence and raising an army. Regiments were formed, shops and depots of supplies were established, ordnance was assembled, and river boats were transformed into a navy.

His little army outnumbered and inadequately equipped, he avoided drawn battles, making numerous surprise attacks in which he captured much-needed arms and medical stores. The federal post at Bayou des Allemands was taken, the federal advance along the Lafourche was stopped, and seventeen hundred Union soldiers surrendered at Berwick Bay.

Taylor early adopted a simple strategy. At every halt he examined the adjacent roads, their direction and condition, distances to cities, general topography, and the country's capacity to furnish supplies. He then reduced the scene with notes to a sketch which he impressed on his memory and on the march always imagined he faced the enemy. "Such slight success as I had in command," he wrote, "was due to these customs."

The discovery of salt mines at Avery Island was a godsend to the Confederacy. General Taylor cured beef at New Iberia and shipped it to the relief of Vicksburg, with corn, molasses, forage, salt, and sugar.

He planned the recapture of New Orleans and had reached Kenner when Vicksburg fell on July 4, 1863, and he was cut off from the Confederacy. In 1864, against overwhelming odds, he was successful in the Red River campaign. In the bloody battles of Mansfield and Pleasant Hill he forced the invaders across the Atchafalaya, after capturing twenty-five hundred men and twenty pieces of artillery.

After a brief furlough with his family at Natchitoches, Taylor was promoted to lieutenant general and was assigned to the department of east Louisiana, Mississippi, and Alabama. He was put in command of General Hood's defeated army but despite prompt and vigorous action could not overcome the demoralization. General Taylor surrendered the last army of the Confederacy east of the Mississippi at Citronelle, Alabama on May 5, 1865.

His estate had been confiscated. He had married Louise Marie Myrtle Bringier in 1851. Two of their five children died of scarlet fever during the war. With the return of peace he divided his time between New Orleans and New York. He visited Washington frequently in an effort to secure the release of imprisoned Confederates. In 1873, he sailed for Europe where he was cordially received. In later years he served as trustee of the Peabody Educational Fund for the promotion of education in the South. He died of dropsy in the home of a friend in New York on April 12, 1879.

Shortly before his death he finished his reminiscences in a book entitled *Destruction and Reconstruction.* His volume attracted wide attention, North and South, for its vivid and unbiased pen portraits of Civil War characters. The book shows marked literary talent and is embellished with wise and lively comment. "The greatest is he," he said, "who commits the fewest blunders." In his modesty, he claimed neither for himself nor for his father any high place in military history. "Although since the days of Nimrod, war has been the constant occupation of men," he wrote, "the fingers of one hand suffice to number the great commanders."

Patrick Ronayne Cleburne

THE FIGHTING IRISH never bred a braver soldier than Patrick Cleburne. He was born in the county of Cork, Ireland, son of a farmer and physician, on March 17, 1828, the birthday of St. Patrick whose name he was given by his Protestant parents. His mother, Mary Ann Ronayne, who died when he was four years old, was descended from Maurice Ronayne, a patriot who resisted the tyranny of Henry IV in 1406.

Young Patrick was instructed by tutors, attended a private school, and at eighteen, apprenticed himself to a druggist. Because of deficiencies in Greek, Latin, and French, he failed to pass the examination set for him in the Apothecaries' Hall, Trinity College, Dublin. Humiliated, he went away to enlist in the 41st Regiment of Infantry.

After three years he purchased his discharge with money from his father's estate and sailed from Queenstown to New Orleans accompanied by his sister Anne and a half brother. Arriving on December 25, 1849, he went on alone to Cincinnati where he worked as a prescription clerk and then moved to Helena, Arkansas, to become part owner of a drug store.

Helena gave seven generals to the Confederate army, the most famed of whom were Patrick Cleburne and Thomas C. Hindman, who came to Helena following the Mexican war. Working together during a yellow fever epidemic that swept the town in 1855, Cleburne and Hindman became fast friends. Cleburne was Hindman's best man at his wedding and once was badly wounded in a street fight in Helena when he came to the aid of Hindman who was attacked by political opponents.

In 1856 Cleburne was admitted to the bar and had achieved a measure of prosperity when the ominous clouds of sectional strife gathered in 1860. Though Arkansans were divided on the burning issues, the majority believed that the federal government was assuming more power than the authors of the Constitution ever intended. Cleburne was an ardent Whig, but when the party adopted the antiforeign policy of the Know-Nothings, he became a Democrat.

He helped organize the Yell Rifles at Helena in 1860, enlisting as a private, and in January, 1861, went to Little Rock to seize the federal arsenal. When Arkansas seceded, the Yell Rifles volunteered, and Cleburne was made captain and then colonel of the 1st Regiment of Infantry.

He spent the winter of 1861 at Bowling Green, Kentucky, where a Confederate army was being assembled by General Albert Sidney Johnston. While drilling and disciplining his men for combat, he was promoted to the rank of brigadier general. His command received its baptism of fire in the bloody battle of Shiloh and thereafter, as long as Cleburne lived, he and his men were distinguished in every battle and campaign in which the gallant army of Tennessee participated.

At Shiloh he won commendation for his valor and skill. Though wounded leading a fierce charge at Richmond, Kentucky, he participated in the battle of Perryville. On December 12, 1862, he was made a major general and gave a good account of himself at Chattanooga. At Chickamauga his command captured a position which had resisted a number of attacks and repulsed Sherman. At Ringgold Gap, at his own peril, he saved Bragg's artillery and wagon train from seizure by pursuing the enemy, for which he received a vote of thanks from the Confederate Congress.

On the basis of his demonstrated superiority as a division commander, he could have been lieutenant general had he not made himself suspect by his early advocacy of using slaves as soldiers and freeing those who rendered faithful service. His attention was called to the fact at the time that this proposed plan might stand in the way of his advancement, but he persisted in putting what he believed to be the good of his adopted country above personal ambition.

At the very beginning of the bitter controversy, Cleburne stated, "As to my position, I hope to see the Union preserved by granting to the South the full measure of her constitutional rights. If this cannot be done I hope to see all the Southern States united in a new confederation and that we can effect a peaceable separation. If both these be denied us, I am with Arkansas in weal or in woe."

Cleburne led a charmed life through shot and shell. At Richmond he was shot through the mouth. At Perryville he was wounded by a cannon shot that killed his horse. He passed through the fierce conflicts of Murfreesboro, Chickamauga, Missionary Ridge, Ringgold Gap, and the battles of the Atlanta campaign unscathed. Finally he fell at Franklin on November 30, 1864, while charging with his men on foot. He died in his stocking feet, having given his boots that cold winter morning to a barefoot soldier.

When Cleburne died, he was only thirty-six. He never married but at the time of his death was engaged to Sue Tarleton, the daughter of a cotton factor in Mobile, "a young maiden of rare accomplishment and intelligence," who, he wrote, after she kept him "in cruel suspense at length consented to be mine." After his death some of his personal belongings were sent to her by his aides and delivered in person by a friend of Helena days who was then living in Selma.

It is probably the way this fighting Irishman would have preferred to go, for he was a dedicated soldier and inspiring leader. Robert E. Lee called him "a meteor shining from a clouded sky." Cleburne once declared in an impassioned and eloquent speech to his command: "If this cause which is so dear to my heart is doomed to fail, I pray heaven may let me fall with it, while may face is turned to the enemy and my arm battling for that which I know to be right."

Zebulon Baird Vance

VANCE came down from the mountain country in 1851 to Chapel Hill to enter the University of North Carolina, clad in ill-fitting homespun clothes and homemade shoes. His fellow students ridiculed his rustic appearance, but North Carolina's future governor, senator, and favorite son had a hankering for books. From his boyhood he had learned his Scott, his Shakespeare, and his Bible.

Zebulon Baird Vance, son of David Vance, a farmer and country merchant, and Mira Margaret Baird, was born in Buncombe County, North Carolina, on May 13, 1830. After attending neighborhood schools, he went to Washington College at the age of fourteen but withdrew on the death of his father, who left a widow and eight children. Vance studied law at the University of North Carolina for one year, received his county-court license to practice in 1852, settled in Asheville, was immediately elected county solicitor, and a year later admitted to practice in the superior court.

But politics was his major interest. Coming on the scene just when the spirit of disunion ran rampant, Vance, who was devoted to the federal Union, began his career as a Henry Clay Whig. When the Whig Party dissolved, he declined to join the rebellious Democratic Party as so many others did, and aligned himself with the newly organized American Party. He served one term in the North Carolina House of Commons and from 1858 until 1861 in the Congress. He was reëlected for a third term on a platform supporting Union measures but was prevented from taking his seat by the secession of North Carolina.

Though upholding the constitutional right of a state to withdraw, Vance opposed the exercise of that right for any cause then existing. He resisted the secession movement until Lincoln called for troops. He then urged North Carolina to support the southern states. When the ordinance of secession was adopted, he organized a company of "Rough and Ready Guards" at Asheville, was elected captain, and was soon on active duty. In August, 1861, he was elected colonel of the 26th North Carolina regiment and led it in the New Bern campaign and in the Seven Days' battle near Richmond.

In the state election of 1862, the conservative wing of the Democratic party, which was critical of the Confederate administration, nominated Vance for governor, and he won by an unprecedented majority. Like Governor Joseph E. Brown of Georgia, he was a statesrighter, even within the Confederacy, refusing to surrender to it the writ of habeas corpus and powers of conscription.

Under his administration, North Carolina conducted an extensive trading business in cotton and naval stores, which were exchanged for supplies abroad. Vance sent agents to England to make purchases, organized a fleet of swift steamers to run the blockade into the port of Wilmington, and distributed materiel to North Carolina soldiers and civilians and to the Confederacy.

When the struggle for Southern independence became hopeless, Vance attempted in vain to negotiate with Sherman as he approached Raleigh and finally surrendered to General Schofield at Greensboro. He was arrested by order of President Johnson on his thirty-fifth birthday and imprisoned in the Old Capitol Prison at Washington until released on parole.

Returning home, Vance formed a law partnership at Charlotte. Finally pardoned, he was elected to the United States Senate, but after a futile effort for two years to have his disabilities under the Fourteenth Amendment removed, he surrendered his certificate of election. Soon thereafter Congress restored to him his citizenship.

In 1876 North Carolina Democrats girded themselves to overthrow the carpetbag Republican regime which had taken over the state government and elected Vance, their popular leader, governor. His administration was distinguished by a revival of railroad building and improvement in the public schools for both races. He repudiated the fraudulent state bonds, adjusted the state's indebtedness, and set the pace for a new era in North Carolina.

At the end of two years of his four-year term, Vance was elected to the United States Senate, where he served until his death on April 14, 1894. He was a prodigious worker, diligent student, and an accomplished advocate. No one excelled him in eloquence. He was endowed with a spontaneous sense of humor and a knack for quick repartee. His voice was soft, musical, and flexible. In all the opportunities and temptations for private gain, his integrity was never questioned.

Vance was an outstanding opposition senator, a determined foe of the internal revenue system, and was outspoken against political corruption. His close application to his work undermined his health and impaired one of his eyes. The operation for its removal in 1891 shattered his nervous system, and he died in Washington. By his first wife Harriet N. Espy, who died in 1878, he had four sons. In 1880, he married Mrs. Florence Steele Martin of Kentucky.

His leadership spanned forty years in which he retained the respect and confidence of the people of his state. He was the perfect public servant. Governor, senator, and statesman, he symbolized the transition from the ante bellum South to the New South that arose triumphant from the ashes of disillusionment and adversity.

Augustus Hill Garland

On May 20, 1861, Arkansas seceded from the Union to become one of the Confederate states. Immediately, its governor, Henry M. Rector, sent out a call for ten thousand volunteers; and thirty thousand responded.

The fiercest battle in Arkansas during the Civil War took place on Pea Ridge, Benton County, on March 7, 1862. Though the Confederates carried the field under General Van Dorn, among their many dead were two Confederate generals. Other battles were at Prairie Grove and at Arkansas Post. When the Union forces won control of the Mississippi River with the fall of Vicksburg on July 4, 1863, war activity west of the river subsided. But Arkansas became a state divided against itself, with the Confederacy operating a state government south of the Arkansas River and the federals in command north of it.

With the surrender of General Kirby-Smith on May 26, 1865, the fighting officially ended in Arkansas, which was placed under military rule. In 1868, following the Congressional Plan of Reconstruction, Powell Clayton, a retired Union veteran, was elected governor on a Republican ticket. As a carpetbag governor, he was neither the worst nor the best among the plunderers who gravitated into the vanquished South to loot the helpless. Clayton instituted martial law and used Negro militia to hunt down Ku Klux Klansmen at a cost of $330,675.

When the Democrats returned to power in 1874, Arkansas was bankrupt. Augustus Hill Garland, who was inaugurated chief executive on November 12, 1874, found "there was not enough money in the treasury to buy sufficient wood to build a fire in the governor's office."

Governor Garland, who was to restore peace and promote prosperity, was born in Tipton County, Tennessee, on June 11, 1832, the son of Rufus and Barbara (Hill) Garland. In 1833 his parents moved to Miller County, Arkansas, where his father died. Subsequently, his mother moved to Washington, the county seat of Hemstead, and in 1837 married Thomas Hubbard. Augustus was educated in Kentucky at St. Mary's College at Lebanon and St. Joseph's College at Bardstown. On returning to Arkansas, he taught school for a time in Sevier County, studied law in the office of his stepfather, and was admitted to the bar in 1856. Six years later he moved to Little Rock and in 1860 was admitted to practice before the United States Supreme Court. He married Virginia Sanders in 1853; she died in 1877.

Active in public affairs, Garland was elected to the secession convention and was one of those who voted against an ordinance to secede. At the second session of the convention, however, after the bombardment of Fort Sumter, he voted with the majority and was one of five delegates elected to the Provisional Confederate Congress. He was chosen representative in the first Confederate Congress, continuing until 1864 when he was sent to the Confederate Senate.

Upon leaving the senate at the end of the war, Garland was asked by Governor Harris Flanagan to open negotiations for federal recognition of the state government. He secured a pardon from President Andrew Johnson and at once applied for the reinstatement of his license to practice before the Supreme Court, which was denied because of the so-called "iron-clad" oath.

An act of Congress on January 24, 1865, had disbarred every one who could not take oath that he had never borne arms against the United States or accepted office in a government hostile to it. Garland contended the act was unconstitutional, ex post facto, and even if constitutional, his disability had been removed by the President's pardon. Both his views were sustained by the Supreme Court.

In 1867, after the Democrats captured the legislature, he was elected to the United States Senate but was denied his seat. When the spurious carpetbag regime was overthrown in 1874 he was elected and inaugurated governor. Among other problems, he inherited a heavy state debt, $4,378,544 of which could not even be accounted for. In 1877 he was again elected to the United States Senate and this time took his seat.

Garland introduced a bill to investigate the effects of the tariff, initiated a measure giving the Mississippi River Commission authority to construct levees, and supported civil service reform.

When President Grover Cleveland appointed him attorney general in his cabinet, it was not surprising that this Confederate was subjected to a congressional investigation which came to naught.

Garland spent a good part of his life overcoming political obstacles and defending the constitution. When he retired from the cabinet, he resumed the practice of law, this time in Washington, D. C., and was fatally stricken there while arguing a case before the Supreme Court on January 26, 1899.

Above all else Garland was the tireless advocate. His was the rare distinction of having served as Confederate congressman and senator, governor of Arkansas, United States senator, and United States attorney general. And through the many upheavals of volcanic times, he deserved, won, and retained the confidence and esteem of God-fearing men.

James Ewell Brown Stuart

POPULARLY known as "Jeb" Stuart, he was the Civil War's most elusive cavalryman. He was born on Laurel Hill plantation, Patrick County, Virginia, on February 6, 1833. His father, Archibald Stuart, was directly descended from an earlier ancestor of the same name, a pioneer of Scotch-Irish stock, who settled in Pennsylvania in 1726 and then moved to Virginia in 1738. Jeb's mother, Elizabeth Letcher (Pannill), was of Welsh extraction.

The seventh of ten children, Stuart received his early schooling at home in Wytheville, attended Emory and Henry College for two sessions, and entered the United States Military Academy in 1850, graduating thirteenth in a class of forty-six. A popular cadet there, he was noted for his religious fervor and frequent fights.

Commissioned brevet second lieutenant in the Mounted Rifles in July, 1854, he received his regular commission in October, joined his command in Texas, was transferred to the 1st United States Cavalry, and spent most of the subsequent six years in Kansas. Here, on November 14, 1855, he married Flora, daughter of Colonel Philip St. George Cooke, after a whirlwind courtship.

Stuart soon disclosed definite aptitude for outpost duty. During the summer of 1859 he went East, in the hope of selling to the war department the rights to a device he had invented for attaching the cavalry sabre to the belt. While in Washington, he was asked to ride in haste to Arlington with a sealed message for Colonel Robert E. Lee, who had been superintendent of the military academy for the last two years of his cadetship. Stuart went with Lee to Harper's Ferry and there identified "Osawatomie" (John) Brown, the obsessed abolitionist he had met in Kansas. Back on the frontier, Stuart wrote Jefferson Davis on January 15, 1861, requesting "a position" in the "Army of the South." While on leave Stuart learned that Virginia had seceded from the Union and immediately resigned from the United States army, in which he was then a captain.

Because of the divided governmental authority at the time, Stuart was doubly commissioned lieutenant colonel of Virginia infantry and captain of Confederate cavalry. At Harper's Ferry, with about three hundred horsemen, he successfully screened a wide front. At First Manassas he protected the Confederate left and with a well-timed charge contributed to the victory. He was made brigadier general on September 21, 1861, and organized an admirable outpost system, to bring to high efficiency his cavalry of twenty-four hundred men.

He accompanied Joseph E. Johnston to the Peninsular campaign and because of his spectacular exploits became a celebrity. Before the Seven Days' battles he was ordered by Lee to reconnoiter McClellan's right flank. He made a complete circuit of the federal army, and when he reported to Lee he brought with him 165 prisoners and 260 horses and mules, with the loss of only one man. He was promoted to major general on July 25, 1862, and placed over the cavalry division of the army of northern Virginia, a command he held until his death.

Stuart proved to be an excellent intelligence officer, combining the highest skill and intrepidity. Lee regarded him as the "eyes of the army." The chief criticism against him was that he moved with too much boldness. In a raid on General Pope's communications he not only seized a large quantity of stores but also obtained documents giving the strength and disposition of the Union forces. He performed brilliantly in actions leading up to and during the battle of Second Manassas. Following Lee's return to Virginia, Stuart on October 9, 1862, set out across the Potomac with eighteen hundred men and four guns to make a raid on Pennsylvania. Riding around the federal enemy, he returned to Virginia via White's Ford three days later with twelve hundred federal horses. He guarded the Confederate right at Fredericksburg and aided Stonewall Jackson at Chancellorsville. Stuart was given command of the 2nd Corps after both Jackson and A. P. Hill were wounded.

One of Stuart's fiercest engagements occurred at Brandy Station before the Gettysburg campaign. He continued to distinguish himself through the winter of 1863-64. With forty-five hundred men he moved to head off Sheridan, who was proceeding South with twelve thousand sabres. Stuart demanded of his weakened horses their last mile of endurance as he turned Sheridan's columns. In the action, however, Stuart, who had never been touched by sabre or bullet in all his encounters, was mortally wounded at close range at Yellow Tavern in front of Richmond and died the next day at the Confederate capital on May 12, 1864.

In keeping with his daring exploits Jeb Stuart was a picturesque soldier. Though his patriotism was above challenge and his private life clean and wholesome, he practiced showmanship. His gray cloak was lined with red; he liked to wear a red flower or ribbon loveknot in the lapel of his jacket; his hat was cocked on one side with a gilt star that held a peacock's plume. He always rode a spirited steed. He encouraged merrymaking in his camp but prohibited drinking, swearing, and loose living; the younger men in the cavalry corps idolized him. Lee regarded him almost as a son and remarked after the war that Stuart was his ideal soldier.

Jeb Stuart, the plumed knight, was only thirty-one when he died. Like his intimate friend, Stonewall Jackson, he rode his war horse into legend and history, ranking as one of America's foremost cavalry commanders. His death marked the beginning of the decline of the superiority which the Confederate horse had enjoyed over that of the Union.

Joseph Wheeler

"FIGHTING JOE" WHEELER was one of the bravest soldiers of all time. During the Civil War he participated in some eight hundred skirmishes and commanded 172 battles. Two horses were shot from under him at the battle of Shiloh, and during other battles a total of sixteen horses were killed while he was riding them. He fought twenty-six engagements in thirteen days. Thirty-six staff officers fell by his side, eight of whom were killed, the others wounded. A list of his engagements is almost a record of the Confederate Army. Yet, he was wounded only three times throughout the war.

Joseph Wheeler was born near Augusta, Georgia, on September 10, 1836, the son of Joseph and Julia Knox (Huff) Wheeler. Both parents were of New England colonial stock. His father, who moved to Georgia in young manhood, was descended from Moses Wheeler of New Haven, Connecticut.

Joseph's mother died when he was five, and, his father having lost his fortune by going security for friends, the lad was sent to a maternal uncle in Connecticut. After receiving a haphazard primary education in the public schools, he was appointed to the United States Military Academy, graduating in 1859.

He was breveted a second lieutenant of dragoons and saw two years' service in the regular army in New Mexico. When the disruption of the Union threatened, he wrote his brother, "If Georgia withdraws and becomes a separate state, I can not, with propriety and justice to my people, hestitate in resigning my commission."

Upon his return to Georgia in 1861, he was initially commissioned a first lieutenant of artillery and immediately promoted to a colonelcy. He fought through the Shiloh campaign and gained such recognition as a disciplinarian and leader that he succeeded to the command of the 19th Alabama Infantry. On July 18, 1862, at twenty-six, he was placed in command of the cavalry of the army of Mississippi.

In the next two and a half years, "Fighting Joe" rose successively to brigadier general, major general, and lieutenant general, with but one specific assignment, the leadership of the cavalry in the western theater of operations. He covered Bragg's advance into and retreat from Kentucky and took a prominent part in the Murfreesboro and Chickamauga campaigns. After Rosecrans' retirement to Chattanooga, Wheeler executed a masterly raid on Union communications. His cavalry participated in the siege of Knoxville and opposed Sherman throughout his long progress to Atlanta, Savannah, and Raleigh. When his forces distintegrated at Joseph E. Johnston's surrender, Joseph Wheeler himself was captured near Atlanta. At twenty-eight, he was the hero of many personal encounters and had earned his sobriquet of "Fighting Joe."

General Robert E. Lee bracketed him with J.E.B. Stuart as one of the two outstanding Confederate cavalrymen. Capable opponents, with superior forces of fine cavalry, never succeeded in mastering him.

After the surrender, Joseph Wheeler became a commission merchant for three years in New Orleans. On February 8, 1866, he married Daniella (Jones) Sherrod of Alabama. In 1868, he moved to Wheeler, Alabama, named in his honor, and engaged in farming and the practice of law.

As the tide of Reconstruction ebbed, he entered politics. He was elected to Congress on June 3, 1882, but as a result of a contest was unseated. He was reëlected on March 3, 1883. He served continuously until his voluntary retirement in 1899. His chief public contribution there was his untiring effort to reconcile the North and South.

At the outbreak of the Spanish-American War, "Fighting Joe" at sixty-two could not resist the call to arms. When reminded that there stood upon the statute books an act prohibiting any man who had borne a commission in the Confederate army from holding one in the army of the United States, he observed that he "reckoned there would be plenty of room in the ranks." So back in uniform as a major general of volunteers, he commanded the cavalry division of Shafter's Santiago expedition, landed in Cuba at Daiquiri to precipitate the engagement at Las Guasimas on June 24, 1898, and despite an illness was present at the battle of San Juan Hill. After the surrender and the repatriation of the bulk of the expeditionary forces, he commanded the convalescent and demobilization camp at Montauk Point, Long Island.

He was then sent to the Philippines to command a brigade. Upon his return to the United States, he was commissioned a brigadier general and retired on his sixty-fourth birthday to live in peace in Brooklyn, New York, until he died on January 25, 1906.

During the Civil War, he found time, in 1863, to write a textbook entitled *Cavalry Tactics.* He was the author of "Bragg's Invasion of Kentucky" in *Battles and Leaders of the Civil War* and a number of treatises, including "A History of the Effect Upon Civilization of the Wars of the 9th Century" and a "Report on the Island of Guam."

Soldier, planter, lawyer, member of Congress, lieutenant general in the Confederate army, major general of volunteers and brigadier general in the army of the United States, a fighter by profession and a patriot by conviction, General Joseph Wheeler is worthy to associate with the heroes of history. Claimed by Alabama as her own, he was chosen, along with J. L. M. Curry, distinguished educator, as favored sons to represent her in Statuary Hall in Washington.

Robert E. Lee

A COURAGEOUS SOLDIER, Christian gentleman, and distinguished educator, Robert E. Lee was the fifth child and third son of Henry "Light-Horse Harry" Lee, famous Revolutionary general, and Anne Hill (Carter) Lee. He was born on January 19, 1807 at Stratford, Westmoreland County, Virginia.

Two signers of the Declaration of Independence, Lee's grandfather Richard Henry Lee and granduncle Francis Lightfoot Lee, had also been born at Stratford. General Lee's wife, Mary Custis, whom he married in 1831, was a great-granddaughter of Martha Washington, and her father's residence, Arlington House, across the Potomac from Washington, had been their own home until the Civil War.

At the age of eleven Robert lost his father; at eighteen he entered the Military Academy at West Point, where he was adjutant of the corps and from which he was graduated second in his class without a demerit. At the outbreak of the Mexican war he was captain of engineers at San Antonio. He joined General Winfield Scott in the Vera Cruz expedition to win the general's lasting confidence and esteem by his capacity on the march. During the various engagements leading to the capture of Mexico City, in one of which Lee was wounded, his regular rank was augmented by three brevets for gallantry to that of colonel. He returned to the United States in 1848 and was supervising the construction of Fort Carroll in Baltimore harbor when appointed superintendent of the Military Academy in 1852. Three years later United States Secretary of War Jefferson Davis approved his transfer from staff to line, and he was commissioned lieutenant colonel of the 2nd Cavalry in west Texas.

He was on leave at Arlington, which he had inherited from his father-in-law, at the time of John Brown's raid on Harpers Ferry and was placed in command of the detachment of marines that stormed the engine house, capturing Brown and his "garrison."

When the lower south seceded in 1861, General Scott, at the instance of President Lincoln, offered Lee the chief command of the United States forces, which he refused. When Virginia seceded, Colonel Lee tendered his resignation and within two days was made commander in chief of the military and naval forces of Virginia. Though Lee had freed the slaves which he had inherited from his father-in-law and had no sympathy for the institution, he wrote his sister at the time that he could not raise his hand against his relatives, his children, and his home.

Lee led his men in a series of battles and campaigns that still serve as models of military strategy and won for him and his army undying fame, even though he lost the war. Ill-equipped and outnumbered, with his men subsisting near the end on a daily ration of a pint of cornmeal and quarter of a pound of bacon, he could not resist the massed pressure of Grant, who broke through his lines at Petersburg. In January, 1865, Lee had been confirmed general in chief of the Confederate States. On April 9, he surrendered what was left of his fighting forces at Appomattox Court House. Of thirty-five thousand troops with which he started, only seventy-eight hundred remained with arms in their hands.

When General Lee appeared among his men after the surrender, mounted on his famous war horse Traveller, they overwhelmed him with regard and sympathy. As a paroled prisoner of war he returned to Richmond; he had no home, for Arlington had been seized by the federal government. The Lees continued to pay rent on a house in Richmond in Confederate money, which the landlord insisted was in the original agreement.

Lee received many tempting offers but accepted the presidency of Washington Academy at a salary of fifteen hundred dollars a year and set off alone for Lexington on Traveller from a farmhouse where he had spent the summer. The buildings, damaged by federal troops, were occupied by four professors and forty-five cadets. The trustees managed to borrow five thousand dollars so the college could open. Through Lee's leadership, and the coöperation of patrons north and south, the academy prospered. In 1867 there were four hundred students enrolled, and the trustees doubled his salary. Lee sought to instill moral and religious ideals in his students. He made many educational innovations and initiated the honor system. He said, "We have but one rule here, and that is that every student must be a gentleman." Washington College changed its name to Washington and Lee University in his honor.

General Lee had applied for a pardon and the restoration of his citizenship on June 13, 1865, but the pardon was never granted. He was indicted for treason and never brought to trial, but America's great examplar continued to live without bitterness. His three sons followed him in the conflict. One son, George Washington Custis Lee, graduated at the head of his class at West Point, was aide-de-camp to Jefferson Davis, major general of a division of the army of northern Virginia, and when General Lee died on October 12, 1870, succeeded his father as president of Washington and Lee University.

No American had a comparable influence on the people of the Confederate states. Physically, morally, and intellectually he was no ordinary man. Of deep religious convictions, he was a true soldier of the cross. His faith in the God of his fathers, his devotion to duty, patient serenity, tolerance of others, all blend into one preëminent personality to form the Southern gentleman. Out of all the carnage and sorrow of that unfortunate conflict, the sublimity of General Lee emerges as both the incarnation of the lost cause and the guiding spirit of the resurgent South.

4

Reconstruction, Reunion, and World Power

Andrew Johnson	Charles Goodnight
Wade Hampton	Henry Woodfin Grady
L.Q.C. Lamar	William Crawford Gorgas
James Zachariah George	Walter Hines Page
Stephen Dill Lee	Woodrow Wilson
Francis Redding Tillou Nicholls	Booker Taliaferro Washington
Henry Watterson	James Buchanan Duke
Edward Douglas White II	Joseph Stephen Cullinan
Benjamin Ryan Tillman	Richmond Pearson Hobson
Quanah Parker	Joseph Taylor Robinson
Henry B. Plant	Harvey Crowley Couch
Henry M. Flagler	Will Rogers
Richard Coke	Rudolph Matas
Jesse Chisholm	Cordell Hull

Andrew Johnson

WHEN Lincoln was assassinated during his second term, Andrew Johnson from Tennessee, the vice-president, became president. A "poor white," born in a shack, in Raleigh, North Carolina, on December 19, 1808, he was the younger son of Jacob Johnson and Mary McDonough. His father, "an honest man, loved and respected by all who knew him," a bank porter and sexton, died when Andrew was three, leaving the mother and two children in a state of poverty.

Andrew, the only president who never spent a single day in a schoolroom, was apprenticed with his brother to a tailor to be worked, fed, and clothed until they were twenty-one. After two years of bondage both boys ran away and a ten-dollar reward was posted for their capture. In 1826 Andrew, together with his mother and stepfather, was in Greenville, Tennessee, where he opened a tailorshop. There at nineteen he married Eliza McCardle, the daughter of a Scotch shoemaker, who assisted him in his reading and writing which he had already undertaken in an effort to educate himself.

With a flare for public speaking and politics, Johnson's career began with his election as alderman of his village. Championing the cause of the working man, he was elected mayor, legislator, state senator, and in 1843 congressman, a post he filled for ten years. Gerrymandered out of his district by a Whig legislature, he ran for governor as a Democrat, was elected in 1853, and four years later won a seat in the United States Senate.

The nation was heading for war when he arrived in Washington. In an era of mass insanity, his was a struggle for the sanctity of the Constitution and the preservation of the Union. Although a Southern Democrat and slaveholder, when the other Southern senators withdrew he alone remained. While the Radical Republicans welcomed him as a powerful ally, Southern extremists thought him a traitor.

In March, 1862, while still senator, Johnson was appointed by President Lincoln military governor of Tennessee. While Johnson was serving efficiently and effectively in this capacity, Lincoln was renominated by the National Union convention, and the same considerations which led that body to drop the party name Republican led to the nomination of Andrew Johnson, a Southern Democrat, as vice-president.

Johnson's health was impaired by a strenuous campaign, and feeling faint at the inaugural ceremonies, he drank three glasses of brandy that went to his head. This gave men of malice something to exploit throughout his tempestuous career. On the morning of April 15, 1865, the day after Lincoln's assassination, Johnson was informed by the cabinet of his accession to the Presidency. In a simple ceremony the oath of office was administered by Chief Justice Chase. Johnson announced that he would retain Lincoln's cabinet intact and pursue his policies.

The assassination, following so closely the collapse of the Confederacy, fired men's emotions. At first Johnson was bitter, but sobered by his commitment to carry out Lincoln's program, he did his utmost to restore peace.

The fall of the Confederacy left the South prostrate and bankrupt with four million freed slaves. The war was over, but there was no peace. Opposition to Lincoln's magnanimous program, already gathering bitter opposition when he was shot, was concentrated upon Johnson. Under the evil genius of Senator Thaddeus Stevens of Pennsylvania, a conspiracy was formed to write one of the most ignominious chapters in American history. The South must be punished, its people persecuted, its aristocracy destroyed, and its former slaves put in command. The Reconstruction amendments were enacted and were ratified by states controlled by former slaves, carpetbaggers, and scalawags. The Civil Rights Act was passed over the President's veto. The police power of the states was usurped by armed federal force, and Freedmen's Bureaus were set up to impose a slavery on Confederates more oppressive than they had ever exercised over their slaves.

The President himself was so completely circumscribed by congressional enactments, so harassed by his foes, and vilified by the Northern press that his usefulness to stem the tide of hate was at an end. His enemies found no good in the man, and his friends were few. Even the purchase of Alaska from Russia was condemned. Impeached in the House for "high crimes and misdemeanors," and tried before the Senate, he came within one vote of being convicted.

A few months later Johnson's term expired, and he returned to Tennessee. When the madness had subsided and Johnson had recovered from an attack of yellow fever, he was reëlected to the United States Senate. Death and the mutations of politics had removed his former enemies. A few faithful friends remained to give to the occasion of his return a belated but dramatic vindication.

Before the stormy session came to an end, Johnson delivered a speech in which he severely attacked President Grant's official record, denounced his aspirations for a third term, and concluded, "Let peace and prosperity be restored to the land. May God bless this people; may God save the Constitution." Johnson returned to his home, where he suffered a paralytic attack and died on July 31, 1875.

PS

Wade Hampton

THE YEAR the Civil War began, Wade Hampton's plantations in South Carolina and Mississippi produced five thousand bales of cotton. With twelve thousand acres in cultivation and nine hundred Negroes he was probably the richest man in the South. His father had been an aide to General Jackson in New Orleans in 1815. His grandfather served with heroism in the American Revolution under Marion and Sumter.

Wade Hampton, the third, was born in Charleston, South Carolina, on March 28, 1818, at the home of his mother's parents. His early years were spent chiefly at Millwood and at Cashier's Valley, his father's summer home in the North Carolina mountains. At Millwood, his father bred blooded horses, and under his training Wade became a noted hunter, an accomplished fisherman, and an excellent horseman. He was a powerful man, six feet in height, broad-shouldered, deep-chested, and strong of limb. When in the saddle he rode so well that he and the horse were one, and he could grip a horse with his knees until it groaned. He had a record of more than eighty black bears killed in the Mississippi swamps with the hunting knife.

Hampton went to school near Millwood, then to Columbia Academy, and in 1836 was graduated from the South Carolina College. At twenty he married Margaret Preston, his half cousin, and after her death in 1855 he married Mary McDuffie, orphaned daughter of a former South Carolina governor. He served in both houses of the South Carolina legislature from 1852 to 1861. He had studied law with no intention of following that profession and after the death of his father devoted himself largely to his plantations.

Hampton opposed slavery as economically unsound, and though he believed secession was within the law, he thought it inexpedient. However, with the firing on Fort Sumter, he gave of himself and his resources to the cause without stint. He organized the Hampton Legion, purchasing much of the equipment out of his own purse. He participated in the battle of First Manassas, where he was wounded for the first of five times in the first two years of combat. He commanded an infantry brigade in the Peninsular campaign and was appointed brigadier general on May 23, 1862. He served under J. E. B. Stuart in the Cavalry Corps of the Army of Northern Virginia and participated in most of his operations from 1862 to 1864. Throughout the war he was in the thick of the fighting and after Stuart's death in May became chief cavalry commander in the Army of Northern Virginia.

After he assumed command, the Confederate Army in Virginia was never again on the offensive, and the supply of horses at his disposal was near the vanishing point. With the exception of his capture of 2,486 beef cattle at Coggins Point, he was on the defensive. In 1865 he was ordered to J. E. Johnston in the Carolinas, where he was promoted to lieutenant general on February 15, 1865 and remained until the surrender to Sherman.

The war had taken the greater part of Hampton's fortune, and though he rejoiced to find many of his former bondsmen in Mississippi ready to go back to work, he was never able to prosper again. He had watched his state's capital, Columbia, captured and burned. He lost two sons in the conflict. The planter beat his plowshare into a sword and made the good fight; then the soldier turned from defeat with equal heroism to help bring order out of chaos. He supported the Reconstruction plan prescribed by Andrew Johnson, but when a radical Congress substituted its more drastic policy, Hampton joined in the general protest and entered vigorously into the 1869 state and presidential campaigns, working to defeat the party responsible for the disaster. Failing in his purpose, he devoted his attention to his private affairs, spending much time in an effort to rehabilitate his Mississippi plantation.

Running for governor in 1876 on a platform of "Reconstruction, Redemption, and Reform," Hampton was elected over the carpetbagger D. H. Chamberlain then in office. Both claimed the election and were inaugurated, with Chamberlain finally yielding to the militant forces of reform in that tempestuous aftermath. In the twenty-five years still left to Hampton, he became the apostle of prosperity and peace to a shattered state. A few swindlers were brought to justice, the tremendous state debt was reduced, and industrial development encouraged.

Not long after Hampton was reëlected for a second term a leg broken on a hunting expedition had to be amputated. While he lay desperately ill, he was elected to the United States Senate and served until 1891 when he was defeated by Benjamin R. Tillman. He became a commissioner of Pacific Railways in 1893, a position he held until three years before his death on April 11, 1902. He lived in Columbia in a house which had been presented to him by the people of South Carolina when his own had burned. When he died twenty thousand mourners followed on foot the bier of the incomparable cavalryman.

He was one of three civilians without previous military training to attain the rank of lieutenant general in the Confederate service, sharing that distinction with Richard Taylor and Nathan Bedford Forrest.

"In all the high companionship of knightly men," wrote Douglas Southall Freeman, "none had exemplified more of character and courage and none had fewer mistakes charged against him."

L.Q.C. Lamar

THE FOURTH of eight children and the namesake of a distinguished father, Lucius Quintus Cincinnatus Lamar was born in Putnam County, Georgia, on September 17, 1825. His uncle, Mirabeau B. Lamar, was the second president of the Republic of Texas.

After preparatory work in the public schools, Lamar entered Emory College, Georgia. He was graduated in 1845 while the college was under the presidency of A. B. Longstreet to whose daughter, Virginia, Lamar was married on July 15, 1847.

Reading law in the office of a kinsman he was admitted to the bar. Lured by the opportunities that a new state offered a young lawyer, he moved to Oxford, Mississippi. His father-in-law had accepted the presidency of the University of Mississippi, and Lamar taught mathematics for a time while establishing his law practice. A member of the bar at twenty-four, two years later this gifted speaker was meeting seasoned politicians in joint debate. At thirty-two he was in Congress, resigning his seat in 1860 to join the Confederacy. In 1861 he accepted a commission as lieutenant colonel in the Confederate Army and saw active service.

Appointed by President Jefferson Davis as special commissioner of the Confederacy to Russia he reached Paris and was recalled. Running a federal blockade he returned to the field of battle as judge advocate with the rank of colonel of cavalry at Richmond.

At the close of the Civil War he accepted the chair of ethics at the University of Mississippi and was in Congress again in 1872. He was in the United States Senate in 1877, was Secretary of the Interior in the Cabinet of President Cleveland in 1885, and in 1888 he was elevated to the Supreme Court of the United States as associate justice.

A man with both the courage of his convictions and the courage of his contempts, his friends were legion on both sides of the Atlantic, from the humblest hovel in Mississippi to the hearthstone of William Makepeace Thackeray in England.

Teacher, scholar, soldier, statesman, jurist, and peacemaker, in that tragic era at the close of the Civil War, he influenced public opinion, North and South, as no other man.

His rise to fame came in Congress in 1874. Senator Charles Sumner of Massachusetts had died, and Lamar was asked to second the motion to devote the day to the memory of this elder statesman. The gallery in the Senate chamber was filled with members of the diplomatic corps and others of note to hear a "fire-eating" Mississippian pay tribute to a South-hating abolitionist.

The hatred of war still rankled . . . the "bloody shirt" still waved . . . the atmosphere of the national Congress was highly charged. The room was as hushed as a death chamber while "the molten silver flowed from the tongue" of a magnetic personality.

"It was my misfortune," said Congressman Lamar, "perhaps my fault, personally, never to have known this eminent philanthropist and statesman. The impulse was often strong upon me to go to him and offer my thanks for his kind and considerate course toward the people with whom I am identified. . . . My regret is therefore intensified by the thought that I failed to speak to him out of the fullness of my heart while yet there was time." It was, someone observed, as if the soul that had departed from Sumner lived in Lamar.

"The South—prostrate, exhausted," he continued, "drained of her life blood, as well as her material resources, yet honorable and true . . . suffers in silence. The North, exultant in her triumph, and elated by success, yet as if mastered by some mysterious spell . . . her words and acts are the words and acts of suspicion and distrust. Would that the spirit of the illustrious dead . . . could speak from the grave to . . . every heart throughout this broad territory: 'My countrymen! Know one another, and you will love one another.' "

When he had finished both sides of the chamber were in tears, and then for the first time since the Civil War, Democrats and Republicans together broke into great applause. The press on both sides of the Mason-Dixon line reverberated with the speech and favorable comment, and a nation overnight became electrified.

L. Q. C. Lamar in a single speech spanned for the first time the deep, dark chasm that stretched between the North and South to reunite a divided people.

"Let us hope," he said, "that future generations, when they remember the deeds of heroism and devotion done on both sides, will speak not of Northern prowess and Southern courage, but of the heroism, fortitude and courage of Americans in a war of ideas, a war in which each section signalized its consecration to the principles, as each understood them, of American liberty and of the Constitution. . . ."

Sublime in his character and of a serenity of soul that rose above pride and prejudice, no other Mississippian reflected such honor or credit upon his South . . . no other statesman reached so deeply into the hearts of his people or carried so far the spirit of American brotherhood to a reunited country.

H.C.

James Zachariah George

PLANTER-STATESMAN James Z. George was not to the manor born; he was a product of the soil, born in obscurity on October 20, 1826, in Monroe County, Georgia, and reared in poverty. His schooling was limited to such learning as the "field schools" of the rural South provided.

At eight James moved with his mother and stepfather from Georgia to Noxubee County, Mississippi. Two years later they settled in Carroll County.

Up from the plow handles, self-educated with borrowed books read before pine-knot fires, James Z. George stepped out of the crowd to assume the intellectual leadership of Mississippi.

Through a special enactment of the state legislature he was admitted to the bar to practice law before he was twenty. As a lad he enlisted in the infantry under Colonel Jefferson Davis in the war with Mexico. The war over, he returned to Mississippi and was married to Elizabeth Young of Carroll County, where they continued to live except for intervals when professional or public duty took them elsewhere.

In 1854, at twenty-eight, he was appointed reporter of the High Court of Errors and Appeals in which office he prepared ten volumes of reports. He was a member of the secession convention of 1861, served in the Confederate Army as captain, colonel, and brigadier general, and was wounded in action, captured, and held prisoner until the close of the war.

As a lawyer James Z. George was preëminent in his day in Mississippi, and the partnership he formed with Wiley P. Harris in Jackson in 1872 established a record that is one of the brilliant chapters in the legal practice of the state.

He was chairman of the Democratic Executive Committee in the critical years of 1875 and 1876, and largely through his fearless leadership there was lifted the yoke of a new kind of slavery that the misfortunes of war had put upon the neck of Mississippi. Appointed judge of the State Supreme Court in 1879, he was chosen chief justice and in 1881 was sent to the United States Senate where he served with distinction until his death in 1897.

The only Democrat to have an important share in framing the Sherman Anti-Trust Law of 1890, he made an unsuccessful effort to exempt agreements among workingmen from the operations of the act.

He published a digest of court decisions through 1870 and left an incomplete manuscript of the *Political History of Slavery in the United States,* which was published seventeen years after his death.

His monumental work, however, was the constitution of Mississippi, adopted in convention in 1890. Into that great instrument he blazed new trails for political freedom and social justice. Through it he achieved racial peace for a war-torn state and set forever in her fundamental law the rights of the common people above special privilege.

His crowning contribution in the United States Senate was in the creation of the United States Department of Agriculture. As a farmer he foresaw the far-reaching influence of such an agency in the service of the Republic.

While James Z. George, with abiding faith in the future of the South, bought lands and prospered, he, more than any other Mississippi statesman of his time, kept the common touch.

His political philosophy he put into a single paragraph during a hectic campaign for the Senate in 1892: "Public life has no charm for me," he said, "beyond the consciousness of having at all times, to the best of my humble ability, worked for the welfare and advancement of the people of Mississippi, and of the whole country. I shall not, therefore, compromise my principles, nor advocate what I know will injure the people, for the poor privilege of occupying a conspicuous place among those who have aided in destroying what I have always endeavored to preserve and advance... the welfare of my countrymen."

James Z. George was no orator. His speech was simple as his dress was plain. But while he spoke softly, without gesture or eloquence, he convinced men readily by the force of his logic and convictions. His honesty was the honesty of the mother earth; his only masters were his God and his conscience.

On June 2, 1931, the state of Mississippi presented to the federal government the statues of Jefferson Davis and James Z. George, her two favorite sons, as her patriotic contribution to the country's select.

There they stand in bronze in Statuary Hall in Washington as they once stood in the flesh, companions in arms at Monterrey in the war with Mexico and in spirit in the Civil War.

As long as the Republic survives and men cherish freedom, these two will continue to share the affections of a people who revere the memory of their heroic dead and proclaim their independence.

To one came the challenge to lead fighting men into battle to the beat of drums, to the other the call to lead a people broken in spirit to the ways of peace.

Soldier, jurist, lawgiver, and statesman, James Z. George, in the fullest sense, was the people's servant; he was Mississippi's foremost reconstructionist.

Stephen Dill Lee

BY ORDERING the first shot fired on Fort Sumter on April 12, 1861, at half past four in the morning, Stephen Dill Lee started the Civil War.

In the course of that bloody conflict he gave a good account of himself. A hundred battlefields testify to his courage and his genius. President Jefferson Davis said that Lee was one of the Confederacy's best soldiers. "I have tried him," he said, "in cavalry, infantry and artillery, and found him not only serviceable but superior in all."

Born at Charleston, South Carolina, on September 22, 1833, Lee grew to young manhood there and was no doubt inspired by the brilliant public record of his distinguished grandfather, Thomas Lee, an able jurist, linguist, banker, and orator.

He entered West Point at seventeen and was graduated in 1854. He saw frontier duty in Texas, Kansas, and the Dakotas, and as assistant adjutant general of Florida took part in the Seminole war. He resigned his commission of first lieutenant in the United States Army after his native state of South Carolina seceded from the Union and cast his lot with the South in 1861. With the collapse of the Confederacy he made his home in Mississippi where he had seen active service during the conflict.

He was married to Regina Blewett Harrison of Columbus, Mississippi, on February 9, 1865. After spending twelve years in the rehabilitation of his plantation, he came out of retirement in 1878 to serve as senator in the state legislature.

In 1880 General Lee became the first president of the Mississippi Agricultural and Mechanical College, now Mississippi State University. Father of industrial education in the South, no other citizen has had such a far-reaching and penetrating influence upon the agricultural and industrial development of the Southern states. Lee advanced in his day a new thought to Southern-bred collegians. He believed that education and manual labor should go together. In making his first report to his Board of Trustees, he said: "All students are required to work from two to three hours a day . . . on the farm, among the stock, in the garden . . . shops or grounds. . . . Our experience shows that students who work . . . stand highest in their classes and enjoy best health. This feature enables our Mississippi boys of real worth and moderate means to be educated at far less expense than they can get an education in any other institution. It also inculcates and retains habits of industry at that period of life when education is being obtained. . . . It makes labor honorable and demonstrates that labor and a high standard of liberal and scientific education are not incompatible, but go hand in hand with the struggle of life, and in developing our industries and resources. . . ."

Lee warned the South that unless its farmers learned the science of modern agriculture their lands would be owned by strangers. "Knowledge is power," he said, "in every department of life—as important to the farmer as the professional man."

General Lee's educational philosophy made a profound impression on the nation. Work was no longer beneath the dignity of educated gentlemen.

He foresaw the part that electricity would play in the industrialization of the South, and in his report of 1893 he wrote, "I deem it most important that the boys of Mississippi be instructed in an electrical laboratory, to fit them for industrial pursuits now just ahead." That same year he began a crusade for an appropriation to equip such a laboratory and provide electric lights for the college grounds and dormitories. At times combating an unsympathetic legislature and the hosts of ignorance, "Old Steve," as he was affectionally called, pioneered with new methods of instruction and introduced departments in the mechanical arts and engineering.

Experiments at the college revealed the surprising fact that cotton seed, which had been a waste and a liability, had a feed and food value, and a new industry emerged from the soil. The first creamery in the Gulf states was established at the college and the foundation laid for a more diversified agricultural development.

Under Lee's leadership the advantages of diversified agriculture and drainage were fully demonstrated and the value of scientific farming definitely proved among a people whose methods were comparatively primitive.

The cultivation of better grasses and the introduction of improved herds changed the agricultural complexion of the "Magnolia State." Graduates went forth with a new faith in farming. The development of this new idea in education spread to other states and created a demand for students to fill positions as teachers, managers of farms and creameries, and professors and instructors in other agricultural colleges and at agricultural experiment stations.

Stephen Dill Lee died in 1908. In the devastation that followed in the wake of Appomattox, with a social order disrupted, an economic system destroyed, and the flower of southern manhood killed or maimed, Lee the soldier became a builder.

H.C.

H.C.

Francis Redding Tillou Nicholls

FEW EVENTS in Louisiana history have been as dramatic as the blow Governor Francis T. Nicholls inflicted upon the state lottery racket in 1888.

The Louisiana Lottery Company had been chartered in 1868 for a period of twenty-five years. In return for the monopoly, the company paid the state forty thousand dollars annually and was exempt from taxation. When the charter was about to expire, the company asked for a twenty-five-year renewal in advance, offering the state one and a quarter million dollars annually.

The offer came at a time when Louisiana was debt-ridden; the state needed money for levees, schools, salaries, and pensions. When an act for the renewal of the charter was passed by the legislature, Governor Nicholls vetoed it and delivered a message of indignation.

Governor Nicholls had lost an arm and a leg in the Civil War and had stumped the state in the bitterest political campaign of its hectic history. Standing before the legislature and emphasizing his words with his one hand, he said, "Gentlemen, I have but one hand, but before I would disgrace it by signing that measure, I would have it torn from my body and carried to Virginia and buried by the side of its mate."

Francis Nicholls was born in Donaldsonville, Louisiana, in 1834. He attended Jefferson Academy at New Orleans and at twenty-one was graduated from West Point.

He served in the Seminole campaign in Florida and then resigned his commission as second lieutenant in the artillery to study law at the University of Louisiana, now Tulane. He quit school before his graduation to fight and win an important case and soon established a reputation at the bar.

With the outbreak of the Civil War he organized a company of volunteers from the parishes of Ascension and Assumption and was rapidly promoted from captain of the Phoenix Guards to brigadier general. He was in the battles of Manassas and Chancellorsville and fought with Taylor's brigade in northern Virginia. After he recovered from the loss of an arm in the battle of Winchester, he gallantly led the Second Louisiana in an engagement in which he lost his foot when his horse was shot from beneath him.

After Appomattox, General Nicholls returned to his home at Napoleonville where he was pursuing the practice of his profession when the state Democratic convention nominated *"all that was left of General Nicholls"* for governor to combat the carpetbaggers.

Both the Democratic and Republican parties claimed the election and two governors were installed, but Nicholls finally prevailed in a contested case that shook the republic. Governor Nicholls faced the crisis of Reconstruction with a statesmanship that drove the scalawags from the state and re-established righteous government in Louisiana.

He returned again to private practice and received an appointment from President Grover Cleveland to the board of visitors for West Point. In 1888, however, the people of the state drafted him to destroy the lottery menace, the corruption of which had reached the political core of Louisiana.

Patriot and statesman, he turned his talents to the rehabilitation of his state. Under his administration the public school system was improved, a state board of education was created, and charitable institutions were supported. The benefits of sound government were reflected in a substantial increase in population, industrial development, and business recovery.

In 1892, Nicholls was appointed chief justice of the Supreme Court of Louisiana. He served nineteen years on the bench with rare distinction. His voluminous reports, lucid and painstakingly elaborate, contributed much to molding constitutional law in Louisiana. His profound wisdom and sense of justice survive as a tradition with the bar of the state. During an era when government and business in Louisiana were rocked by war, Reconstruction, legislative and social reforms, and an epidemic of yellow fever, the leadership of Francis Nicholls brought order out of political chaos.

In a moral and economic crisis, Nicholls was a stabilizing influence; he inspired confidence and respect. He protected the lives, property, and liberties of the people under democratic government and put a new emphasis upon efficiency in high place.

Under his enlightened leadership on the field of battle, at the public forum, and on the bench, men were shown again that character is the eternal torch by which the fires of fearless patriotism are rekindled.

Patriot, statesman, and jurist, Nicholls retired from the bench only in his last illness at the age of seventy-seven. He died within a year to live in the hearts of his people as a public servant whose long career was marked by the enviable and steadfast attributes of true greatness . . . courage, kindness, and integrity.

Henry Watterson

IN THE heyday of personal journalism, when Horace Greeley, Joseph Pulitzer, and Whitelaw Reid were American household names, Henry Watterson, editor of the Louisville *Courier-Journal,* was well in the forefront of the fourth estate.

"Marse Henry" was born in Washington, D.C., on February 16, 1840, the son of Harvey Magee Watterson and Talitha (Black) Watterson. His father was a member of Congress from Tennessee. A small, sickly child, he made periodic journeys to the family estates. Except for a few terms at the Protestant Episcopal Academy in Philadelphia, his schooling was informal, but he was an avid reader and absorbed much through his association with educated people. Henry gave early promise of becoming a pianist, but a weak left hand and the loss of vision in his right eye put an end to cultivating his talent.

Throughout a colorful career "the Colonel" was constantly close to the changing political picture. As a child in the House, playing at page with the consent of a doting father, he was on the floor when John Quincy Adams was stricken and carried from his seat to die.

Henry had visited the Hermitage with his father and had sat on Andrew Jackson's knee. He knew all the presidents from Jackson to Harding, and though he died in Harding's time, he already numbered Calvin Coolidge, Herbert Hoover, and Franklin D. Roosevelt among his acquaintances. As a reporter for the *Daily States* in Washington, he reported the inauguration of Abraham Lincoln. A Unionist by conviction, although he eventually became a secessionist and Confederate soldier, he was drawn strongly to Lincoln; some of his best known writings were devoted to the Great Emancipator.

Though offered a commission as private secretary to United States Secretary of War Simon Cameron, Watterson went home, determined to write in peace until the war was over. But he found himself too much alone. "The boys were all gone to the front, and the girls were . . . all crazy," so he joined the Confederate army and was in and out for four years. He was on the staff of General Leonidas Polk until he fell ill, then worked on a propaganda newspaper in Nashville.

After the fall of Nashville, he was appointed editor of the state newspaper at Chattanooga, which he named the *Rebel* and turned into an organ for the Confederate army. While editing the *Rebel* he met his future business partner, Walter N. Holdeman, proprietor of the *Louisville Courier,* who, being an ardent Southern sympathizer, had suspended his newspaper and retired behind the Confederate lines. As editor of the *Rebel* Watterson first displayed the pungent prose that made him famous.

As the Union army moved on Atlanta, the publication of the *Rebel* was discontinued. After serving Generals Albert Sidney Johnston and John Bell Hood in various staff capacities, Watterson was an editor in Montgomery, Alabama. After the war ended, he took an editorial job on the Cincinnati *Evening Times.*

On December 20, 1865, he married Rebecca Ewing of Nashville and in 1867 they went to London. Upon his return he filled assignments on the Nashville *Republican Banner* and Louisville *Daily Journal,* before joining Holdeman in a merger that brought the *Courier-Journal* into existence.

The newspaper was one day old when the young editor began crusading for a restoration of Southern home rule. He sponsored Governor Samuel Jones Tilden of New York as the hope of the Democratic Party for president and a reunited country, and he took advantage of a Congressional vacancy to serve in the House as a Tilden advocate. Except for Lincoln, Tilden was the editor's only public hero. When Rutherford B. Hayes won the election, Watterson returned to his editorial career, never again to hold office. He never expressed more than temporary fealty to any presidential nominee or White House incumbent. He was critical of Grover Cleveland, opposed William Jennings Bryan, and in supporting McKinley for president almost destroyed the *Courier-Journal.*

Watterson deplored Wilson's appointment of Bryan as Secretary of State. He contributed a series of philippics against Theodore Roosevelt, "The Man on Horseback." He attempted to prevent the nomination of Wilson in 1912, and when criticized later for his opposition to Democrats and Wilson's League of Nations, he reminded his critics that "things have come to a hell of a pass when a man can't wallop his own jackass." He was, however, awarded a Pulitzer prize for his editorials hailing the declaration of war against the Central Powers.

Watterson sold his control of the *Courier-Journal* in 1918 as a result of the suppression of a Watterson editorial, and he retired to amuse himself writing "*Marse Henry*": *An Autobiography.* He died at Jacksonville in December, 1921, at the age of eighty-one.

He had an amazing zest for life and for convivial conversation. His drooping mustache, brief goatee, bushy eyebrows, and high-pitched voice were familiar to America's millions who knew him to be a fearless editor and hard worker. In his late years, "Marse Henry" became pessimistic over the nation's future because of the triumph of national prohibition and equal suffrage, championed by those whom he had ridiculed as "red-nosed angels" and "Crazyjanes." He died believing that civilization might collapse "in seventy years" because of the prevailing godlessness.

Edward Douglas White II

"I, EDWARD DOUGLAS WHITE, do solemnly swear that I will administer justice without respect to persons, and do equal right to the poor and to the rich, and that I will faithfully and impartially discharge and perform all the duties incumbent on me as chief justice of the United States, according to the best of my abilities and understanding, agreeably to the Constitution and laws of the United States."

Thus on December 19, 1910, Edward Douglass White was elevated from associate justice of the Supreme Court to chief justice of the United States.

Edward was born on a farm in LaFourche Parish, Louisiana, on November 3, 1845. He attended Mount St. Mary's College in Maryland, the Jesuit College in New Orleans, and Georgetown College in the District of Columbia. He left college at sixteen to enlist as a private in the Confederate Army. In the Battle of Port Hudson, north of Baton Rouge, he was taken prisoner in 1863 and was paroled.

At the close of the Civil War he read law in New Orleans in the office of Judge Edward Bermudez on Royal Street and at twenty-three was admitted to the bar. He rose rapidly in his profession, was elected to the state senate in 1874, was appointed associate justice of the State Supreme Court in 1879, and was elected to the United States Senate from Louisiana in 1891.

White was appointed associate justice of the United States Supreme Court by President Grover Cleveland in 1894, was elevated to the office of chief justice of the United States by President William Howard Taft in 1910, and at the time of his death in 1921 had served twenty-seven years on the nation's highest tribunal.

In the state legislature White was closely identified with the anti-lottery movement, and he worked ardently for the construction of levees along the Mississippi. On that memorable day of September 14, 1874, he carried a musket and assembled with others at the Clay statue on Canal Street to participate in the demonstration that finally broke the back of carpetbag rule in Louisiana.

White fought for a protective tariff on sugar in the United States Senate. As a justice of the United States Supreme Court his one passion was the Constitution. During his term he wrote opinions in seven hundred cases.

His judicial philosophy classified him neither as a liberal nor as a conservative. As he construed the law, in keeping with his oath of office and the light of understanding, he usually found himself somewhere between the extremes.

In delineating the character of a colleague, Judge White inadvertently disclosed his own judicial ideals: There was a "fixed opinion on his part as to . . . the Constitution . . . no thought of expediency, no mere conviction about economic problems, no belief that the guarantees were becoming obsolete or that their enforcement would incur popular odium ever swayed his unalterable conviction and irrevocable purpose to uphold and protect the great guarantees with every faculty which he possessed."

In 1895 the Supreme Court rendered three decisions that gave rise to popular criticism. One decision was in favor of the Sherman Anti-Trust Act; another held the Federal Income Tax of 1894 void in part; the third upheld the power of the federal government to issue injunctions in labor disputes. Judge White dissented in the income tax case. Through the heated controversy that raged, Judge White's harmonizing personality did much to reconcile differences of opinion on the bench.

Coming from the only state whose laws are based upon the Napoleonic Code, Judge White brought to the Supreme Court a knowledge of both civil and common law.

He sat upon the bench in suspicious and explosive times. The country had not fully recovered from the Civil War, and he became a stabilizing factor in a nation politically and socially shell-shocked.

A man of great bulk, broad mind, and big heart, he presided over the Supreme Court with a dignity that inspired confidence and respect. A tireless worker, he accelerated the machinery of the Court to make a record that won the praise of both bench and bar. He was gracious, genial, lovable, and popular. He was a man of learning, integrity, and judicial temperament.

Upon the horizon of humanity there looms now and then a man of justice; he always comes out of the crowd, for he must be the product of experience. Unbiased, he does not let prejudice, personal opinion, nor political consideration deter him in the interpretation of the law, in keeping with his oath and the Constitution. Edward Douglas White was such a man. At the age of two he was orphaned; at sixteen he was baptized with fire on the field of battle. He served in the legislature and Senate. In his most useful years he wore the robes of our highest court. When he died in 1921 he had discharged his duties faithfully and impartially, according to his ability and understanding and the Federal Constitution.

Soldier, senator, statesman, planter, and jurist, only now and then is a man with such conviction and devotion to the public weal recorded in the pages of political history.

Benjamin Ryan Tillman

After the Reconstruction period in the postwar south, a new political power sprang from the soil. Dirt farmers, as distinguished from planters, became articulate and alert through eloquent advocates. They were the spiritual descendents of the Patrons of Husbandry and Farmers' Alliances. Their spokesmen, colorful characters, were men like Tom Watson of Georgia, Jeff Davis of Arkansas, and "Pitchfork Ben" Tillman of South Carolina. These leaders of the "rednecks" and "hillbillies," called rabble rousers and demagogues, served their appointed purpose at a time when the little farmer and small tradesman were at loose ends in a shattered economy.

"Pitchfork Ben" Tillman humbled Wade Hampton, the gallant warrior and assumed political control of the electorate of the Palmetto Palm state. Governor and United States senator, he was born on August 11, 1847, in Edgefield County, South Carolina, the youngest of the seven children of Sophia (Hancock) and Benjamin Ryan Tillman. His ancestors had settled in South Carolina before the American Revolution.

His father, a farmer and innkeeper, died when Ben was two. Two brothers were war casualties; two others were killed in personal encounters; one died with fever. His brother George, a lawyer and politician, killed a bystander in a gambling feud in 1856 and as a consequence served two years in the penitentiary. Ben aided his mother in the management of her many slaves, studied in a local private school, and in 1861 entered Bethany, a rustic neighborhood academy. An apt student in English and Latin, he left school in 1864 at the age of seventeen to join the Confederate Army. Because of an illness which incapacitated him for two years and resulted in the loss of an eye, he was discharged from the service.

On January 8, 1868, Tillman married Sallie Starke of Georgia, by whom he had seven children. They cultivated a four-hundred acre, red-earth farm adjoining his mother's property from which they eked out a bare living for seventeen years.

He participated in the Hamburg and Ellenton Riots in 1876 when white men were forced to resort to violence to take command of their government which had fallen into the reckless hands of scalawags and carpetbaggers. Moved by his reverses as a farmer, Tillman forced himself on the attention of his fellow citizens. In a rousing speech at Bennettsville in 1885, he asserted that the farmers were being betrayed by lawyers and merchants. He demanded that the state undertake a system of agricultural education and through letters to the Charleston *News and Courier,* arraigned the rulers of the state and urged the farmers to organize.

To the surprise of many citizens, he organized the Farmers' Association, and almost captured control of the state government. Thomas Green Clemson, upon his death in April, 1888, left a site and an endowment for a proposed state college. During the following summer, Tillman so awakened the rural masses that he was able to force the governor and legislature to accept the Clemson bequest.

The farmers became convinced that Tillman was the only man who had "the brains, the nerve and the ability to organize the common people against the aristocracy," and he was their candidate for the Democratic nomination for governor in 1890. In an exciting and bitter campaign, he was nominated and elected, and subsequently reëlected. He became the complete master of the political fortunes of South Carolina.

In the face of bitter opposition, Tillman called a constitutional convention to initiate reforms. Clemson College was opened in 1893, and Winthrop College, a normal and industrial school for women, two years later. Taxes for public education were increased, representation in the legislature was reapportioned, and congressional districts were redrawn. He had written into the constitution a provision for educational and property qualifications to make the disfranchisement of Negroes legal. He created a state railroad commission and set up a state dispensary for the sale of alcoholic beverages.

In defeating Wade Hampton for the United States Senate in 1890, Tillman gained national fame; he called Hampton the "Grand Mogul" and his political foes the "Brigadiers." "Send me to Washington and I'll stick a pitchfork into his ribs," he said of Grover Cleveland. Aspiring to the Democratic nomination for president in 1896, he ruined his chances by his violent denunciation of Cleveland.

In the United States Senate, "Pitchfork Ben" favored naval expansion and the war with Spain. He opposed the annexation of Hawaii and the Philippines and Theodore Roosevelt's Panama policy. He attacked the "armor trust" for making excess profits out of the government and exposed the machinations of the steel magnates in the Senate and on the Chautauqua platform. He served in the Senate until his death on July 3, 1918, and exercised control over the state's vote at national Democratic conventions.

When Tillman suffered paralytic strokes in 1908 and 1910, his influence was already on the wane. His state dispensary, a pet project, became corrupt and was abolished. The state supreme court which he had created decided against him in a contest with his daughter-in-law for the guardianship of his two grandchildren.

Across the state house grounds in Columbia, "Pitchfork Ben" Tillman and Wade Hampton, worthy protagonists, dirt farmer and planter, face each other in monumental stone. There they stand, these favorite sons of South Carolina, in silent and mutual contemplation, sharing the respect and affections of the people of South Carolina.

H.C.

Quanah Parker

BORN SOMEWHERE within the Comanche country, probably in 1845, Quanah Parker was the son of Peta Nokoni, chief of the Quahadas, the most warlike of the Comanches. His mother, Cynthia Ann Parker, was white, a great-granddaughter of one of the signers of the Declaration of Independence. Captured by the Comanches as a child in 1835 during a raid on Texas settlers she finally became the wife of Nokoni.

During one of Nokoni's buffalo hunting expeditions in 1860, Cynthia Ann was retaken by Texas Rangers and restored to her own people. Separated from family and Indian friends and unhappy in strange surroundings, she soon died of a broken heart.

Upon the death of Nokoni, Quanah was forced to shift for himself. Bold, skilled, and alert, at the age of twenty-one he organized a band of his own. At the close of the Civil War the government wanted to place the Plains' tribes on reservations in Oklahoma. When they met in council at Medicine Lodge, Kansas, in 1867 to form a treaty for the purpose, Quanah refused to take any part in it.

The Comanches were a nomadic people, dependent on the buffalo for food and robes, and to abandon the hunt for the confinement of a reservation was to destroy their freedom; so they joined forces with the Kiowas, Apaches, Cheyennes, and Arapahoes in self-defense. Horse stealing, raids on white settlements, and fights with federal troops were frequent. Quanah in particular terrorized the frontier while the government waged a relentless campaign for seven years to crush his tribal confederation.

In the spring of 1874, as chief of the Comanches and the recognized leader of the other hostile tribes, Quanah made a last bold attack on the white invaders. Angered over the destruction of their herds, Quanah led seven hundred tribesmen against a party of twenty-eight buffalo hunters camped at Adobe Walls, Texas. Unable to resist powder and lead with spears and arrows, the Indians were defeated in a bloody fight that lasted all day. Many were killed, and Quanah was among the wounded.

The Plains' tribes were finally conquered, Quanah being the last to surrender. He led his brave little band of four hundred disarmed Quahadas into Fort Sill, Oklahoma, on June 2, 1875. As the leader of his people, the savage then became a civilizer. Despite opposition among his own people he adapted himself to the new conditions immediately and became a power and influence on the reservation in southwestern Oklahoma.

Quanah fostered building and agriculture. While he spoke English and Comanche and knew the sign language, he was illiterate. Believing that the best method to learn the white man's ways was through the association of their children, he favored public schools for both white and Indian children.

For a number of years after coming to Fort Sill, Quanah and his followers lived in their tepees, but in the fall of 1890 he built a commodious house of twelve rooms, fifteen miles west of Lawton. While he rode the range for others for a time, he finally raised cattle on his own, cultivated his broad acres, and prospered. A shrewd businessman, he was at one time the richest Indian in the nation. By leasing surplus pasture lands to stockmen he added to the tribal income in "grass money."

He could not be prevailed upon by federal commissioners to choose one of his seven wives. Under the tribal law he felt they were as much his responsibility as his twenty children. While he discouraged extravagance and dissipation, missionaries could not prevail upon him to forsake the religion of his ancestors.

Quanah traveled much, usually accompanied by Too-nicey, his favorite wife. He visited his mother's people in Texas, journeyed to Mexico many times, and toured the country. As chief and ambassador for the Comanches and their allies, he made frequent trips to Washington. He was appointed one of the four judges of an Indian court on the reservation in 1888. He rode in the inaugural procession of President Theodore Roosevelt and named a son for him.

He was tall, straight, and strong. Despite his white, blond mother, his complexion was bronzed and dark. He had heavy, raven-black hair and gray eyes. Those who knew him in his prime testify that when aroused his expression was ferocious. In his days of peace, however, his personality mellowed, and he became genial and jovial. He was famed for his forthright frontier tales and picturesque speech.

Quanah became ill while visiting Cheyenne friends near Hammon, Roger Mills County, Oklahoma, in 1911, and he died from pneumonia upon his return home, following a hard journey by rail and hack. As he reached his trail's end, an old medicine man ministering the last tribal rites prayed "Father in Heaven, this our brother is coming."

A year before he died he had removed the remains of his mother from Texas to Oklahoma. He was buried by her side, their dust reunited in a little Indian cemetery at Post Oak Mission, five miles north of Cache. Quanah Parker had a tender sentiment for his white mother's memory. At maturity he took her family name, and one of his daughters he called Cynthia Ann. He often said he and his mother would finally meet in the same paradise.

Henry B. Plant

WHEN HENRY BRADLEY PLANT began buying and building railroads in Florida in 1879, much of the state was inaccessible and so sparsely populated that it contained no city with as many as ten thousand inhabitants.

Henry Plant first visited Florida in 1853 with his wife, who had been ordered there by her physician. Located near Jacksonville, which was then an obscure hamlet, he became impressed by Florida's salubrious climate and the latent opportunities the state provided for diversified development. Plant the tourist soon became Plant the builder, as he turned his rare talents to the transformation of his adopted state.

He was born in Branford, Connecticut, on October 27, 1819, the son of a farmer. His father died when he was six, and his mother took him to live in New Haven, Connecticut.

Here he attended a private school, and his grandmother, who wanted him to become a clergyman, offered him an education at Yale. Impatient to strike out on his own, however, he took a job as captain's boy and deck hand on a steamboat that plied between New York and New Haven. Among other duties he handled express parcels, a business then in its infancy. He organized an express company which was later absorbed by the Adams Express Company, and when the business was transferred from steamboats to railroads, he was retained and put in charge of the New York office.

In 1854, one year after his wife's health had been restored, he became general superintendent of his company for the territory south of the Potomac and Ohio Rivers. In an area in which transportation facilities were inadequate, he overcame many difficulties in the expansion of his company's business.

When the Civil War threatened in 1861, the company feared the confiscation of its southern properties and organized the Southern Express Company, a Georgia corporation, composed of southern stockholders, with Plant as president. The company served as agent for the Confederacy in collecting tariffs and transferring money. Following a serious illness in 1863, Plant went to Europe for a forced vacation, returning home by way of Canada.

At the close of the Civil War, most of the railroads of the South were physically and financially crippled, and following the depression of 1873 many were in bankruptcy. With confidence in the eventual recovery of the South, Plant became keenly interested in its need for transportation. He bought the Atlantic & Gulf and the Charleston & Savannah Railroads at foreclosure sales. With these as a nucleus, he began building a system along the Atlantic seaboard which, twenty years later, included fourteen railway companies with 2,100 miles of track, several steamship lines, and a number of hotels.

With the coöperation of others, among whom was Henry M. Flagler, he organized the Plant Investment Company in 1882, a holding company for the joint management of the various properties under his control. So that Florida orange growers might have better shipping facilities to reach northern markets, he reconstructed and lengthened several smaller railroad properties within the state.

In 1882 Plant acquired the South Florida Railroad, a line extending from Sanford to Kissimmee, and by 1884 had extended it to Tampa. He made Tampa, a village of six hundred population, the home port for a new line of steamships that sailed to Havana, and he erected a two and a half million dollar hotel for the accommodation of tourists.

Railroad extensions from Plant's branch lines, within five years, opened up what became one of the world's most productive citrus and phosphate regions. The Pinellas Peninsula was incorporated into his transportation network, and St. Petersburg, an unimportant village in 1890, soon bloosomed into a resort city of national importance.

In the areas that his railroads opened up and served, homeseekers followed; tourists became residents. Citrus groves, truck farms, mines, cigar factories, sponge plants, and other industries multiplied. Resort building and agricultural and industrial development produced a diversified prosperity.

Following Plant's death on June 23, 1899, his railroad properties were consolidated to form the Atlantic Coast Line and were extended to Fort Myers.

Equipped with a strong physical constitution and a man of temperate habits, Henry B. Plant was in harness until he was almost eighty. As a resourceful, tireless servant in the cause of state building, he made a permanent contribution to the prosperity and happiness of the Sunshine State. The foundation of his great wealth made it possible for his son to make many substantial gifts to hospitals and other institutions.

The rapid growth of Florida in population and wealth and the expansion of trade in states tributary to his system made Henry B. Plant a factor of power and influence. A man of rare vision, he had the capacity to project his dreams into actualities. He pioneered in the transformation of Florida from a romantic wilderness into a playground and workshop. He is a part of that select company of the dreamers and builders of the Republic.

H.C.

H.C.

Henry M. Flagler

BORN AT Hopewell, New York, of German descent on January 2, 1830, the colorful career of Henry Morrison Flagler unfolds like a magic carpet. The son of a Presbyterian preacher, cradled in poverty, he overcame want and woe to achieve fame and fortune.

With the blessings and prayers of righteous parents, young Flagler left the district school at fourteen to strike out for himself. Empty handed, journeying by boat or afoot, he finally made his way to Republic, Ohio, where he took a job in a country store at five dollars a month with board. Employed later in a store at Fostoria, he saved enough by the time he reached twenty, to set himself up as a grain commission merchant at Bellevue. When he had amassed a small fortune of fifty thousand dollars he moved to Saginaw, Michigan, to manufacture salt. Losing his entire capital in the venture and embarrassed by heavy obligations, he returned to Ohio to reënter the grain business at Cleveland.

Here he cultivated the acquaintance of John D. Rockefeller, bookkeeper for a commission merchant, through whom Flagler had often marketed grain. Rockefeller was pioneering in oil, and the partnership of Rockefeller, Andrews & Flagler was formed in 1867, their refinery to become in 1870 the Standard Oil Company.

Next to Rockefeller, Flagler was the strongest man in the organization. Rockefeller said of him: "For years and years this early partner and I worked shoulder to shoulder; our desks were in the same room. We both lived on Euclid Avenue a few rods apart. We met and walked to the office together, walked home to luncheon, back again after luncheon, and home again at night. On these walks, when we were away from the office interruptions, we did our thinking, talking and planning together."

Throughout the hectic history of Standard Oil, Henry M. Flagler was active in its management, and he retained his official connection with the company until near the end of his life, resigning as vice-president in 1908 and as director in 1911.

Flagler visited Florida in 1883 and was impressed by its latent wealth and its limited transportation and hotel facilities. The total railroad mileage in Florida in 1880 was only 518 miles. In 1886 Flagler purchased the Jacksonville, St. Augustine and Halifax River Railroad, along with several shorter lines and consolidated them, with many improvements, into the Florida East Coast Railway. In 1892 construction was started south from Daytona. Palm Beach was reached in 1894 and Miami, then but a clearing in the jungle, in 1896.

Flagler extended the system to Key West in 1912; fifty miles of track were constructed through the Everglades, and 106 miles veritably spanned the sea. As causeways, viaducts, and drawbridges were built from key to key, the distance from Miami to Cuba was shortened, with steamers and ferries delivering passengers and loaded freight cars from Key West to Havana. Partially destroyed by the September storm of 1934, this structure of stone and steel was converted into a scenic highway.

Flagler dredged the harbor at Miami, establishing steamship lines that plied between Miami and Key West and Nassau.

Already having erected a chain of palatial hotels in St. Augustine, Ormond, Palm Beach, and Miami, he built two in Nassau. His investments in Florida exceeded forty million dollars.

While Flagler converted sand-swept beach and wasteland into playgrounds and gardens, he gave encouragement to the development of citrus fruit orchards and truck farms. While cities and health resorts sprang into existence at his magic touch, Florida produced a striking transformation in the personality of this captain of industry.

In his economic struggle from poverty to riches, self-discipline had developed within him a cold indifference to the needs of others. He had worked hard and played little. In Standard Oil he had served under a stern commander and was shrewd, practical, and ruthless. The making of money had been his all-consuming purpose.

Florida, however, challenged the better side of his genius, mellowed his spirit, and completely changed his attitude toward society. As promoters colonized the country he became keenly interested in the individual success of homeseekers who followed his leadership in the great migration. His personal concern for the welfare of employees on his railroad was returned with an admiration as loyal as it was sincere.

Flagler built schools, churches, and hospitals, always insisting that his endowments be anonymous. He read extensively in his declining years and while sensitive regarding his deafness enjoyed the fellowship of friends. He died on May 20, 1913 at the age of eighty-three at White Hall, his home at West Palm Beach, leaving the bulk of his great fortune to his third wife.

Clerk, capitalist, builder, and humanitarian, Henry M. Flagler had diverted his great wealth and rare talents to the development of his adopted state. He foresaw as no other man of his time the limitless possibilities in the soil and climate of the "Land of Sunshine and Flowers." He helped make the Fountain of Perpetual Youth of which Ponce de Leon had dreamed and the El Dorado which De Soto had sought, living realities. Out of his faith, wealth, and zeal, he performed an industrial miracle, and gave Floridians an enthusiasm they have never lost.

Richard Coke

In 1860 Texas was primarily rural, with cotton farming its chief commercial occupation. Since most of its settlers had come from the Cotton South, which had embraced the cause of Texas annexation, it was natural for Texans to cast their fortunes with the Confederacy. An ordinance of secession was ratified by popular vote in 1861. Governor Sam Houston, who refused to subscribe to an oath supporting the constitution of the Confederacy, was forced from office and was succeeded by Lieutenant Governor Edward Clark.

Geographically protected from the theatre of conflict, Texas saw few major engagements, but all able-bodied men, from sixteen to sixty, were called to the colors, and the sixty-five thousand sons she contributed to the cause, including "Terry's Texas Rangers," fought on every front. About two thousand Texans enlisted in the Union Army. Texas also supplied quantities of cotton, sugar, molasses, beef, and ammunition to the Confederate armies.

The most famous encounter was the repulse of a federal force of five thousand men attempting a landing at Sabine Pass. Lieutenant Dick Dowling and his forty-seven men captured two federal gunboats and took three hundred fifty prisoners without losing a man. Galveston was captured by federal forces on October 9, 1862 and recaptured by the Confederates on January 1, 1863. The last battle of the Civil War, a Confederate victory, took place at Palmito Ranch, near Brownsville, on May 12, 1865, and was fought after General Lee had surrendered.

Reconstruction began favorably for Texas. With her great potentials of land, timber, cotton, and cattle, her people were returning to peace and prosperity when the Congressional Reconstruction Act of 1867 brought an end to the "loyal" white man's government and the carpetbaggers, scalawags, and military importations took over.

As with every other Southern state, the aftermath of Reconstruction in Texas was turmoil, bankruptcy, and despotism. The conservative citizens were triumphant in 1874, and the political plague ended when Governor Richard Coke took possession of the office of governor.

Richard Coke was born in Williamsburg, Virginia, on March 13, 1829. He received his early education in the common schools, entered William and Mary College in 1845, and was graduated with honors. He read law, was admitted to the bar, and came to Texas in 1850, carrying his library on horseback. He hung out his shingle in Waco, a town less than a year old, and before he was thirty was recognized as one of the leading lawyers of the state.

In 1852 Coke married Mary Elizabeth Horne of Waco. In 1858 he was appointed by Governor Harden R. Runnels a member of a commission to induce the Indians, who were harassing settlers on the frontier, to remove to the Indian Territory. In the crisis of 1860, he was a member of the secession convention. In 1862 he raised an infantry company which became a part of the 15th Texas Regiment, and as captain served throughout the war in Arkansas, Louisiana, and Texas.

When Coke returned to Waco to resume the practice of law in 1865, he was appointed district judge and later one of the associate justices of the Texas State Supreme Court. He served for one year when he was included in the forced removal of state officials by General Philip H. Sheridan, under the Reconstruction Act.

As the Democratic nominee for governor in 1873, he was elected over E. J. Davis, the Republican, by a vote of two to one. The Republican state supreme court declared the election void, and when the newly elected legislature assembled, Governor Davis stationed Negro militia in the statehouse and appealed to President U. S. Grant to interfere. When Grant refused, Coke was inaugurated on January 15, 1874.

Governor Coke brought order out of chaos. He curtailed the expenses of government, reduced taxes, and made a new start on the public school system. A new state constitution was drafted and adopted. Coke was reëlected for another term but soon after inauguration was elected United States senator.

As senator, he sought federal protection for the frontiers and funds to deepen the state's harbors. He opposed federal aid to schools and fought the protective tariff. He seconded the efforts of Senator John H. Reagan to bring interstate railways under federal control and worked for the passage of the Interstate Commerce Act in 1887. He supported the free coinage of silver and sought the repeal of the iniquitous Force Acts directed against the South.

After serving for three terms in the Senate, Coke declined to stand for reëlection and retired to his home in Waco in 1894, near which he had an extensive plantation and where his useful career ended with his death in May, 1897.

A worthy member of the bar of his state, a qualified judge, constructive governor and senator, he was a man of spotless integrity, endowed with uncommon common sense and faithful to every public trust reposed in him. In the era of recovery that followed the political blight of Reconstruction, he was peacemaker and protector. His private life and political record have weathered the years to receive the praise of those dedicated to the cause of good government.

H.C.

Jesse Chisholm

THE SPANIARDS who sought gold in the Southwest left a legacy in horses and cattle. "Escapees" from their expeditions multiplied by the millions on the grassy plains to enrich Texas with its longhorns and wild mustangs, each essential to the other.

During the Civil War four million head of cattle were driven to the Mississippi River to supply the Confederate Army. And after the war, over a period of twenty years, ten to twelve million cattle were driven out of Texas to northern markets over the Jesse Chisholm Trail, the Goodnight-Loving Trail, or Dodge City Trail.

Jesse Chisholm, pathfinder and peacemaker, was of Scotch-Cherokee descent and was born in Tennessee about 1806. At fifteen he moved with his parents and other Cherokees to Arkansas.

At twenty-three, he joined a party of adventurers to the Kansas country in search of gold. The following year he served as guide and interpreter in the Leavenworth-Dodge expedition along the Red River to make peace treaties with the Plains tribes. He helped open a road from Fort Smith to Fort Towson in the same country when the Choctaws were moved from Mississippi. For forty years his name appears in frontier history as trader, interpreter or trail-blazer.

He was not only familiar with the universal sign language of the Indians but had mastered fourteen tribal dialects as well, and his services were indispensable to explorer and surveyor. At a council in 1853 he served as general interpreter for eight participating tribes. He was so familiar with the customs, habits, and speech of the Comanche Indians that through his coöperation the first written words of the Comanche language were compiled.

Primarily, however, Jesse Chisholm was a trader. He established several posts in the Indian Territory and in 1858 located six miles west of what is now Oklahoma City. But in his trading ventures he usually chose the trail. He preferred to load his wagons and packhorses with coffee, tobacco, sugar, clothing, and tools and barter with the Indians for skins and furs in their villages and tepees. He moved among the fiercest tribes in complete security, even when they were at war with the whites. He was trusted and respected by red men and white men alike, for they shared implicit confidence in his integrity.

In 1861 Captain Albert Pike of Arkansas, Confederate commissioner, pressed Chisholm into service in negotiating treaties with the western tribes. The task not one to his taste, he joined the fugitive Creeks in Kansas. In 1862 he moved among the Wichitas who in seeking asylum had also fled the Territory, and among them he erected a post on the banks of a creek in Kansas which still bears his name.

The Civil War had demoralized business and disturbed the tribes. With the encouragement of the Indians, Chisholm turned south in 1865 on another trading trip into the Territory. Joined by J. R. Mead, a fellow trader and one of the founders of Wichita, Kansas, he followed a route known later as the Chisholm Trail. It originated near San Antonio, Texas, and ran north through Oklahoma to Abilene, Kansas.

Over this trail, at the close of the war, thousands of cattle moved from Texas to northern markets. Stagecoaches, couriers and the march of soldiers followed. And, finally, railroads and highways paralleled his track through the wilderness, along which cities sprang to spread and prosper.

Along with Black Beaver, the Delaware chief, he had been instrumental in persuading the Comanche and Kiowa chiefs to attend peace councils at Wichita in 1865 and at Medicine Lodge in 1867. His influence with the tribes was such that when he died they scattered "like so many frightened quail."

A man of piety and good judgment, to the Indians he became a patriarch and friend. While he usually prospered in his precarious pursuits, his charities and the uncertainties of the frontier often kept him impoverished. But his credit was high with the supply merchants, and he was never without the good will of his many customers. He ransomed no less than nine children held in bondage by the Indians and adopted them. He married twice and had six children, but his favorite was Vincente, a captive Mexican whom he ransomed from the Comanches with two hundred dollars' worth of merchandise.

Jesse Chisholm was for a time engaged in the manufacture of salt in Blaine County, Oklahoma, where he established a trading business in 1866. It was at this post that he became ill with cholera morbus from eating bear grease poisoned by being melted in a brass kettle, and he died on March 4, 1868. The mortal remains of this restless man were buried on the banks of the North Canadian River at Little Mound near the trail he had often trod. There a few miles east of Greenfield, Oklahoma, school children have erected a modest marker for his rustic shrine.

Nothing more completely reveals the genuine character of this traveler-trader than his creed, which he faithfully kept: "No man ever came to my camp hungry, and went away unfed, or naked and departed unclad. All my life I have tried to live at peace with my fellowman and be a brother to him. The rest, I leave with the Great Spirit, who placed me here and whom I trust to do all things well."

D. SHOURDS

Charles Goodnight

At the time of the Civil War there were two animal kingdoms in Texas: the Spanish longhorns grazed the Nueces and Rio Grande Valleys and the buffalo roamed the northern plains.

Introduced by the Spanish, the wild longhorns multiplied but were of little value before the Civil War. Texas ranchmen claimed three million head but were without a market. Cattle were slaughtered for their hides and tallow. When the Union Stockyards were built in Chicago in 1865, however, they began moving north to rail connections.

Texas cotton farmers learned to ride wild horses and herd wild cattle, and the picturesque cowboy appeared on the American scene. With his ten-gallon hat, high-heeled boots, wiry little mustang, and graphic vernacular peculiar to the range and trail, this lanky, hard-bitten individualist became a national institution. On the heels of the vanishing buffalo, cowmen with their lariats, sombreroes, bandanas, and chuck wagons drove Texas steers to market.

The open range was doomed in 1871 when a young hardware salesman introduced barbed wire into Texas. Sheepherders and farmers, called "nesters," began to fence in the open ranges, and ranches, pastures, and improved breeds were introduced to create a cattle economy.

Richard King, a steamboat captain, founded the King Ranch in 1853 at Kingsville, and the ranch experimented with breeds to originate the famous Santa Gertrudis. The first major ranch in west Texas was established in the Panhandle by Charles Goodnight in 1876.

Cattleman extraordinary, Charles Goodnight, born in Kentucky on March 3, 1836, came of a long line of pioneers. His great-grandfather, Michael Goodnight, had emigrated from Germany to Rockbridge County, Virginia. While Charles was still a child his father died. His mother remarried, and the family moved to Texas in 1846, settling upon the Milam County frontier. At nine Charles rode a young white-faced colt bareback all the way from Illinois to Texas. Saddles were made for men, and he learned at a tender age the sting of horse sweat in a galled crotch.

The lad was hunting beyond the frontier at thirteen, was in the cattle business at twenty, and moved to Palo Pinto County in northwest Texas. At twenty-four he was guiding Texas rangers; at thirty he blazed trails two thousand miles in length; at forty he established a range three hundred miles beyond any other settlement; at forty-five he dominated twenty million acres of range country. At ninety he was an international authority in the cattle industry and dreaming of greener pastures.

With the outbreak of the Civil War, Goodnight mustered in with the Frontier Regiment of Texas Rangers, participating in many encounters. After the war ended, he located on the Pecos River, established Texas cattle ranches in southern New Mexico and Colorado and a permanent range in Arkansas. He blazed trails to Kansas, Colorado, and Wyoming.

In 1876, the panic caught the ranches overstocked, and Goodnight crossed three hundred miles of wilderness with a herd of sixteen hundred cattle to settle in the Palo Duro Canyon in the Texas Panhandle. Here he formed a partnership with John George Adair, of Rothdair, Ireland, and began the development of the great JA Ranch which soon embraced nearly a million acres of land grazing one hundred thousand head of cattle.

Goodnight crossed Shorthorn and Hereford stock with his longhorns to develop one of America's finest beef herds. He roped buffalo calves from which he raised a herd, crossed the buffalo with the Polled Angus cattle to produce the cattalo, a new breed. He crossbred the wild turkey and raised hybrid hogs.

He fought outlaws for forty years, cultivated the Comanches under Quanah Parker, and made friends with the Kiawas, Pueblos, and Taos. He initiated the first Panhandle stockmen's association, introduced purebred cattle, supported the first frontier schools, and later at the town of Goodnight in West Texas founded Goodnight College which in 1917 became a public high school.

In 1871 he had married Mary Ann Dyer, and after her death in 1926 he married on March 5, 1927, at the age of ninety-one, Corinne Goodnight of Butte, Montana. A son by this marriage did not survive. He died at the age of ninety-three, universally recognized as the most colorful cowman of the West.

Colonel Goodnight was massive of frame; his tremendous head, set forward on his broad shoulders, was crowned with a great shock of hair, and he wore a patriarchal beard. His penetrating eyes pierced through the shadows of shaggy brows, and his legs were bowed from having spent years in the saddle. He was profanely eloquent. It is doubtful if any other Texan so thoroughly mastered the techniques of open country scouting or had a deeper understanding of cowhands and cattle.

Old Blue, his favorite lead-steer that led many a herd over his trails to market, he refused to sell. In the museum at West Texas State College at Canyon, the widespread horns of Old Blue are on exhibit. And Old Charlie, a huge bull buffalo, long the mascot of the college and once a member of Goodnight's herd, stands mounted within the college entrance. Not far from this historic setting, Goodnight brought his first wagon train from the plains in 1876, and nearby at Palo Duco Canyon he founded the old JA Ranch.

As Old Blue led his herds, Colonel Goodnight was for forty years an active and enlightened leader in the Panhandle. Vigorous and aggressive and forthright until the last day of his life, he died holding truth to be above all orthodox creeds, hating hypocrisy, and despising liars and cow thieves.

Henry Woodfin Grady

As FACILE with pen as he was fluent of speech, Henry W. Grady, editor and orator, was the most prophetic and eloquent spokesman of the South in his time.

He was born in Athens, Georgia, on May 24, 1850, the first of three children of William S. and Anne Elizabeth (Gartrell) Grady. His father, a man of large estate, organized and equipped a company for the Confederacy and went off to Virginia where he was promoted to colonel and killed in action at Petersburg while leading his men. Grady reached young manhood during Reconstruction, when the South was ringed with federal soldiers and at the mercy of the carpetbaggers, scalawags, and ex-slaves.

Grady had every educational opportunity. He attended Athens' schools, was graduated from the University of Georgia, and after a course of law at the University of Virginia returned home, married Julia King in 1871, and edited the *Courier* at Rome. Forbidden by his employer to denounce corruption in local politics, he bought the town's two other papers and as publisher of the *Daily-Commercial* crusaded until it collapsed. With two other men, Grady founded the Atlanta *Herald* in which he lost what was left of his patrimony. In 1879 Cyrus W. Field lent him twenty thousand dollars to buy a one-fourth interest in the Atlanta *Constitution*.

The born journalist was soon in his full stride as he shattered the postwar despair that gripped most of the South. His pungent philippics on politics, the diversification of crops, the development of industries, and a solution of the Negro question were widely read and quoted. Through his daily columns and farm weekly, Grady reached the hearts and hearthstones of a receptive audience.

Invited to address the New England Club in New York, Grady spoke with all his frankness, feeling, and magnanimity. The twenty-minute speech electrified the nation and did more to reunite the country than all the orations and editorial effusions that had occupied the attention of the public since the war. Never did a message come at a more opportune time. The people of the South, defeated and dejected, emerging from their long, agonizing ordeal, were still under suspicion and the pressures of the prejudiced. Grady depicted the footsore, Confederate soldier, ragged, half-starved and heavy hearted, enfeebled by want, woe and wounds, returning from Appomattox, to find his house in ruins, his farm devastated, his stock killed, his slaves free, his money worthless, and his credit destroyed. He then reviewed what his hero in gray had accomplished as he rose from sackcloth and ashes, proud and triumphant. He payed tribute to Abraham Lincoln and pleaded for mutual sympathy and patience in the creation of an indissoluble union of American states and for the imperishable brotherhood of a reunited country.

The press of the nation throbbed, and Grady was famous overnight. He addressed multitudes to become the South's acknowledged leader. He spoke on "The South and Her Problems" in Dallas; "The Solid South" at Augusta; "Against Centralization" at the University of Virginia, and on "The Race Problem in the South" at Boston. He believed that the color problem could not be solved by law or resolved by fiat or force, and appealed for patience. Grady became the somnolent South's insistent arouser, directing the imagination and genius of her sons to capitalize more fully upon her natural resources and native talent that they might make the most of their unparalleled opportunities.

He portrayed their plight with homespun wit and wisdom. He described a burial in Pickens County, Georgia, saying the grave was dug through solid marble, but the marble headstone was from Vermont. The burial was in a pine thicket, but the coffin came from Cincinnati. An iron mountain overlooked the scene, but the coffin nails and screws came from Pittsburgh. Hard woods and metals abounded, but the corpse was hauled in a wagon which was made in South Bend. The country so rich in undeveloped resources furnished nothing for the funeral but the poor man's body and the grave in which it awaited judgment. And the corpse was lowered to rest on coffin bands from Lowell and carried nothing into the next world as a reminder of his home in this save the halted blood in his veins, the chilled marrow in his bones, and the thud of the dull clods that fell on the lid of his casket.

He was without an equal among younger men of the South. A master of humor and pathos, he was the practical dreamer, with his head in the stars and his feet on the ground. Short in stature, solidly built, he was endowed with a rich, melodious voice and a magnetic personality. He thawed out the coldest unbelievers and cracked the crust of the most chronic skeptics. Millions hung upon his words as he wrapped the mountains, valleys, forests, and farms with his scintillating genius and exposed their hidden wealth. Deeply religious and strong of faith, he used neither tobacco nor alcohol and served as the young man's model.

Henry W. Grady was stricken with pneumonia on his way home from his Boston speech and died upon his return on December 23, 1889, when he was only thirty-nine. Millions mourned his untimely passing. A living meteor had come out of the darkness for a brief span to light up the hearts and hopes of mankind.

William Crawford Gorgas

IN THE extermination of the yellow fever mosquito in Panama, Dr. William Crawford Gorgas made possible the Panama Canal.

Sanitarian and surgeon general of the United States Army, he was the son of Josiah Gorgas and Amelia (Gayle) Gorgas and was born at Toulminville, near Mobile, on October 3, 1854. His father was a war veteran of the Mexican War, an officer in the United States Army, and later chief of ordnance for the Confederacy. His mother was the daughter of Judge John Gayle, a former congressman and governor of Alabama. At the collapse of the Confederacy his father for four years managed a blast furnace, then became vice-chancellor of the University of the South at Sewanee, Tennessee, and for a time president of the University of Alabama.

During the Civil War the Gorgas family lived at Richmond where young William saw ragged Confederate soldiers marching through its streets with bare feet, and witnessed the entrance of Union troops as his father evacuated the city in the company of President Jefferson Davis. For some time after that William refused to wear shoes, and the lad of eleven summers aspired to become a soldier.

With frequent changes of residence and the confusion of war times, William's early education was irregular. He graduated from the University of the South in 1875, but his heart was set upon a military career. Unable to obtain an appointment to West Point, he decided to get into the army by way of a medical degree.

Gorgas entered Bellevue Hospital Medical College in New York and after three years of financial distress was graduated in 1879. Following an internship, he was appointed to the medical corps of the United States Army. In 1883 he married Marie Cook Doughty of Cincinnati, Ohio. In the line of duty for twenty years, Gorgas occupied posts in Texas, North Dakota, and Florida. For ten years preceding the Spanish-American War he was located at Fort Barrancas, Pensacola Bay. Stricken with yellow fever at Fort Brown, Texas, he became immune to the disease and was thereafter frequently drafted for service where the fever was prevalent to conduct experiments on this puzzling malady.

When American troops occupied Havana in 1898, Gorgas was placed in charge of a yellow fever camp at Siboney. He was later appointed chief of sanitation and cleaned up the city. In spite of these precautions the scourge spread. When the board of which Walter Reed was head gave proof that the stegomyia mosquito (specifically, the *Aëdes Aegypti*) was a carrier of yellow fever, Gorgas applied more effective prevention measures. Gorgas destroyed the breeding places around homes of this highly domesticated insect, isolated the sick, and screened their houses. He rid a pestilential city of fever and won an international reputation.

When the Panama Canal was projected, Gorgas was moved to Washington where he applied himself to a study of yellow and malarial fevers in relation to the canal problem. The failure of the French to complete the project had at last been traced to mosquito infestations. He visited the Suez Canal and Panama and in 1904 commenced his work in the Canal Zone. Though superiors at first opposed his efforts, a serious epidemic prompted official coöperation, and Gorgas rid the Canal Zone of yellow fever. President Theodore Roosevelt appointed him a member of the commission charged with construction of the Canal. The cities of Panama and Colón became models of cleanliness, and Gorgas was recognized as the world's foremost sanitation expert.

In 1903 Gorgas was called into service by the Transvaal Chamber of Mines to visit South Africa to make recommendations for the control of pneumonia among Negro workers in the Rand mines. While engaged in this work, he was notified of his appointment as surgeon general of the army, and upon his return to the United States was made a major general. The International Health Board enlisted him as an adviser and in 1916 sent him with a staff of assistants on a tour of inspection into South and Central America. In World War I he was head of the army's medical service until after the Armistice.

The International Health Board commissioned him to investigate the presence of yellow fever on the west coast of Africa in 1920. After attending the International Hygiene Congress in Brussels, he returned to London where he had a stroke and died on July 3, 1920. His funeral was held in St. Paul's Cathedral, and the body was returned to the United States to rest in Arlington Cemetery.

During his last illness, General Gorgas was visited by King George who knighted him. He had been decorated by a number of foreign governments; scientific societies and associations welcomed him into their fellowship, and colleges and universities awarded him honorary degrees

Trim and athletic, he retained through life a compact physique and alert mind. In his mellowing years a shock of gray hair and white mustache enhanced his patriarchal appearance. Persistent in purpose, he was gentle of temperament, amiable, optimistic, and unassuming. Although he was showered with praise, his modesty was matched only by his professional skill.

Gorgas made possible the construction of the Panama Canal. More than any other man of his time he was instrumental in making the South and the tropics more livable by conquering malaria and yellow fever.

Walter Hines Page

ON JUNE 28, 1914, Gavrillo Prinzip, a Bosnian Serb terrorist, assassinated Archduke Francis Ferdinand, heir to the Austrian throne, and his Duchess of Hohenberg, at Sarajevo, now in Yugoslavia, and set up a chain reaction that precipitated World War I.

Woodrow Wilson, the scholar-statesman, was president at the time, and his diplomatic representatives at European capitals were Thomas Nelson Page, man of letters, ambassador in Rome; Dr. Henry van Dyke, poet, at the Hague; Brand Whitlock, novelist, at Brussels; and Walter Hines Page, journalist, in London.

Walter Hines Page was born at Cary, North Carolina, on August 15, 1855. His father, Allison Page, although the owner of a few slaves, disapproved of the institution of slavery and was a strong Unionist; he undoubtedly influenced the views of his son. From his mother, Catherine Frances Raboteau, Walter inherited an appreciation of good books.

Walter attended local schools, the Bingham Academy at Mebane, and entered Trinity College (now Duke University) in 1871. Two years later he transferred to Randolph-Macon College, Ashland, Virginia. There he fell under the influence of Thomas Randolph Price, a Greek and English scholar, who instilled in him a devotion to English literature and an enthusiasm for England.

Page entered Johns Hopkins University under a fellowship when it opened in 1876 but abandoned Greek scholarship for a career in journalism. He joined the St. Joseph *Gazette* in Missouri as a cub reporter in 1880 and in five months was editor. After an extensive tour of the South, he prepared a series of penetrating articles on his observations for newspaper syndication; they were well received. He joined the New York *World* with a roving assignment and later served as its literary critic and editorial writer.

In 1883, Page launched a crusade for the reconstitution of the South, having acquired control of the Raleigh *State Chronicle.* He advocated improved educational facilities for whites and Negroes, promoted scientific farming, the development of new industries, greater opportunities for the common man, and better roads, and discouraged Confederate hero worship. His paper, however, was a financial failure, and he was obliged to abandon it in 1885 and return to New York.

It was not until he joined the business staff of the *Forum,* in 1887 that Page's talents came to full fruition. He soon acquired the direction of the publication and converted what was a moribund monthly into a lively review. His success led to an invitation to become associate editor of the *Atlantic Monthly,* and three years later he was its editor in chief. Page's next venture in journalism was as a partner in the new publishing house of Doubleday, Page & Company, and the following year he founded *The World's Work,* of which he became editor in 1913. The periodical encouraged educational, agricultural, industrial, and sanitary improvements in the South.

A Jeffersonian Democrat, Page became an early advocate of the candidacy of his old friend, Woodrow Wilson, for the presidency of the United States. With two others he raised three thousand dollars to employ a publicity agent to arrange a speaking tour for Wilson, and he was instrumental in Wilson's nomination and election. When Wilson offered him the ambassadorship to Great Britain in 1913, he readily accepted for he believed it would give him the opportunity to promote Anglo-American ascendancy in world affairs. His engaging personality, culture, and sympathy for England speedily won for him a warm welcome in London. He worked harmoniously with the President in eliminating causes of friction between the two nations in connection with the Panama toll question. And so highly did Wilson value Page's services that when the ambassador suggested resigning for financial reasons, the President prevailed upon his friend, Cleveland Dodge, to add twenty-five thousand dollars a year to what the government provided for the embassy.

After war broke out Page and Wilson gradually drifted apart. Page had little patience with the President's desire for strict neutrality. He construed the war as a brutal assault on democractic civilization by Prussian militarism and thought the United States should at least have given the Allies limited support. When Germany sank the "Lusitania," he believed that we should have severed diplomatic relations and prepared for war. An inexperienced diplomat, and pro-British to begin with, Page easily fell under the influence of his great friend, Lord Edward Grey, British Foreign Secretary, and Wilson suspected when Page expressed an opinion that it was also Grey's.

When the United States finally entered the war, Page rejoiced, interpreting it as a vindication of his own position. He urged active participation and hoped that world leadership for the English-speaking nations would come with peace. The strain of increased work, along with an attack of nephritis undermined his health, and he was forced to resign. He returned to the United States, and died at Pinehurst, North Carolina, on December 21, 1918, a war casualty, survived by his widow, Willia Alice (Wilson) Page, whom he had married in 1880.

In addition to Walter Hines Page's voluminous correspondence, rich in literary quality and good humor, he was the author of three books, *The Rebuilding of Old Commonwealths, A Publisher's Confession,* and *The Southerner.*

Woodrow Wilson

THE EIGHTH native Virginian to become president of the United States, Thomas Woodrow Wilson, was born at Staunton on December 28, 1856. His father, Joseph R. Wilson, was a Scotch Presbyterian minister, and his mother, Janet Woodrow, born in Carlisle, England, was the daughter of a Scotch minister.

Wilson spent his youth in Augusta, Georgia, Columbia, South Carolina, and Wilmington, North Carolina. He attended Davidson College, was graduated from Princeton University in 1879, and studied law at the University of Virginia, receiving his degree in 1881. He practiced law at Atlanta, then entered Johns Hopkins for postgraduate work in political science. He was associate professor of history and political economics at Bryn Mawr College, also served as a lecturer at Johns Hopkins, and as professor of political economics at Wesleyan University.

At Wesleyan, Wilson completed his book *The State,* an analysis of various forms of governments, which established his reputation as a scholar and political philosopher. In 1890 he was called to Princeton as professor of jurisprudence and political economy, and two years later was elected president of the university.

Wilson's innovations, especially his preceptorial system and the quad plan, were resisted by faculty and alumni; the first would provide opportunity for individual instruction, the latter coördinate the intellectual life of the college. He believed the mind should be developed by using it rather than stuffing it. His ideal university would give the scholar the prestige he deserved and reduce social and athletic activities to a secondary place. His revolutionary efforts singled him out as a champion of the underdog, and New Jersey politicians began to wonder if this fighting doctor of philosophy would not make a good vote getter. So the professor was nominated for governor on the Democratic ticket, was elected, and served from 1911 to 1913. During his term the state passed a primary election law, a corrupt practices act, and employers' liability legislation.

Because of Wilson's reform record, as president of Princeton and governor of New Jersey, he was nominated for president by the Democratic party in 1912. With the Republicans divided between the factions led by Taft and Roosevelt, the eloquent scholar was elected. Inaugurated in 1913, the first two years of his administration were marked by passage of the Federal Reserve Act, the Underwood-Simmons Tariff, and the Clayton Anti-Trust Act, and the Federal Trade Commission was created.

President Wilson withdrew from the Chinese financial consortium and deprecated economic imperialism and territorial aggrandizement. He sought to make amends to Colombia on the Panama Canal question, and adopted a policy of "watchful waiting" in the controversy with Mexico. With the shock of World War I in 1914, he urged his fellow citizens to be "impartial in thought as well as in action." Despite many aggravations, he strove to maintain American neutrality and national peace in explosive times. "There is such a thing," he said, "as a man being too proud to fight." He was reëlected for a second term mainly on the slogan, "He kept us out of war."

Wilson endeavored to protect American lives and property in revolutionary Mexico and fought for America's traditional rights on the high seas. His sharp warnings to Germany led to the resignation of his Secretary of State, William Jennings Bryan, who was a pacifist. The President protested British interference with our shipping, and when the Germans started unrestricted submarine warfare, he broke diplomatic relations with Germany. After four American ships had been sunk with many lives lost, he appeared before Congress to ask for a declaration that a state of war with Germany existed, which was voted on April 6, 1917. The nation's overseas force ultimately numbered two million men.

Wilson's war strategy was to crush German autocracy that the world might be "safe for democracy." In the declaration of his famous "Fourteen Points" essential to peace, he became a spokesman for the Allies. Immediately after the Armistice on November 11, 1918, he sailed for France to attend the Paris Peace Conference. In a triumphant tour of Europe, he was hailed as the prophet of hope and the apostle of peace. With the signing of the Treaty of Versailles, June 28, 1919, the first World War came to an official end.

The Treaty, which included the League of Nations, was yet to be approved by the United States Senate, where it met with bitter opposition and was not ratified. In making a national speaking tour to win public favor for a referendum in support of the League Wilson suffered a stroke at Pueblo, Colorado, and returned to Washington paralyzed, a victim of his lost cause. His retirement from the public scene was overshadowed by a lingering illness and the cold resistance of the American public to his international aims and ideals. After he was stricken he made only one public appearance, at the inauguration of his successor, President Harding. Broken in body, depressed in spirit, he died on February 3, 1924.

Wilson was twice married, first to Ellen Louise Axson on June 24, 1885, and after her death to Mrs. Edith Bolling Galt. Each came into his life when she was most needed, one to inspire him in his youth, the other to comfort him in his many sorrows.

During his Presidency the Panama Canal was opened, the federal income tax constitutional amendment was ratified, the country went dry with prohibition, and women's suffrage became a fact. Though the crusading scholar did not realize his dream of world peace, wherever men have the vision to pursue that high purpose, he will be remembered as the preëminent prophet of a better world.

Booker Taliaferro Washington

HENRY WATTERSON, former editor of the Louisville, Kentucky, *Courier-Journal,* said of Booker T. Washington: "No man, since the war of the sections, has exercised such beneficent influence and done such real good for the country—especially to the South."

Born a slave on James Burrough's plantation at Hale's Ford, Franklin County, Virginia, on April 5, 1856, he was the son of Jane Ferguson, a cook. His father is believed to have been a white man from a neighboring plantation. In his book, *Up From Slavery,* Washington describes the one-room cabin with dirt floor and open fireplace where his mother and her three children lived.

Soon after the emancipation his stepfather, Washington Ferguson, removed the family to Malden, near Charleston, West Virginia. His mother secured a copy of Webster's *Blueback Spelling Book,* and Booker mastered the alphabet. He divided his time between work at a salt furnace and his studies until at seventeen he entered Hampton Institute, Virginia. Though his tuition was paid by a friend of the principal, he earned his other expenses as school janitor. He learned the trade of brick-mason, graduated in 1875, went as a waiter to a summer hotel in Connecticut, then returned to Malden to teach in a school for Negro children.

Afterward he gave the postgraduate address at Hampton and, speaking on "The Force that Wins," created such a favorable impression that he was called to take charge of the night school and Indian dormitory there while serving as secretary to the principal.

In 1881 the legislature of Alabama appropriated two thousand dollars to start a normal school for the education of Negro teachers. George C. Campbell, a banker, merchant, and former slaveholder and Lewis Adams, a mechanic and ex-slave, both of Tuskegee, wrote to Hampton Institute for a teacher and Washington was recommended.

The school opened with forty pupils in a dilapidated shanty near a Negro Methodist Church. Washington was principal and professor of mental and moral science. Under his untiring efforts for thirty-four years, Tuskegee Normal and Industrial Institute soon took a place of prominence in the field of Negro education.

He taught his students the dignity of labor and to "live on the farm off the farm." From 1884, when he addressed the National Educational Association, he was in much demand as a public speaker. His addresses were striking for their sincerity, simplicity, and good humor. His English was that of the Bible, and he spoke with conviction. Whether before members of a Southern legislature, a Negro teacher's convention, or the Harvard Alumni Association, he emphasized an education fitted for life, the need of keeping close to nature, and cultivating the respect of one's neighbors.

His epochal speech at the Cotton States and International Exposition at Atlanta, Georgia, on September 18, 1893, brought him national recognition as the leader of his race. He was the most outstanding exponent of interracial coöperation and understanding. His views were opposed at times by the Negro "intellectuals," who felt that he underemphasized political rights. But he was more interested in making the race worthy of the franchise, and in improving its economic lot. His was a utilitarian philosophy . . . the practical school of thought. When he started at Tuskegee, the Alabama Negro was on a sow-belly, corn-pone, collard-greens, cotton economy.

He brought a young Negro scientist, George Washington Carver, to Tuskegee to take charge of the Agricultural department. Carver, an ex-slave, had worked his way through the State College at Ames, Iowa. For forty years Carver carried on his scientific experiments at Tuskegee. In his efforts to improve the lot of the southern farmer, he won fame for his scientific discoveries about the peanut and the sweet potato, "the lifesavers of the south."

The school that Washington had started in a shack was an institution when he died; it had a hundred buildings and 1,537 students and 197 faculty members, all Negroes; and it taught thirty-eight trades and professions. It owned two thousand acres of land locally and had an endowment of two million dollars.

Washington was married three times, first, in 1882, to Fannie N. Smith of Malden, who died in 1884; second, in 1885, to Olivia A. Davidson of Ohio, who died in 1889; third, in 1893, to Margaret James Murray of Mississippi.

In addition to lectures at home and abroad, Washington wrote, among other books, *The Future of the American Negro, Sowing and Reaping, Up From Slavery,* which was translated into eighteen languages, *Working with the Hands, The Negro in Business,* and with R. E. Park *The Man Farthest Down.*

No Negro of his generation enjoyed more universal respect. And with all the honors he received at home and abroad, he never lost his becoming humility. He had a simple solution for his people, expressed in the phrase, "Cast down your buckets where you are." When he died on November 14, 1915, he was buried at Tuskegee. A bronze statue on the campus there shows Washington lifting the scales from the eyelids of the Negro slave. Among quotations from his speeches inscribed at its base is a characteristic saying: "No man, black or white, from North or South, shall drag me down so low as to make me hate him."

James Buchanan Duke

WITH THE Civil War over, Washington Duke returned on foot to his farm near Durham, North Carolina, to find it had been swept clean by the invading army except for two blind mules and a shed of leaf tobacco that had been overlooked by the enemy.

Washington Duke had opposed slavery, had voted for Lincoln, but had served as orderly sergeant for the Confederacy. His two sons, Ben and Buck, age ten and nine, respectively, helped their father pound out the "light tobacco" with hickory sticks in a log barn; it was then put in sacks labeled "Pro Bono Publico." Hitching their blind mules to a wagon, supplied with rations, and with a half dollar in capital, they struck out to peddle their product. From this humble start sprang a multimillion dollar industry.

James Buchanan Duke was born on his father's small farm on December 23, 1856. His mother, Artelia (Roney) Duke died in his infancy. A child during the war, in his teens through Reconstruction, he was early inured to want and woe.

Father and sons, having met with ready sales on their initial venture, purchased more tobacco, built a larger log house for its manufacture, and had so prospered by 1872 that they had sold 125,000 pounds and were as substantial as any local factor in the industry.

Buck for a time attended the academy in Durham and was quick with figures. He then went to a Quaker boarding school, now Guilford College, but was soon back home persuading his father to let him go to Eastman Business College in Poughkeepsie, New York, to learn bookkeeping. This was the extent of his schooling except for a little tutoring by an aunt.

His love was the farm and the factory, and when he was fourteen he was manager of the Negro boys in the sheds; at eighteen he became a partner in the firm of W. Duke & Sons and already knew the business from the ground up. Buck worked twelve to fourteen hours a day and developed early into a rawboned, ruddy, young giant. He had large feet and was pigeon-toed almost to the point of deformity . . . a tobacco-chewing hillbilly, who emerged from the pine woods to become an industrial genius.

In 1881 Buck Duke began making cigarettes. He first imported Russian and Polish Jews to roll them by hand, then later installed Bonsock machines. The public still believed that only sissies and dudes smoked cigarettes—Duke himself despised them—but by pouring out hundreds of thousands of dollars in advertising, sales mounted, and by 1889 Duke was supplying half the country's total production. He bought his tobacco cheap, processed it efficiently, advertised extensively, and undersold his competition.

Soon the five principal cigarette manufacturers were engaged in the celebrated "tobacco war." Finally, in 1890, all were merged into the American Tobacco Company, with twenty-five million dollars in capital and Duke as president. Tobacco became big business. In 1895, the combination began aggressively to absorb companies making all-tobacco cigarettes, cheroots, smoking and chewing tobacco, and snuff. An attempt made to gain control and oust Duke failed. In 1898 a combination of plug manufacturers formed the Continental Tobacco Company, with seventy-five million dollars in capital, and Duke was made president. The American Snuff Company, the American Cigar Company, and the American Stogie Company came into existence, and Duke entered the retail field with the United Cigar Company. His combinations ultimately controlled one hundred fifty factories with a capitalization in excess of half a billion dollars. In 1911 the United States Supreme Court, after five years of litigation, ordered the American Tobacco Company dissolved as a combination in constraint of trade. Only Buck Duke, who had put his empire together, could take it apart, which he did by setting up the separate companies that had formed the original merger into competitive units.

Duke plunged into the development of the water power of Southern Piedmont in 1904 and formed the Southern Power Company, the world's pioneer major hydroelectric system. Within twenty years it supplied power to over three hundred cotton mills, factories, and cities.

In the heyday of Duke's rise from peddler to tobacco and power tycoon, he became infatuated with a pleasure-loving, young divorcee, Mrs. William D. McCredy. She was entranced by his manliness, and he was intrigued by her vivacious charm. When he was forty-eight and she forty-two, they married but were divorced soon after. In 1907 Duke married Mrs. Nanaline Inman of Atlanta; they had one daughter, Doris.

In 1924 Duke created a trust fund, composed principally of his holdings in the Southern Power Company, to be used for endowing Duke University in North Carolina, for medical services in the two Carolinas, and for the relief of Methodist churches and ministers and orphans. When he died on October 10, 1925, he left even a richer legacy in multiplied industries and payrolls in a diversified economy.

James Buchanan Duke was forceful in appearance and manner, and he exuded confidence. He started out at the age of nine peddling Pro Bono Publico tobacco from a wagon with two blind mules, and more than any other man he influenced the tobacco smoking, chewing, and dipping habits of the whole world.

He said of his competitors, "While they eat and talk, I work." And to those who would succeed, he suggested, "Walk when you are young, so that you can ride when you are old."

Joseph Stephen Cullinan

THOUGH THE EXISTENCE of petroleum deposits in the United States had been reported as early as 1627, the first producing oil well was brought in by Colonel Edwin L. Drake at Titusville, Pennsylvania, on August 27, 1859. The search for petroleum began when men were prophesying that whale oil for illumination purposes would soon be a thing of the past and the world would be pitched into perpetual darkness.

Oil was first discoverd in Texas in Nacogdoches County by Lynis T. Barrett in 1866; in Corsicana, in 1896; near Jennings, Louisiana, in 1901; in El Dorado, Arkansas, in 1920; in Yazoo County, Mississippi, in 1939; and in Mobile County, Alabama, in 1955. But oil and gas first came richly into their own as the south's prime energizers with the discovery of the Spindletop at Beaumont, Texas, on January 10, 1901.

Patillo Higgins, persistent dreamer and father of Spindletop; John H. Galey, famed wildcatter; and Joseph Cullinan, financial wizard, were among the many pioneers in oil and gas in Texas.

Joseph Cullinan, born at Sharon, Pennsylvania, on December 21, 1860, was of Irish parents who had emigrated from County Clare. He was the eldest son and second of eight children of John Francis and Mary (Considine) Cullinan. His father being an impecunious oil worker, Joseph was forced to leave public school at the age of twelve to help support a large family. Employed by the Standard Oil Company, then a small concern, "Buckskin Joe," as he was called, got firsthand experience in drilling, laying pipe lines, assembling tank forms, and constructing refineries. He had been promoted to the position of manager of the company's natural gas division when he resigned in 1896 to go into business on his own manufacturing oil tanks at Washington, Pennsylvania. He married Lucie Halm of Lima, Ohio, on April 14, 1891, and they had five children.

His reputation was such that the officials of Corsicana, where an oil well had come in while they were drilling for water, called upon him to survey the field's potentialities. With the financial backing of Standard Oil Company officials, Cullinan established the first Texas pipe line and refinery. His J. S. Cullinan & Company became later the Magnolia Petroleum Company. Though primarily producers of illuminating oil, he and his brother, Dr. M. P. Cullinan, demonstrated the feasibility of oil as a locomotive fuel on a St. Louis & Southern Railroad engine. They also experimented successfully with methods of asphaltic paving.

In 1901, when the Lucas gusher blew in on Spindletop mount near Beaumont with a flow of one hundred thousand barrels a day, Cullinan sold out at Corsicana and formed a fifty thousand dollar corporation to refine and market it. His Texas Fuel Company, that went into operation in January, 1902, proved to be inadequate to cope with the situation; so the Texas Company was organized in March with a capitalization of three million dollars, which absorbed the assets of Cullinan's Company.

The Texas Company was a one-man show, and Cullinan ran it pretty much from the field. When it had become a major concern with five refineries, a fleet of freight cars and ocean-going tankers, and assets exceeding sixty million dollars, its eastern directors secured approval of the board to move the executive headquarters to New York. Cullinan considered this decision in violation of his original understanding and resigned.

Oil still his primary occupation, he formed the Farmers Oil Company which later consolidated with twenty subsidiary companies into the American Republics Corporation, a holding company, the assets of which grew from thirty thousand dollars in 1916 to seventy-four million dollars in 1927, with control over two million acres of oil land. And still Cullinan found time to become president of the Galena-Signal Oil Company in 1919.

In a bitter fight among stockholders who challenged his leadership, he resigned in 1928. The American Republics Corporation was placed in receivership during the depression, but Cullinan became president again in 1936.

The mark of the genius of this resourceful speculator was left in three major oil companies he created: Texas, Magnolia, and American Republics. He sought an answer to the industry's massive overproduction problems in 1928 by advocating federal control and the appointment of Herbert Hoover, or some other suitable person, as an oil "czar" to coördinate the efforts of producers and agencies.

Of diverse interests, Cullinan held high office in the National Rivers and Harbors Congress, the American Liberty League, and the Mount Rushmore National Memorial Commission. He was one of the original members of the Food Administration, headed by Herbert Hoover in 1917, and served with him on the Commission for Relief in the Belgium Educational Foundation. He died of pneumonia while a guest in the home of Hoover at Palo Alto, California, on March 11, 1937.

Tall, handsome, daring, and restless, radiating confidence, Joseph S. Cullinan was a Texas oil man in the truest tradition. He pioneered in an industry that completely changed the economy of the nation and the map of the world. He had a simple but practical philosophy: "Doubts and fears," he said, "are man's worst enemies. As long as a man doesn't know he can't do it, he can go ahead and do anything."

H.C.

Richmond Pearson Hobson

DURING THE Spanish-American War, the Spanish fleet, under Admiral Cervera, slipped through the waiting American squadrons into Santiago harbor. Rear Admiral William T. Sampson devised a scheme of sealing up the enemy's vessels by sinking a ship at the narrowest part of the channel. Assistant Naval Constructor Richmond Pearson Hobson, with seven men, volunteered to blow up the collier "Merrimac" and bottle up the fleet.

About 2:00 A.M. on June 3, 1898, the "Merrimac" was in position, but with her steering gear damaged by heavy enemy bombardment, she went out of control and was sunk by the combined fire of shore batteries, torpedoes from Spanish vessels, and finally by torpedoes set off by Hobson. He and his crew miraculously survived the explosion. They were taken from a floating raft by Cervera in person and were imprisoned for a time in Morro Castle, where they were courteously treated until exchanged for other prisoners in July. Hobson's heroism brought this strange war into immediate public focus as a unifying event to offset the prevailing criticism over haphazard military operations, the embalmed beef scandal, and friction within the service. The emotions of the American people overflowed, and Hobson's return to this country touched off a patriotic revival that swept the nation.

Hobson was born in Greensboro, Hale County, Alabama, on August 17, 1870, the second son of seven children of James Marcellus and Sarah Crown (Pearson) Hobson, the grandson of Richmond Mumford Hobson, chief justice of the North Carolina Supreme Court.

At an early age Richmond had already given some promise of distinction. He was described as precocious and serious minded. After preliminary study in private schools, he entered Southern University in Greensboro at the age of twelve where he remained for three years. From the university he went to the United States Naval Academy, graduating at the head of his class in 1889. There he rated higher educationally than he did socially. He was ostracized by his classmates for meticulously reporting their misdemeanors, as duty required, and only one man is supposed to have spoken to him for two years. When a midshipman proposed that communication be resumed, Hobson refused on the ground that he had enjoyed his isolation and the silence.

No doubt this experience left its scars. In a novel he wrote, *Buck Jones at Annapolis* (1907), the hero, for similar causes, is clapped into Coventry, "a punishment beyond anything conceived of elsewhere." Possibly, his secluded experience at the academy prompted him to choose the Construction Corps rather than the usual line duty in the navy.

Following his graduation, his midshipman's cruise, and a stint in the Navy Department, Hobson went to Paris to obtain a degree at the *Ecole d' Application du Génie Maritime.* After five years of active service at Annapolis, in navy yards, and at sea as a naval constructor with the fleet, he was ordered to the "New York," which was soon to become the flagship of Rear Admiral Sampson, in the blockade of Cuba during the war with Spain.

His exploit in the sinking of the "Merrimac" electrified the nation. Hobson became a national hysteria. When at a reception in Chicago he kissed a cousin, multitudes of women across the country wanted the same privilege. By the time the twenty-eight-year-old, handsome hero reached Denver on his triumphant tour, five hundred women were given the traditional Hobson salute.

A brave and intelligent young man, capable of unusual gallantry, he could not easily cope with the adulation of the multitudes. When the burst of mass enthusiasm subsided, he resigned from the service in 1903 and devoted the rest of his life to promoting through political action, ceaseless publicity, and organized effort the ideas and causes that commanded his intensified interest. These interests were many and varied: American naval supremacy, which he actually believed to be "the will of God"; the prohibition of alcohol, which he called "a protoplasm poison"; the suppression of narcotics, designated by him, "the modern pirates."

He was elected to Congress in 1900 on an anti-railroad platform and served four terms. In 1914 he lost a hard-fought race for the United States Senate to Oscar W. Underwood, despite strong backing from progressives and prohibitionists. In Congress he was "a nervous . . . dramatic guerilla fighter for causes." In one of these causes, the effort to create a chief of naval operations, his services were invaluable. However, in his suspicion and hatred for Japan, his manifest destiny role for American naval supremacy, and in national leadership in the promotion of international peace, he was regarded by many as a kind of public nuisance.

Hobson had married Grizelda Houston Hull of Tuxedo Park, New York, on May 25, 1905. He died of a heart attack on March 16, 1937.

Richmond Pearson Hobson appeared on the American scene at a propitious period. He fired the imaginations of millions of Americans to become a uniting and healing influence in a nation still divided against itself.

In belated recognition of his services to his country, he was awarded the Congressional Medal of Honor in 1933 for his work of thirty-five years before and was designated a rear admiral on the retired list.

Joseph Taylor Robinson

HE WAS born in a log house on a farm northwest of Lonoke, Arkansas, on August 26, 1872, the ninth child and fourth son in a family of eleven children. His father, James Madison Robinson, a country physician, Baptist minister, and farmer, had moved to Arkansas from New York State in 1844. His mother, Matilda Jan (Swain) Robinson, was part Indian, and born in Columbia, Tennessee.

"Joe T." Robinson, by which name he became known to millions of Americans, had little formal schooling but had applied himself so diligently to self-instruction that he was issued a certificate to teach school at the age of seventeen. After teaching for two years, he attended the University of Arkansas for two sessions, leaving at the age of twenty to read law in the office of Judge C. Trimble in Lonoke; he was admitted to the bar three years later.

He had already been elected to the state legislature, serving for one term only, when he abandoned the practice of law in 1902 at the age of thirty to become a successful candidate for Congress. He served for five successive terms.

In 1912, Robinson was elected governor of Arkansas, and when Senator Jeff Davis died in 1913, Robinson was chosen by the state legislature to fill his seat, which he occupied until his death on July 7, 1937. Within one year he was congressman, governor, and senator.

Dedicated to the public service, Joe T. Robinson was elected Senate Democratic leader in 1923 and reached the high point of his extraordinary political career in 1928 when he was nominated for vice-president on the Democratic Party ticket with Al Smith.

A strong internationalist, Robinson was often a delegate of the United States at such international meetings as the Inter-Parliamentary Union (1921, 1923, and 1924) and the London Naval Conference in 1930. He fought continuously for American membership in the World Court. During the administration of President Woodrow Wilson, he favored the League of Nations and ratification of the Treaty of Versailles without reservations. In 1917, he took sharp issue with those senators who opposed the declaration of war.

As congressman, Robinson aligned himself with the moderately progressive members, favoring federal regulation of railroads, of child labor, and trading in cotton futures. He supported the income tax and women's suffrage constitutional amendments and advocated a large navy, the establishment of parcel post service and postal savings, and the reduction of foreign immigration by a rigid literacy test.

As United States senator, under Republican administrations, Robinson opposed high protective tariffs, the tax-cutting program of Secretary of the Treasury Andrew Mellon, and exorbitant political campaign expenditures. He advocated increased veterans' benefits and federal flood control for the Mississippi River and its tributaries. He refused to support Senator George Norris' plan for federal power development at Muscle Shoals, but later under President Franklin D. Roosevelt he piloted passage of the New Deal's Tennessee Valley Authority Act through the Senate.

During the short time he was governor of Arkansas, Robinson directed an active session of the legislature, which enacted a corrupt practices act, the establishment of a bureau of labor statistics, a revision of the state banking laws, and an authorization for the building of dams across non-navigable streams for hydroelectric power.

An able leader and forthright spokesman for his party, Robinson was most effective as a behind-the-scenes worker. Although the only major piece of legislation which bears his name is the Robinson-Patman Act of 1936, designed to eliminate price discrimination tending to promote monopoly or reduce competition, his legislative labors are concealed behind the names of others.

Robinson's party loyalty was most pronounced in his efforts to push through the Senate Roosevelt's Judiciary Reorganization Bill providing for the appointment of an additional Supreme Court justice for each septuagenarian remaining on the bench. This so-called "pack the court" measure was most unpopular and failed to pass. The senator was fatally stricken with a heart attack in the midst of the court fight and died in his Washington apartment.

Robinson was married to Ewilda Gertrude Miller of Lonoke on December 15, 1896. They had no children but contributed to the education and welfare of many.

Although generally identified as a southern conservative, during the political efforts of the New Deal Robinson did yeoman's service under two Democratic administrations that were anything but conservative. An impressive personality, bulky in stature with a powerful voice, he was a popular speaker before political and business conventions, farmers' meetings, and manufacturers' associations.

He occupies a high place among Arkansas' political select. Robinson may not have had the popular appeal of Arkansas' Senator Jeff Davis, whose political credo was, "I am a Hard Shell Baptist in religion; I believe in footwashing, saving your seed potatoes, and paying your honest debts." But Robinson, the one-time plow boy, became an enlightened and dedicated political leader and a worthy public servant.

Harvey Crowley Couch

HE WAS born on a hillside farm in Calhoun County, Arkansas, the son of an itinerant Methodist minister who preached on Sunday and farmed during the week. He went to work in his teens; his first job was firing a cotton-gin boiler at fifty cents a day.

Later he was paid two hundred dollars a year to clerk in a country store and picked up a little change on the side running a laundry basket agency on commission; he was later employed as a mail clerk on a railroad at a monthly salary of seventy-five dollars. He borrowed thirty dollars to start a telephone line in a village, expanded it into a system serving towns in four states, and at thirty-four years sold his company for one and a half million dollars.

Harvey Crowley Couch was born on August 21, 1877, the son of Thomas C. Couch and Nanie (Heard) Couch. Of Welch extraction, his great-grandparents were born in Georgia.

Born during Reconstruction, Harvey started life unpropitiously, but he plowed, milked, and "slopped" hogs and grew in strength. Resourceful from the beginning, he built flutter wheels on the banks of creeks as a child to saw wood with water power, and after seeing his first railway train he improvised a toy track down a hill.

When Harvey was seventeen, his father's health failed, and the family moved to Magnolia, Arkansas. Oversized, nearly six feet tall, he was assigned to the fifth grade with boys of twelve and thirteen. Wearing a hickory shirt and homespun suit made by his mother, with other boys in white shirts and "store-bought" clothes, Harvey endured his embarrassment for a month, when he confided to his teacher that he felt out of place and was going to quit and go to work.

His teacher, Pat M. Neff, who later became governor of Texas and president of Baylor University, belittled the ridicule of Harvey's classmates, suggested that he try to make two grades in one, and wrote on the blackboard a lesson Harvey never forgot: "A quitter never wins, and a winner never quits." He inspired Harvey with the thought, "Men like you have built empires." In later years Harvey Couch often said, "Next to my mother, Pat Neff has influenced me more than any other person. . . . He touched me with his great personality."

Harvey was a pupil under Neff for two years when the helplessness of his father made it necessary for him to go to work to support the family. Fortified with what he had mastered in *McGuffey's Readers* and a Blue-back Speller and fired with the irrepressible urge to get somewhere and be somebody, he went forth to achieve fame and fortune.

Starting empty-handed, he built a telephone line from Bienville, Louisiana, to Magnolia, Arkansas, while he continued his mail run. By the time he was thirty-four, his telephone system, which he sold to the Bell interests, covered several states.

He then bought two small electric plants at Arkadelphia and Malvern, Arkansas, contracted with a sawmill to supply current, and connected the two towns with a transmission line. This was the birth of the Arkansas Power & Light Company, with headquarters at Pine Bluff. Properties were purchased in other cities in Mississippi and Louisiana. A power station was built at Sterlington, Louisiana, and natural gas was used for generating power. Couch bought millions of dollars worth of electrical equipment on open account. He constructed Remmel Dam on the Ouochita River to generate the first hydroelectric power in Arkansas, and his expanding utilities were consolidated with the Electric Bond & Share Company. Carpenter Dam was built and Lake Hamilton formed near Hot Springs. He borrowed five hundred thousand dollars to form the state's first rural electrification project.

Having pioneered in communication and electrification, Harvey Couch next ventured into the business of transportation. He bought the Louisiana & Arkansas Railroad on which he once had been a mail clerk and merged it with the Kansas City & Southern to form a major railway system under the management of his brother Charles Peter Couch.

Harvey Couch married Jessie Johnson of Athens, Louisiana, on October 4, 1904, and they had one daughter.

In 1932, during the depth of an economic depression, President Herbert Hoover organized the Reconstruction Finance Corporation. He appointed Harvey Couch as a director, and he continued to serve under President Franklin D. Roosevelt as chairman of the corporation. In this strategic position his wide experience was felt in every part of the country during a period of national recovery.

Countless calls were made upon him in the public service, and his leadership helped initiate an industrial revolution in the Deep South. At the time of his death on July 30, 1941, he was identified officially with many industrial and commercial enterprises and was active in a number of charitable and educational institutions.

He was the indefatigable worker and persistent student. He educated himself by asking questions and became one of the best-informed men in the country. He had an abiding faith in the people of the South and confidence in its future. Though he could pinch his pennies and was often a hard trader, he wanted to help the little man. He had earned his own way the hard way. "Success in life depends in part on the kind of friends one makes," he said, "make friends and be true to them."

Will Rogers

THE METEORIC career of Will Rogers provides one of the most amazing tales of individual achievement.

He was born on an obscure ranch in the Indian Territory in 1879, between what is now Oologah and Claremore, Oklahoma. When he crashed in a plane in the Arctic in 1935 he was the most widely and favorably known American citizen.

He was the son of pioneering parents each of whom was partly Cherokee, and his father operated a trading post among the Osages and raised cattle. His mother wanted him to become a preacher.

Will's formal education was limited to a short session at a boarding school and a brief spell at a military academy. Cowboy that he was, he could not confine his restless spirit to a classroom nor substitute a uniform for chaps with comfort. So Will abandoned school, raised a herd of cattle on his own, sold it at a profit, and started out to see the world.

At twenty-one he sailed for the Argentine by the way of England and punched cattle on the pampas. With itching feet and an irresistible urge to see strange places he shipped on a cattle boat to Capetown where he found a job breaking in wild horses. Joining a wild west show he worked his way from Africa to New Zealand, Australia, China, and Japan, finally reaching San Francisco. He returned to Oologah to woo and marry Betty Blake after having spent three years seeing the world.

He tramped with a troupe through the southwest, covered the World's Fair at St. Louis in 1904, and at twenty-six was star roper in a wild west show in Madison Square Garden.

He graduated from the tent to the theater, followed vaudeville with his own company for five years, and in 1907 was on Broadway in Ziegfeld's Follies with his lariat and wisecracking monologue.

From the legitimate stage he entered silent pictures. His first show was *Laughing Bill Hyde*. Although he starred in many silent films, it was in sound pictures that he really came into his own. After his first "talkie," *They Had to See Paris,* he became the great American favorite in *Lightnin', Connecticut Yankee, State Fair, David Harum, Judge Priest,* and *Steamboat Round the Bend.*

With the strides of radio he became one of its most popular artists. In 1930 he broadcast a series of fourteen fifteen-minute talks for which he was paid three hundred fifty dollars a minute.

His literary achievements were as well received. At the time of his death his paragraphs were running in three hundred fifty daily and two hundred Sunday newspapers. At three thousand dollars a week he was one of the highest paid syndicate writers in the history of journalism, with an audience of forty million readers.

He was author of a number of books, the first of which *Rogerisms,* appeared in 1919. His "Letters of a Self-Made Diplomat to His President," published in the Saturday Evening Post in 1926, almost split the nation's sides with laughter.

He went about the whole world as an ambassador of good will, and while he talked with kings he kept the common touch. No other man was in such demand as an after-dinner speaker.

His philanthropies ran into the millions as he gave without stint of his money, time, and talent. He barnstormed the country for the Salvation Army and the American Red Cross. He raised money for storm sufferers, the drought destitute, and flood victims.

World citizen and privileged character, he flew about the earth to subdue the great with his inexhaustible wit and piercing satire. He gave John D. Rockefeller a dime, ridiculed the Prince of Wales in London, and imitated President Calvin Coolidge over the air.

He stepped out of the crowd when men were torn with strife and conquered the world with his spontaneous sallies. He disclosed the childish vanities of men and helped a despondent people to weather the Great Depression by poking fun at it.

He exposed the silly shams of posing statesmen and pious frauds and exploded the big conceits of little men with concentrated mirth. He captivated a continent with his philosophical exaggerations.

Those who knew him find it difficult to circumscribe his genius or portray his boundless personality. The combination of the Scotch, Irish, and Indian in him created a new type for the discriminating biographer.

Cowboy, actor, comedian, commentator, author, humorist, philosopher, and humanitarian, Will Rogers was a man of many parts.

Made of the common clay, fashioned from the rarest mold of modern times, he had the uncommon touch of reaching alike the mind of peasant and prince, plutocrat and pauper. He knew the heart of mankind and spoke the language of every race and tongue.

Blessed with that divine gift of human sympathy and understanding, he so debunked his generation that the millions who laughed while he lived wept when he died.

"His life was gentle, and the elements
So mix'd in him that Nature might stand up
And say to all the world, 'That was a man!' "

Rudolph Matas

WHEN HE DIED in New Orleans on September 23, 1957, at the age of ninety-seven, Dr. Rudolph Matas was recognized internationally as the world's foremost surgeon.

He was born in Bonnet Carre, St. John's Parish, Louisiana, on September 12, 1860. His father and mother, who came from the Spanish province of Catalonia, returned to Spain shortly after Rudolph's birth. In 1867, they returned to the United States, and Rudolph had his preliminary education at Soule College in New Orleans and at the San Juan Institute in Matamoras, Mexico. His father, Dr. N. Heru Matas, an oculist, had profited during 1862–63 trading in contraband and running cotton through the Union blockade.

Rudolph enrolled in the Medical School of the University of Louisiana (now Tulane) in the fall of 1877 and received his doctor of medicine degree in 1880. While still an undergraduate, he won a two-year internship at Charity Hospital in New Orleans and was appointed to the Yellow Fever Commission to Cuba in 1879 as interpreter, clerk, and miscroscopist. In 1882, he was called to Mier, Mexico, to treat an epidemic of yellow fever.

While an intern he assisted in the first laparotomy performed using Listerian techniques. Dr. Joseph Lister's antiseptic methods in performing operations was being introduced from England.

Appointed in 1886, Dr. Matas remained Demonstrator of Anatomy at Tulane until he was appointed Professor and Chairman of the Department of Surgery, a position which he held until he retired in 1927.

A pioneering surgeon and physician, Dr. Matas was first to differentiate between typhoid and malarial fever in Louisiana, first to use intravenous saline infusions on surgical patients, first in the United States to perform a surgical operation on a patient under spinal anesthesia, and among the first to identify appendicitis as a condition that could best be treated by surgery. He was first to perform an endoaneurysmorrhaphy on May 6, 1888.

The recognized father of vascular surgery, he saw his fame spread. The "Matas operation," a surgical treatment of enlarged veins and arteries, was his discovery and invention and has long been a standard surgical technique, saving countless lives and adding years to the usefulness of many men and women.

Dr. Matas operated occasionally until he was eighty-seven, and was active in medical circles until he was past ninety; he achieved many of his triumphs after the loss of one eye. His span of life extended just short of a century during which he was the dean of a group of famed physicians and surgeons, including Drs. Edmond Souchon, Stanford Emerson Chaillé, Joseph Jones, T. G. Richardson, and Carrol Allen, that made New Orleans a medical center.

When Dr. Matas' mother and sister who lived with him for years returned to Spain in the early nineties, he engaged Mrs. Adrienne Landry, a widow, as his housekeeper, and she later became Mrs. Matas.

He contributed countless monographs to his profession on surgical subjects and was the author of numerous articles in medical journals. He made extensive reports before the Southern Surgical and Gynecological Association in 1900 and the American Surgical Association in 1902. He possessed a phenomenal memory, was a fluent extemporaneous speaker, and commanded the confidence of his contemporaries. He was an indefatigable student and inspiring teacher; one of the most effective articles ever written for medical students was his "Soul of the Surgeon."

Dr. Matas was one of the founders of the American College of Surgeons in 1913, was its president in 1925, and was awarded an honorary fellowship in 1952. He was president of the American Surgical Association in 1909 and president of the International and Gynecological Association in 1910. He received the first Certificate of Merit awarded by the American Medical Association, was a member of all outstanding surgical societies of the world, and was awarded many honorary degrees by universities at home and abroad.

While he still lived, a portrait medallion of him was placed in the Touro Infirmary on the occasion of his forty-sixth year with that institution, much of the time its chief surgeon. In a deserved citation in recognition of his unselfish civic service, he was awarded the *Times-Picayune* Loving Cup in 1941.

With all the honors that were conferred upon him throughout a long and active career, he remained humble and grateful. He described himself as a "plain American citizen and doctor who has tried faithfully all his life to discharge his obligations to his family, to his fellows, and his country with conscientious fidelity." He could remember when his patients of the Louisiana bayous paid their doctor's bills with strings of fish, baskets of crabs, and sacks of oysters and when he achieved fame and fortune his friends were legion among the lowly and the elite.

Dr. Rudolph Matas was a brilliant scholar and accomplished linguist, using English, French, Spanish, German, and Italian with fluency. He was an eminent scientist, astute clinician, and dedicated doctor. He was conversant in literature, art, music, and sports; his distinguished contemporary, Dr. Will Mayo, said he was the world's best educated physician. He was deep-minded and big-hearted, and his personality was a happy compound of ideas and ideals. He was the kind of man Hippocrates, Greek "father of medicine," had in mind when he described the duties and obligations of a physician in his famed oath.

Cordell Hull

TENNESSEE'S STATESMAN and peacemaker, Cordell Hull, was born in Overton County, on October 2, 1871, in a rented log cabin with holes for windows. He was the son of William Hull, a farmer and trader, and Elizabeth (Riley) Hull; both parents were of Anglo-Saxon extraction and of Revolutionary stock. One of five sons, "Cord" wore homespun and home-made shoes. The sons all helped on the farm and as they grew older rafted logs down the river to the Nashville market. Hull's industrious and resourceful father left an estate of three hundred thousand dollars when he died. During the conflict of the states, he had an eye shot out by a "yankee bush-wacker." After the war, old Hull found his man and with true mountain vengenance shot him down.

Young Hull won a debate at the Willow Grove rural school, arguing that Columbus deserved more credit for discovering America than did Washington for defending it. Impressed, his father sent him to a neighborhood academy in Celina and afterwards to Kentucky Normal at Bowling Green and National Normal University at Lebanon, Ohio. He read law in offices in Celina and Nashville, attended Cumberland University, obtained his degree in 1891, and opened his law office in Celina.

Hull had made his political debut at nineteen when he was elected chairman of the Clay County Democratic Convention. Two years later he was elected representative in the state legislature. As captain of a company of Tennessee United States Volunteers in the Spanish-American War, he arrived in Cuba after the war was over. He returned to Celina to resume his law practice, and then moved to Gainesboro, where he was appointed to the Circuit bench.

Hull was elected to Congress in 1906 and served his district until the 1920 Republican landslide. He was made chairman of the national Democratic Party and was returned to Congress in 1922 when he won a seat in the United States Senate, which he occupied until appointed Secretary of State in the cabinet of President Franklin D. Roosevelt in 1933.

Jeffersonian in his political philosophy, Hull believed that the key to liberty was expressed in the principles of the Declaration of Independence. He was also a political disciple of Woodrow Wilson, in sympathy with the ideals Wilson defined in his New Freedom. He was serious-minded, meditative, frail, and gentle, in appearance the benign Southern gentleman of the old school. He never had occasion to use it, but his intimates said he always carried a long knife.

In Congress, Hull concentrated on statistics and tax legislation, and he was a fanatic advocate of a federal income tax. After the enactment of the Sixteenth Amendment in 1913, he became the author of the first income tax law and later drafted inheritance and estate tax legislation. He believed the protective tariff to be "the king of evils." As Secretary of State he initiated the reciprocal trade agreements enacted by Congress in 1934. He believed that trade retaliation and discrimination were obstacles to world peace. Ultimately trade agreements were made with thirty-seven nations and colonies. Hull also promoted the federal support of a program for the exchange of foreign students and professors.

Though disappointed in the failure of the London Economic Conference in 1933, Hull directed his efforts to the Latin American field. Fortified with President Roosevelt's declaration of the Good Neighbor Policy, he attended the Montevideo Conference in 1933. With world tensions accumulating he began warning the nation of impending peril. Mussolini's aggressions in Africa, Hitler's in Europe, and the revolution in Spain led him to advocate rearmament and the accumulation of strategic war materiel.

The Pan American Conference was held at Buenos Aires in 1936, followed by conferences at Lima, Panama City, and Havana. With World War II raging in Europe, Hull helped pilot through Congress the Lend-Lease Act of 1940 and urged aid to Russia. Hull's wrath reached an all-time high when the Japanese made their sneak attack on Pearl Harbor while he was in conference with their envoys.

He was ignored by Roosevelt in military meetings with our Allies in Casablanca, Cairo, and Teheran. He did not always see eye to eye with the President; he was not in accord with his spendthrift policies, and he believed in a balanced federal budget.

In August, 1943, Hull attended a conference at Quebec with President Roosevelt and Winston Churchhill. He presented the draft there of a trusteeship system for a peace that later took form in the United Nations' organization. Though in poor health, he took his first airplane flight to Moscow and presented to the four nations represented there a declaration which they signed in support of a postwar international organization to keep the peace. Broken in health he could not attend the San Francisco conference of 1945, but Roosevelt called him the "father of the United Nations." Among many awards Hull received the Nobel Peace Prize in 1945. He was too sick to make the trip to Oslo, and divided half the award money with his wife, Rose Frances Whitney, to whom he was married in 1917.

In his declining years Hull wrote his memoirs, and Vanderbilt University in 1951, as a living monument to his memory, established the Cordell Hull Foundation for International Education, an association devoted to "World Peace, Trade and Understanding." Hull died in July 1955.

Index